300 Low-Carb
Slow Cooker Recipes

300 Low-Carb
Slow Cooker Recipes

Healthy Dinners That Are Ready When You Are!

Dana Carpender

FAIR WINDS
PRESS
BEVERLY, MASSACHUSETTS

© 2011 Fair Winds Press
Text © 2011 Dana Carpender

First published in the USA in 2011 by
Fair Winds Press, a member of
Quayside Publishing Group
100 Cummings Center
Suite 406-L
Beverly, MA 01915-6101
www.fairwindspress.com

15 14 13 12 11   1 2 3 4 5

ISBN: 978-1-59233-497-1

Digital edition published in 2011
eISBN-13: 978-1-61058-152-3

Library of Congress Cataloging-in-Publication Data available

Printed and bound in Canada

The information in this book is for educational purposes only. It is not intended to replace
the advice of a physician or medical practitioner. Please see your health care provider before
beginning any new health program.

For my sister Kim,

who works way too hard,

and loves her slow cooker.

contents

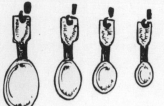

Introduction: My Journey to Slow Cooker Mastery

I have a confession: When my editor, Holly, suggested I write a low-carb slow cooker book, I balked. Oh, I knew it would be popular—many readers had written me asking for a slow cooker book. I just wasn't thrilled at the idea of a couple of months of slow cooked dinners. I'd made some slow cooked meals that were pretty good, but overall, it seemed to me that most slow cooked food was not brilliant. Too many dishes seemed to be waterlogged, mushy, and insipid. Furthermore, so many slow cooker recipes seemed to rely on high-carb canned cream soups—indeed, many slow cooker books seemed to think that "put food in pot, dump in condensed cream of mushroom soup, and cook on low until you come home from work" was a recipe—but not in my book, figuratively or literally!

So I resisted for quite a while, but those e-mails saying, "Please, please, write us a slow cooker book!" were piling up in my inbox. I needed to write a slow cooker book! But it was clear I had to get better at slow cooking.

Well, my mom is a retired librarian, and I learned years ago that if you want to learn something, you need to look it up. So I went to Amazon.com and read reviews of slow cooker books to determine which were drawing raves. I then read the books that got the best reviews, gleaning what I could from them of the tricks of making slow cooker food as appealing as possible, both in taste and texture. Not surprisingly, my slow cooker performance took a remarkable upturn!

I also got an idea of what slow cookers do well. Obviously, they're not for anything that you want to come out crispy and brown, but if what you need is slow, moist cooking, a slow cooker will do it better than any other appliance. Preparing soups and stews and braising are obvious slow cooker strengths, but I also learned that a slow cooker is terrific for cooking anything that needs to be baked in a water bath (sometimes called a bain-marie)—custards, in particular. I was thrilled to discover that my slow cooker did the best job ever of roasting nuts and seeds, and it's perfect for hot beverages for parties and hors d'oeuvres that would otherwise need a chafing dish.

I was very surprised to learn that cooking fish in my slow cooker worked well. You can't leave it for hours and hours because fish overcooks easily. But just an hour or so of the gentle heat of the slow cooker leaves fish tender, moist, and succulent. Do try it when you have an hour to get dinner on the table, even if you mostly use your slow cooker to cook supper while you're out of the house for hours.

I also had a few spectacular failures. (Don't even ask about the brussels sprouts!) But overall, I was pleased to discover that with a few simple considerations in mind, slow cookers can turn out truly wonderful food.

About Slow Cookers

By the time I finished this project, I owned three slow cookers. All of them are Rival Crock-Pots, the original slow cooker. (Crock-Pot is a brand name. All Crock-Pots are slow cookers, but not all slow cookers are Crock-Pots.) The Crock-Pot, as the original, is pretty much the gold standard of slow cookers. The heat comes from all around the crockery insert, rather than only coming from the bottom. If you have one of the slow cookers that has the heating element only on the bottom, you'll have to experiment a bit with these recipes to see if the times are correct.

The "low" setting on a Rival Crock-Pot is around 200°F (93°C) (just above, actually, because things will boil eventually at this setting, and the boiling point is 212°F [100°C]), and the "high" setting is around 300°F (150°C). If you have another brand of slow cooker that lets you set specific temperatures, keep this in mind. If you have another brand of slow cooker and you're not sure what temperature the settings will give (look in the booklet that came with it for this information), you can fill the slow cooker with water, heat it for 2 hours on low, and test the water's temperature with a kitchen thermometer, but this is a lot of trouble. I'd probably just use the low and high settings and keep mental notes on how meals turn out.

A good thing about the original Crock-Pot is that the crockery insert lifts out of the base. This allows it to be refrigerated, microwaved (if your microwave is big enough), and—most important—put in the dishwasher. *Do not* put your slow cooker in the dishwasher if the crockery cannot be separated from the heating element! Nothing electric should ever be submerged in water.

My slow cookers range in size. The smallest holds 2½ quarts (2.4 liters), the middle-sized holds 3 quarts (2.8 liters), while the big one holds 5½ quarts (5 liters). The 5½-quart can easily hold enough food for 8 people. It's the obvious choice if you have a big family or like to cook enough to have leftovers for future meals. The 3-quart is the most common size. If you have a family of 4, it should be about right. If you have this size, figure you'll need to halve recipes that make 6 to 8 servings. The 2½-quart is great for making dips, hot hors d'oeuvres, and hot beverages, but it is a bit small for family cooking.

Another consideration: My 5½-quart Crock-Pot will fit a 6-cup (1.4 L) casserole dish, 8-inch (20 cm) springform pan, and a standard Bundt pan opening up many new cooking options. If you have a smaller unit and want to make custards, cheesecakes, and other dishes that call for inserting a dish or pan, you'll have to find dishes that will fit. It's easier with a bigger slow cooker.

Keep in mind that slow cookers come in round or oval shapes. You'll want a round slow cooker, instead of an oval, so you can insert a round glass casserole or a springform. Sadly, a big, round slow cooker takes the most storage space. I know of no good way around this.

Some Things I've Learned about Slow Cooking

- Browning meat or poultry before putting it in the slow cooker upgrades vast hordes of recipes. Yes, it takes time and dirties up a skillet. But the flavor and texture that browning bring are worth it, worth it, worth it. Often I'll have you sauté your vegetables, too.

- It's important to keep liquids to the minimum that will make the recipe work, especially in recipes that have a lot of vegetables. All of the liquid that cooks out of the food while slow cooking will accumulate in the pot because no evaporation occurs. It's easy to end up with very watery food. This rule does not apply to soups, of course.

- Because of this accumulation of liquid, it's a good idea to use concentrated flavors. In particular, you'll find that in many of these recipes I use both broth and bouillon concentrate to make what amounts to a broth that is double-strength or more.

- Sometimes it's a good idea to transfer the liquid from the slow cooker to a saucepan and boil it hard till it's reduced by half. Half the volume means double the flavor.

- It's generally best to use lean cuts of meat, and you'll see I've often used skinless poultry, too. This is because fat that becomes crackling and succulent in the oven makes slow cooker food unbearably greasy. This makes slow cooking a great way to cook some of the leaner and tougher cuts of meat that you might not want to roast. It also makes slow cooking a good cooking method for those of you who are watching calories as well as carbs. It can even save you money—often tough and bony cuts of meat are cheap.

- For some strange reason, vegetables cook more slowly in a slow cooker than meat does. If you put vegetables on top of the meat in your slow cooker, you may find that they're still crunchy when the rest of the dinner is done. Put the ingredients in the pot in the order given in the recipes in this book.

- For this reason, too, it's best to cut vegetables into fairly small pieces. You'll find I've told you what size to cut things, for the most part. If the recipe says ½-inch (13 mm) cubes, and you cut your turnips in 1½-inch (3.8 cm) cubes, you're going to have underdone turnips.

- It's never a bad idea to spray your slow cooker with nonstick cooking spray before putting the food in it. I don't always do this, though I've specified it where it seems a particularly good idea. But I can't think of a situation in which it would hurt.

Things That Other Slow Cooker Books Seem to Think Are Terribly Important, But Don't Seem Like a Big Deal to Me

- Several books wanted me to use only whole spices, such as whole peppercorns or coarse-cracked pepper, whole cloves, whole leaf herbs, etc., etc. I used what I had on hand. I got tasty food.

- A few books felt that you shouldn't season your slow cooker food until the end of cooking time. I do often suggest that you add salt and pepper to taste at the end of the cooking time, but other than that, our seasonings go into the pot with the food. I've never had a problem with this.

- Some books were emphatic about the size of the slow cooker. This matters some; you can't put 4 quarts (3.8 L) of soup in a 3-quart (2.8 L) slow cooker, and if you're only making a small batch of dip, you probably shouldn't use a 5½-quart (5 L) pot. But some cookbooks predicted dire results if I didn't fill my slow cooker at least halfway. I often filled my big slow cooker less than halfway. I got tasty food.

About Timing

The biggest reason for the popularity of slow cookers is what I call "time-shifting"—the fact that they allow you to cook dinner at some time other than right before you eat it, so you can eat soon after you get home from work. Because of this, many slow cooker books tell you to cook most of their recipes for 8 hours or more. They figure you'll be away that long.

Unfortunately, I find that many dishes get unbearably mushy and overdone if they cook that long. I've tried to give the cooking times that I feel give the best results, which may not be the time that fits with your workday. These can generally be extended by an hour without a problem, but extending them by 2, 3, or more hours may well give you a very different result than I got.

A better idea is to do all your prep work the night before—cooking dinner after dinner, as it were. Then lift the filled crockery insert out of the base and stash it in the fridge overnight. The next morning, pull it out of the fridge, put it in the base, and turn it on, just before you leave the house. Starting with chilled food will add 1 to 2 hours to your cooking time. If you do this, don't heat up the base before putting the chilled crockery insert in! You may well crack the crockery.

If you need to extend your time even further, consider getting a timer. You should be fine letting your food wait 2 hours before the timer turns on the slow cooker—3 if the food is straight out of the fridge when the crockery goes in the base. It's a better idea to delay the starting time than to turn the pot off early because retained heat will cause the food to continue cooking even after the pot is turned off. Ask the nice people at your local hardware store about a timer you can plug things into. If you're just now acquiring your slow cooker, there are units available with time-delayed starters built in.

On the other hand, if you want to speed up a slow cooker recipe, you can do so by getting the contents warm before putting the crockery insert in the base. The crocks for two of my three slow cookers fit in my microwave. I have, on occasion, microwaved the full crock on medium heat until it was warm through before putting the crock in the base to continue cooking. This cuts a good hour off the cooking time.

You can, of course, also use the high setting when the low setting is specified. This will cut the cooking time roughly in half. However, I find that for most recipes low yields better results. If you have the time to use it when it's recommended, I suggest you do so.

If you're going to be around for a while and leave the house later, you could cook on high for an hour or so and then switch to low when you leave. Figure, again, that each hour on high is worth 2 hours on low.

The size of your slow cooker relative to your recipe will somewhat affect the cooking time. If you have a 5½-quart (5 L) slow cooker and the food only fills it ¼ full, you can likely subtract 1 hour from the cooking time. Conversely, if the food fills your slow cooker to within an inch of the rim, you can add an hour.

Ingredients: Common and Not-So-Common Ingredients

Here are a few ingredients I thought needed a little explanation:

- **Beer**—One or two recipes in this book call for beer. The lowest carbohydrate beer on the market is Michelob Ultra, but I don't much like it. Still, it should be okay for cooking. Miller Lite and Milwaukee's Best Light are better, and they have only about 0.5 grams more carb per can.

- **Black soybeans**—Most beans and other legumes are too high in carbohydrates for many low-carb dieters, but there is one exception. Black soybeans have a very low usable carb count, about 1 gram per serving, because most of the carbs in them are fiber. Several recipes in this book call for Eden brand canned black soybeans. Many health food stores carry these. If yours doesn't, I'll bet they could special order them for you. Health food stores tend to be wonderful about special orders.

  I wouldn't recommend eating soybean recipes several times a week. I know that soy has a reputation for being the Wonder Health Food of All Existence, but there are reasons to be cautious. For decades now, soy has been known to be hard on the thyroid, and if you're trying to lose weight and improve your health, a slow thyroid is the last thing you need. More alarmingly, a study done in Hawaii in 2000 showed a correlation between the amount of tofu subjects ate in middle age and their rate and severity of cognitive problems in old age. Because scientists suspect the problem lies with the soy estrogens that have been so highly touted, any unfermented soy product, including canned soybeans, is suspect.

This doesn't mean we should completely shun soybeans and soy products, but we need to approach them with caution and eat them in moderation. Because many low-carb specialty products are soy-heavy, you'll want to pay attention there, too. Personally, I try to keep my soy consumption to 1 serving a week or less.

- **Blackstrap molasses**—What the heck is molasses doing in a low-carb cookbook?! It's practically all carbohydrate, after all. Well, yes, but I've found that combining Splenda with a very small amount of molasses gives a good, brown-sugar flavor to all sorts of recipes. Always use the darkest molasses you can find. The darker it is, the stronger the flavor, and the lower the carb count. That's why I specify blackstrap, the darkest, strongest molasses there is. It's nice to know that blackstrap is also where all the minerals they take out of sugar end up. It may be high-carb, but at least it's not a nutritional wasteland. Still, I use only small amounts.

  Most health food stores carry blackstrap molasses, but if you can't get it, buy the darkest molasses you can find. Most grocery store brands come in both light and dark varieties.

  Why not use some of the artificial brown-sugar flavored sweeteners out there? Because I've tried them, and I haven't tasted one I would be willing to buy again. Caution: Splenda brown sugar blend contains sugar.

- **Broths**—Canned or boxed chicken broth and beef broth are very handy items to keep around and certainly quicker than making your own. However, the quality of most of the canned broth you'll find at your local grocery store is appallingly bad. The chicken broth has all sorts of chemicals in it and often sugar as well. The beef broth is worse. It frequently has no beef in it whatsoever. I refuse to use these products, and you should, too.

  However, there are a few canned or boxed broths on the market worth buying. Many grocery stores now carry a brand called Kitchen Basics, which contains no chemicals at all. It is packaged in quart-size boxes, much like soy milk. Kitchen Basics comes in both chicken and beef. Health food stores also have good quality canned and boxed broths. Both Shelton and Health Valley brands are widely distributed in the United States.

  Decent packaged broth will cost you a little more than the stuff that is made of salt and chemicals but not a whole lot more. If you watch for sales, you can often get it as cheaply as the bad stuff, so stock up. When my health food store runs a sale on good broth for 89 cents a can, I buy piles of it!

One last note: You will also find canned vegetable broth, particularly at health food stores. This is tasty, but because it runs much higher in carbohydrates than chicken and beef broths, I'd avoid it.

- **Bouillon or broth concentrates**—Bouillon or broth concentrate comes in cubes, crystals, liquids, and pastes. It is generally full of salt and chemicals and doesn't taste notably like the animal it supposedly came from. It definitely does *not* make a suitable substitute for good quality broth if you're making a pot of soup. However, these products can be useful for adding a little kick of flavor here and there—more as seasonings than as soups. For this use, I keep them on hand. I now use a paste bouillon concentrate product called Better Than Bouillon that comes in both chicken and beef flavors. I find it preferable to the granules or cubes.

- **Carb Countdown**—When I wrote the original edition of this book, the Atkins Boom of 2003 was still going strong, and grocery stores were carrying a lot of low-carb specialty products, some dubious, other quite useful. Carb Countdown, a carbohydrate-reduced milk put out by Hood Dairy, was one that I found very useful, and accordingly I used it in several recipes.

  Things have changed. Hood still makes the product, though they long since renamed it Calorie Countdown. However, far fewer stores are carrying it than were when the original edition came out. If you can find Calorie Countdown near you, great! If not, here are some possible substitutions, and their carb counts:

LC-Milk: As I write this, a company called LC Foods has just introduced a powdered low-carb milk product called LC-Milk. Because it's powdered, it is easy to ship and easy to store. You simply combine the powder with water and heavy cream, and chill, though I'm thinking for a slow cooker recipe the chilling part would be unnecessary. Sufficient powder to make 1 cup (235 ml) of milk, or 10 teaspoons, has 1 gram of carb, with 1 gram of fiber, for 0 grams usable carb. The cream adds 1 gram of carb. The two combined have 192 calories per cup. The mix has no lactose, though there would be a little in the cream. LC-Milk is available from www.holdthecarbs.com, and may well be carried by low-carb online retailers by the time this sees print.

Half-and-half: 10 grams of carbohydrate per cup. Of the substitutes available at your grocery store, this will likely give a result most similar to the original recipe. (For international readers: Half-and-half is a mixture of half milk, half heavy cream.) Adds 187 calories over the Carb Countdown.

Heavy cream: 7 grams carbohydrate per cup. Obviously, this will give a richer result. Adds 684 calories. On the other hand, I've long since started trying to get 75 percent of my calories from fat, and I consider butterfat to be a healthful food. Your call.

Heavy cream and water, in equal parts: This works well in many recipes, and of course it gives a lighter result than pure cream. Simple third-grade arithmetic tells me you'll get 3.5 grams of carbohydrate, and an extra 342 calories per cup.

Almond milk: I've been playing around with almond milk recently, and I like it. It's now widely available in big grocery stores; look for it near the soy milk. (I would *not* use soy milk. I try to minimize my soy consumption. I'm unconvinced the stuff is safe.) Keep in mind that almond milk comes in sweetened and unsweetened varieties; obviously you want the unsweetened kind. The brand I've been getting has just 1 gram of carbohydrate per cup, with 1 gram of fiber, for 0 grams usable carb, so this would be your lowest carb option. It's also far and away the lowest calorie choice, at just 35 calories per cup. It will, however, have a somewhat different flavor than dairy—mild and pleasant, but different. This is also a lactose-free choice.

Milk: You know—just milk. It's 12 grams of carb per cup, so it's the highest carb choice, but in a recipe that makes, say, 5 or 6 servings, that's not disastrous. I'd recommend whole milk. Butterfat is nutritious, and it certainly tastes better than the low-fat stuff. It's an extra 22 calories per cup.

Final note: I've heard from some readers that their grocery stores dropped Carb Countdown, but started re-stocking Calorie Countdown due to customer requests. So, it doesn't hurt to ask.

- **Cauliflower**—You'll notice a certain reliance on cauliflower in this book, both in the form of "Fauxtatoes" (see recipe page 343) and in the form of Cauli-Rice (see recipe page 343). This is because many slow cooker recipes make wonderful gravy, and it's a shame not to have a side dish to help you eat it. (Indeed, traditional slow cooker recipes show a similar dependence on potatoes, rice, and noodles.)

  You can skip the cauliflower if you like. Or you can substitute tofu shirataki noodles.

By the way: If cauliflower (or another suggested garnish or side dish) isn't mentioned in the ingredient list, it's merely suggested and it's not included in the nutritional analysis for the dish. If it is in the ingredient list, it has been included in the analysis.

- *Chili garlic paste*—This is a traditional Asian ingredient, consisting mostly, as the name strongly implies, of hot chiles and garlic. If, like me, you're a chile-head, you'll find endless ways to use the stuff once you have it on hand. Chili garlic paste comes in jars, and it keeps for months in the refrigerator. It is worth seeking out at Asian markets or in the international foods aisle of big grocery stores.

- *Chipotle peppers canned in adobo sauce*—Chipotle peppers are smoked jalapeños. They're very different from regular jalapeños, and they're quite delicious. Look for them, canned in adobo sauce, in the Mexican foods section of big grocery stores. Because you're unlikely to use the whole can at once, you'll be happy to know that you can store your chipotles in the freezer, where they'll keep for months. I just float my can in a bowl of hot tap water for 5 minutes till it's thawed enough to peel off one or two peppers and then put it right back in the freezer.

- *Erythritol*—This is one of the polyol or sugar alcohol sweeteners, and the one I use most often. Unlike maltitol, which is widely used in commercial sugar-free sweets, erythritol has very little gastrointestinal effect. It also has the lowest absorption profile of all the sugar alcohols, so it has virtually no usable carbohydrate, while I generally count half a gram for maltitol. My local health food stores all carry erythritol, but again, you can buy it through CarbSmart.com or Amazon.com if you can't find it locally.

  You can substitute xylitol, another polyol rapidly growing in popularity. Be aware, however, that it is profoundly toxic to dogs, so don't let your pooch sneak a bite.

- *Fish sauce or nuoc mam or nam pla*—This is a salty, fermented seasoning widely used in Southeast Asian cooking, available in Asian grocery stores and in the Asian food sections of big grocery stores. Grab it when you find it; it keeps nicely without refrigeration. Fish sauce is used in a few (really great) recipes in this book, and it adds an authentic flavor. In a pinch, you can substitute soy sauce, although you'll lose some of the Southeast Asian accent.

- *Garlic*—I use only fresh garlic, except for occasional recipes for sprinkle-on seasoning blends. Nothing tastes like the real thing. To my taste buds, even the jarred, chopped garlic in oil doesn't taste like fresh garlic. We won't even *talk* about garlic powder. You may use jarred garlic if you like—half a teaspoon should equal about 1 clove of fresh garlic. If you choose to use powdered garlic, well, I can't stop you, but I'm afraid I can't promise the recipes will taste the same either. One quarter teaspoon of garlic powder is the rough equivalent of 1 clove of fresh garlic.

- *Ginger root*—Many recipes in this book call for fresh ginger, sometimes called ginger root. Dried, powdered ginger is *not* a substitute. Fortunately, fresh ginger freezes beautifully. Drop the whole ginger root (called a hand of ginger) into a resealable plastic freezer bag and toss it in the freezer. When time comes to use it, pull it out, peel enough of the end for your immediate purposes, and grate it. Ginger grates just fine while still frozen. Throw the remaining root back in the bag and toss it back in the freezer.

  Ground fresh ginger root in oil is available in jars at some very comprehensive grocery stores. I buy this when I can find it without added sugar, but otherwise, I grate my own.

- *Granular Sucralose*—Since *15 Minute Low-Carb Recipes* was first published, sucralose, best known by the trade name Splenda, has gone off-patent. There are now dozens of knock-offs and store brands, and there's no reason not to use them instead of the name brand. Do look for one that measures cup-for-cup like sugar. Be wary of brown sugar blends and other sucralose blends; these have sugar in them. And remember that because of the maltodextrin used to bulk it, granular sucralose has about 24 grams of carbohydrate per cup—the *0 carb* figure is an artifact of the teeny serving size listed on the label.

- *Guar and xanthan gums*—These sound just dreadful, don't they? But they're in lots of your favorite processed foods, so how bad can they be? They're forms of water soluble fiber, extracted and purified. Guar and xanthan are both flavorless white powders, and their value to us is as low-carb thickeners. Technically speaking, these are carbs, but they're all fiber—nothing but.

  Those of you who read *500 Low-Carb Recipes* know that I used to recommend putting your guar or xanthan through the blender with part or all of the liquid in the recipe to avoid lumps. You may now happily forget that technique. Instead, acquire an extra salt shaker, fill it with guar or xanthan, and keep it handy. When you want to thicken the liquid in your slow cooker, simply sprinkle a little of the thickener over the surface *while stirring*, preferably with a whisk. Stop when your sauce, soup, or gravy is a little less thick than you want it to be. It'll thicken a little more on standing.

Your health food store may well be able to order guar or xanthan for you if they don't have them on hand. You can also find suppliers online. Of the two, I slightly prefer xanthan.

- **Ketatoes**—Ketatoes, a low-carb instant mashed potato substitute, has sadly passed from our midst. However, at this writing there is a similar product available called Dixie Carb Counters Instant Mashers that works exactly the same as Ketatoes in my recipes, at least the ones I've tried it in. **Anywhere you see "Ketatoes" in this book, think "Dixie Carb Counters Instant Mashers," and you'll be fine.** You can get 'em through the low carb etailers, and even through Amazon.com. I get mine from CarbSmart.com. Yes, I have a relationship with them. No, I will not get a kickback if you order some Instant Mashers.

- **Low-carb tortillas**—These are becoming easier and easier to find. I can get them at every grocery store in town. If you can't buy them at a local store, you can order them online. They keep pretty well. I've had them hang around for 3 or 4 weeks in a sealed bag without getting moldy or stale, so you might want to order more than one package at a time.

  I use La Tortilla Factory brand because they've got the lowest usable carb count of any I've found, just 3 grams. They're mostly made of fiber! Beware: I have recently seen "low-carb" tortillas with deceptive packaging. The listed serving size turned out to equal only half of one tortilla. That's not a serving, as far as I'm concerned!

- **Low-sugar preserves**—In particular, I find low-sugar apricot preserves to be a wonderfully versatile ingredient. I buy Smucker's brand and like it very much. This is lower in sugar by *far* than the "all fruit" preserves, which replace sugar with concentrated fruit juice. Folks, sugar from fruit juice is still sugar. I also have been known to use low-sugar orange marmalade and low-sugar raspberry preserves.

- **Splenda**—Be aware that Splenda granular that comes in bulk, in a box, or in the new "baker's bag" is different than the Splenda that comes in the little packets. The Splenda in the packets is considerably sweeter. One packet equals 2 teaspoons granular Splenda. All these recipes use granular Splenda.

- **Sriracha**—This is a Southeast Asian hot sauce, and it's taking over the world—*Bon Appetit* magazine declared it The Ingredient of the Year for

2010. Find Sriracha in the international aisle of big grocery stores or in Asian markets—look for the bright-red sauce with the rooster on the bottle.

- **Sugar-free imitation honey**—This is a polyol (sugar alcohol) syrup with flavoring added to make it taste like honey. The two brands I've tried, one by HoneyTree and the other by Steele's, are not bad imitations.

  Sugar-free imitation honey is becoming more and more available, and it is a useful product. I can get sugar-free imitation honey here in Bloomington at Sahara Mart, my favorite source of low-carb specialty products, and I've heard from readers that Wal-Mart now carries it. For that matter, many of the low-carb e-tailers carry Steele's brand of imitation honey. It shouldn't be too hard to get your hands on some.

- **Sugar-free pancake syrup**—This is actually easy to find. All my local grocery stores carry it—indeed, many have more than one brand. It's usually with the regular pancake syrup, but it may be shelved with the diabetic or diet foods. It's just like regular pancake syrup, only it's made from polyols (sugar alcohols) instead of sugar. I use it in small quantities in a few recipes to get a maple flavor.

- **Tofu Shirataki**—Finally! There's a genuinely low carb noodle. Shirataki are a traditional Japanese noodle made from a root called kojac or *konyaku*, sometimes mistakenly translated *yam* or *yam bean*. The konjac root is a rich source of a fiber called glucomannan, and it is that glucomannan fiber that forms the bulk of shirataki noodles.

  Shirataki come in two basic varieties: traditional shirataki and tofu shirataki. Traditional shirataki are translucent and gelatinous and very . . . well, Asian. They're good in Asian dishes but pretty weird in Western-style recipes. Tofu shirataki are white, considerably less chewy, and good in a wide variety of applications. My local health food stores carry them in three widths: fettuccini, spaghetti, and angel hair. I keep the fettuccine and spaghetti widths on hand.

  Shirataki come pre-hydrated in a pouch full of liquid. This makes them perfect for our super-quick recipes because you don't have to cook them, only drain and heat them. Snip open the pouch and dump them in a strainer in the sink. You'll notice the liquid smells fishy; you'll want to rinse them. After that, I put them in a microwaveable bowl and give them 90 seconds on high. More liquid will cook out of them, so I drain them again, heat for another

90 seconds, and drain yet a third time; then I add whatever sauce I like. This keeps the liquid cooking out of the noodles from diluting the sauce.

Shirataki keep up to a year in the fridge, so feel free to stock up.

- **Vege-Sal**—If you've read my newsletter, *Lowcarbezine!*, or my previous cookbooks, you know that I'm a big fan of Vege-Sal. It's a salt that's been seasoned, but don't think "seasoned salt." Vege-Sal is much milder than traditional seasoned salt. It's simply salt that's been blended with some dried, powdered vegetables. The flavor is quite subtle, but I think it improves all sorts of things. I've given you the choice between using regular salt or Vege-Sal in many recipes. Don't worry, they'll come out fine with plain old salt, but I do think Vege-Sal adds a little something extra. Vege-Sal is made by Modern Products, and it is available in health food stores.

chapter one

Slow Cooker Snacks and Hot Hors D'oeuvres

Slow cookers are mostly used for cooking dinner while you're out of the house, but they have other uses, such as keeping hors d'oeuvres and dips hot through your whole party! Plus your slow cooker will do the best job of roasting nuts ever. Here are some ways you can make your slow cooker the life of the party.

Glazed Chicken Wings

Put out a pot of these and a big ole pile of napkins and watch your guests eat!

> 3 pounds (1.4 kg) chicken wings
> 1/2 cup (168 g) sugar-free imitation honey
> 1/2 cup (12 g) Splenda
> 1/2 cup (120 ml) soy sauce
> 2 tablespoons (28 ml) oil
> 2 cloves garlic
> 2 tablespoons (28 g) *Dana's No-Sugar Ketchup* (see recipe page 332) or
>   purchased low-carb ketchup

Cut the chicken wings into "drummettes." Season them with salt and pepper and put them in your slow cooker.

In a bowl, stir together the honey, Splenda, soy sauce, oil, garlic, and ketchup. Drizzle the mixture over the wings and stir them to coat. Cover the slow cooker, set it to low, and let it cook for 6 to 8 hours.

Yield: 8 servings, each with: 144 calories, 10 g fat, 10 g protein, 2 g carbohydrate, trace dietary fiber, 2 g usable carbs. (Analysis does not include the polyols in the imitation honey.)

Maple-Mustard Wings

3 pounds (1.3 kg) chicken wings

Salt and pepper

1/4 cup (80 g) sugar-free pancake syrup

1/2 cup (125 g) *Dana's "Kansas City" Barbecue Sauce* (see recipe on page 335)

2 tablespoons (22 g) brown mustard

1 garlic clove, crushed

1 teaspoon lemon juice

If you didn't buy your wings already cut up, cut them into drummettes. (If you stash the bones in the freezer to make bone broth, add the pointy wing tips to the bag; they're wonderful.) Salt and pepper your wings and lay them on your broiler rack. Now broil them, 4 to 5 inches (10 to 13 cm) from the heat, maybe 4 to 5 minutes per side.

While they're broiling, mix together everything else.

When the wings are browned a bit, use tongs to transfer them to the slow cooker. Pour the sauce over them and stir to coat.

Cover the pot, set on low, and let them cook for 4 to 5 hours. Serve from the slow cooker, with plenty of napkins!

Yield: If 5 people share these, each will get: 368 calories, 25 g fat, 28 g protein, 6 g carbohydrate, 1 g dietary fiber, 5 g usable carbs. (Analysis does not include the polyols in the sugar-free pancake syrup.)

Cranberry-Barbecue Meatballs

Boring old ground turkey does a Cinderella turn and comes to the party in this dish!

2 pounds (900 g) ground turkey

2 eggs

4 scallions, minced

2 tablespoons (28 ml) soy sauce

1/4 teaspoon orange extract

1/2 teaspoon pepper

1 teaspoon Splenda

1/4 cup (60 ml) oil

1 cup (250 g) low-carb barbecue sauce (see recipe page 335 or purchase)

1 cup (120 g) cranberries (These are strictly seasonal, but they freeze well.)

1/4 cup (6 g) Splenda

In a big mixing bowl, combine the turkey, eggs, and scallions.

In another bowl, mix together the soy sauce, orange extract, pepper, and 1 teaspoon Splenda and pour into the bowl with the turkey. Now use clean hands to smoosh it all together until it's very well blended. Make 1-inch (2.5 cm) meatballs from the mixture.

Heat half the oil in a big, heavy skillet over medium heat. Brown the meatballs in a few batches, adding the rest of the oil as needed. Transfer the browned meatballs to your slow cooker.

In a blender or food processor with an S-blade, combine the barbecue sauce, cranberries, and 1/4 cup (6 g) Splenda. Run it until the berries are pureed. Pour this mixture over the meatballs. Cover the slow cooker, set to low, and let it cook for 5 to 6 hours. Serve hot from the slow cooker with toothpicks for spearing!

Yield: 48 meatballs, each with: 44 calories, 3 g fat, 4 g protein, 1 g carbohydrate, trace dietary fiber, 1 g usable carbs.

Colombo Meatballs with Jerk Sauce

Colombo is the Caribbean version of curry, and jerk is the notoriously fiery barbecue marinade from Jamaica. The heat of this recipe is best controlled by choosing your hot sauce wisely. Use Tabasco sauce, or Louisiana hot sauce, and they'll be spicy. Use Jamaican Scotch Bonnet sauce, or habanero sauce, and they'll take the top of your head right off!

1 pound (455 g) ground lamb

1 egg

1/4 cup (40 g) minced onion

1/4 teaspoon ground coriander

1/4 teaspoon ground turmeric

1/8 teaspoon anise seed, ground

1 clove garlic, minced

1/4 teaspoon dry mustard

2 teaspoons lemon juice

1/2 teaspoon Splenda

1/2 teaspoon salt

2 tablespoons (28 ml) olive oil

1 bay leaf

1/4 cup (40 g) minced onion

1 teaspoon ground allspice

1 tablespoon (8 g) grated ginger root

1 tablespoon (15 ml) soy sauce

1/4 teaspoon dried thyme

1/4 teaspoon ground cinnamon

1 tablespoon (1.5 g) Splenda

2 cloves garlic, crushed

1/4 cup (60 g) low-carb ketchup

1 tablespoon (15 ml) lemon juice

1 tablespoon (15 ml) lime juice

1 1/2 teaspoons hot sauce

In a big mixing bowl, add the lamb, egg, 1/4 cup (40 g) minced onion, coriander, turmeric, anise seed, minced garlic, dry mustard, 2 teaspoons lemon juice,

$^1/_2$ teaspoon Splenda, and salt. Using clean hands, moosh it all together till it's well blended. Then make 1-inch (2.5 cm) meatballs, pressing them together firmly.

Heat the oil in a big, heavy skillet over medium heat and brown the meatballs in two batches. Drop the bay leaf in the bottom of the slow cooker and then put the meatballs on top of it.

Mix together the second $^1/_4$ cup (40 g) minced onion, the allspice, ginger, soy sauce, thyme, cinnamon, 1 tablespoon (1.5 g) Splenda, crushed garlic, ketchup, 1 tablespoon (15 ml) lemon juice, lime juice, and hot sauce. Pour this sauce evenly over the meatballs. Cover the slow cooker, set it to low, and let it cook for 3 hours. Remove the bay leaf. Serve hot from the slow cooker.

Yield: 35 servings, each with: 48 calories, 4 g fat, 2 g protein, 1 g carbohydrate, trace dietary fiber, 1 g usable carbs.

Easy Party Shrimp

How easy is this? Yet your guests will devour it. If you can't find the crab boil spices in the spice aisle at your grocery store, ask the fish guys. They should know where it is.

> 1 envelope (3 ounces, or 85 g) crab boil spices
> 12 ounces (355 ml) light beer
> 1 tablespoon (18 g) salt or Vege-Sal
> 4 pounds (1.8 kg) easy-peel shrimp or frozen shrimp, unthawed

Drop the crab boil spice net bag in your slow cooker and pour in the beer. Add the salt or Vege-Sal and stir. Add the shrimp. Add just enough water to bring the liquid level up to the top of the shrimp. Cover the slow cooker, set it to high, and let it cook for 1 to 2 hours until the shrimp are pink through. Set the pot to low.

Serve the shrimp straight from the slow cooker with low-carb cocktail sauce, lemon butter, or mustard and mayo stirred together for dipping. Or heck, serve all three. This is enough shrimp for a good-sized party, at least 15 or 20 people, if you're serving it as an hors d'oeuvre/party snack.

Yield: 20 servings, each with: 101 calories, 2 g fat, 18 g protein, 1 g carbohydrate, 0 g dietary fiber, 1 g usable carbs. (Analysis does not include any dipping sauces.)

Zippy Cocktail Dogs

Here's an easy way to jazz up little cocktail wieners.

> ¼ cup (60 g) *Dana's No-Sugar Ketchup* (see recipe page 332) or purchased
> low-carb ketchup
>
> ¼ cup (6 g) Splenda
>
> ½ teaspoon blackstrap molasses
>
> 1 teaspoon Worcestershire sauce
>
> ¼ cup (60 ml) bourbon
>
> ½ pound (225 g) cocktail-size hot dogs

In a large bowl, stir together the ketchup, Splenda, molasses, Worcestershire sauce, and bourbon.

Put the hot dogs in the slow cooker and pour the sauce over them. Cover the slow cooker, set it to low, and let it cook for 2 hours; then uncover and cook for 1 more hour. Serve with toothpicks for spearing.

Note: If you can't get cocktail-size hot dogs, use regular hot dogs cut in chunks. They're not as cute, but they should taste the same!

Yield: 6 servings, each with: 158 calories, 11 g fat, 5 g protein, 4 g carbohydrate, trace dietary fiber, 4 g usable carbs.

Horseradish Smokies

My husband loved these!

> 1 pound (455 g) small smoked sausage links
>
> 1/4 cup (60 g) *Dana's No-Sugar Ketchup* (see recipe page 332) or purchased low-carb ketchup
>
> 1/3 cup (8 g) Splenda
>
> 2 tablespoons (30 g) prepared horseradish
>
> 1/4 teaspoon blackstrap molasses

Put the sausage in your slow cooker.

In a bowl, mix the ketchup, Splenda, horseradish, and molasses. Pour the sauce over the sausage. Stir to coat the sausage. Cover the slow cooker, set it to low, and let it cook for 3 hours. Serve the sausage hot from the slow cooker with toothpicks for spearing.

Yield: 8 servings, each with: 193 calories, 17 g fat, 8 g protein, 1 g carbohydrate, trace dietary fiber, 1 g usable carbs.

Orange Smokies

Put these out at your next Super Bowl party and watch people eat!

> 1 pound (455 g) small smoked sausage links
>
> 1/4 cup (60 g) *Dana's No-Sugar Ketchup* (see recipe page 332) or purchased low-carb ketchup
>
> 1/4 cup (60 ml) lemon juice
>
> 2 tablespoons (3 g) Splenda
>
> 1/4 teaspoon orange extract
>
> 1/4 teaspoon guar or xanthan (optional)

Put the sausage in your slow cooker.

In a small bowl, stir together the ketchup, lemon juice, Splenda, and orange extract. Thicken the mixture just a little, if you think it needs it, with guar or xanthan. Pour the sauce over the sausage. Cover the slow cooker, set it to low, and let it cook for 3 hours. Keep the sausages hot in the slow cooker to serve.

Yield: 8 servings, each with: 193 calories, 17 g fat, 8 g protein, 1 g carbohydrate, trace dietary fiber, 1 g usable carbs.

Tuna and Artichoke Stuffed Mushrooms

I actually came up with this recipe, which was a big hit at my Toastmasters Club Christmas party by the way, because I wanted to figure out the method of baking stuffed mushrooms in a slow cooker. It worked great and frees up your oven for other things. It also lets you get the hot hors d'oeuvres in early, so you can field other pre-party details. You may well find yourself baking all your stuffed mushrooms this way.

1 can (14 ounces, or 390 g) artichoke hearts

3 scallions

1 can (7 ounces, or 200 g) tuna in water, drained

3 ounces (85 g) cream cheese, softened

8 ounces (225 g) shredded Italian cheese blend

3 tablespoons (42 g) mayonnaise

1/2 teaspoon pepper

1/4 cup (15 g) minced fresh parsley

1/4 teaspoon hot sauce or to taste

2 pounds (900 g) mushrooms

Drain and chop the artichoke hearts and throw them in a mixing bowl. Slice up the scallions, including the crisp part of the green shoot, and add them to the bowl. Add the drained tuna. Add the cream cheese, Italian cheese blend, mayo, pepper, parsley, and hot sauce and mash it all up with a fork until everything is evenly blended.

Wipe your mushrooms clean and remove the stems. Reserve the stems for some other purpose, like making an omelet or topping a steak. (Or you could add them to one of the mushrooms recipes in the *Slow Cooker Sides* chapter.) Now stuff the artichoke and tuna mixture into the caps.

Put a basket-type steamer in your slow cooker. Arrange a layer of mushrooms on it. Now take a piece of nonstick aluminum foil, also called *release foil*, and perforate it in several places with a fork to let liquid drip through. Fit it down on top of the first layer of mushrooms. (You'll probably have to make a hole in the middle for the stem of the steamer to poke through.) Put another layer of mushrooms on this. Repeat with a second layer of foil and a third layer of mushrooms. My big slow cooker fit all of my mushrooms in three layers.

Slap on the top, set the cooker to low, and let it go for 4 to 5 hours. You can serve your mushrooms out of the slow cooker if you want to keep them warm, or you can use a spoon to transfer them to a platter.

Yield: This served a party of at least 15 people. Assuming 15 servings, each will have: 142 calories, 10 g fat, 10 g protein, 5 g carbohydrate, 1 g dietary fiber, 4 g usable carbs.

Bacon-Cheese Dip

Bacon and cheese together—it makes you glad to be a low-carber, doesn't it?

16 ounces (455 g) Neufchâtel cheese, softened, or light or regular cream cheese

2 cups (225 g) shredded cheddar cheese

2 cups (230 g) shredded Monterey Jack cheese

1/2 cup (120 ml) Carb Countdown dairy beverage

1/2 cup (120 ml) heavy cream

2 tablespoons (22 g) brown mustard

1 tablespoon (10 g) minced onion

2 teaspoons Worcestershire sauce

1/2 teaspoon salt or Vege-Sal

1/4 teaspoon cayenne

1 pound (455 g) bacon, cooked, drained, and crumbled

Cut the Neufchâtel cheese or cream cheese in cubes and put them in your slow cooker. Add the cheddar cheese, Monterey Jack cheese, Carb Countdown, cream, mustard, onion, Worcestershire sauce, salt or Vege-Sal, and cayenne. Stir to distribute the ingredients evenly. Cover the slow cooker, set it to low, and let it cook for 1 hour, stirring from time to time.

When the cheese has melted, stir in the bacon.

Note: Serve with cut-up vegetables, fiber crackers, or other low-carb dippers.

Yield: 12 servings, each with: 505 calories, 44 g fat, 25 g protein, 2 g carbohydrate, trace dietary fiber, 2 g usable carbs. (Analysis is exclusive of dippers.)

Awesome Sauce aka Provolone and Blue Cheese Fondue

That Nice Boy I Married took one bite and said "Awesomesauce!" And so it is. This can be a party snack, but we like it as a light supper.

        6 ounces (170 g) cream cheese

        12 ounces (340 g) provolone cheese

        4 ounces (115 g) blue cheese

        1 clove garlic

        ½ cup (120 ml) heavy cream

        ½ cup (120 ml) dry white wine

Crush the garlic and put it in the bottom of the slow cooker. Cube the cream cheese and put it in. Then cube the provolone, put that on top of the cream cheese, and add half the blue cheese on that. Add the heavy cream and wine, cover the pot, set to low, and let it cook for a good two hours.

Open up the slow cooker. You will find a gloppy mess. Do not panic. Take your stick blender and blend it until the whole thing is smooth. That's it. It now will keep for at least a couple of hours on low or on the serve setting. When you're ready, set out the slow cooker of *Awesome Sauce*, plus veggies to dip. We dipped with green pepper strips, blanched asparagus, canned quartered artichoke hearts, well-drained, and marinated mushrooms, but I can think of a dozen more veggies that would be good with this. Indeed, it's hard to think of anything that wouldn't be good with this!

Yield: If 12 people share this, each will get: 224 calories, 19 g fat, 11 g protein, 2 g carbohydrate, trace dietary fiber, 2 g usable carbs. (Analysis is exclusive of vegetables.)

Bagna Cauda

The name of this traditional Italian dip means "hot bath," and that's just what it is—a bath of hot, flavored olive oil to dip your vegetables in. Believe it or not, our tester Maria Vander Vloedt's kids really liked this!

    1 cup (235 ml) extra-virgin olive oil
    ¼ cup (55 g) butter
    3 cloves garlic, minced
    2 ounces (55 g) canned anchovies, minced

Combine everything in a small slow cooker. Cover the slow cooker, set it to low, and let it cook for 1 hour.

Note: Serve with vegetables. Fennel, pepper strips, cauliflower, mushrooms, celery, canned artichoke hearts, and lightly steamed asparagus are all traditional choices.

Yield: Per batch: 2448 calories, 267 g fat, 17 g protein, 3 g carbohydrate, trace dietary fiber, 3 g usable carbs. (It's hard to know how to divide this into servings, and it's unlikely you'll end up eating it all, even with a big group. After all, you can't scoop up a tablespoon (15 ml) at a time of hot olive oil. So here's the stats for the whole potful. Notice that carb count!)

Hot Artichoke Dip

This is my slow cooker version of the ubiquitous hot artichoke dip that appeared in *500 Low-Carb Recipes*. Using a slow cooker, the dip stays hot till it's gone!

    1 cup (225 g) mayonnaise

    1 cup (100 g) grated Parmesan cheese

    1 clove garlic, crushed

    8 ounces (225 g) shredded mozzarella cheese

    1 can (14 ounces, or 390 g) artichoke hearts, drained and chopped

Add everything to your slow cooker, stir it up well, and smooth the surface. Cover the slow cooker, set it to low, and let it cook for 2 to 3 hours.

Serve with low-carb crackers and/or cut-up vegetables.

Yield: 8 servings, each with: 339 calories, 33 g fat, 11 g protein, 2 g carbohydrate, 1 g dietary fiber, 1 g usable carbs. (Analysis is exclusive of crackers and vegetables.)

Hot Crab Dip

Hot crab, hot cheese, garlic—what's not to like?

    1 cup (225 g) mayonnaise

    8 ounces (225 g) shredded cheddar cheese

    4 scallions, minced

    1 can (6 ounces, or 170 g) crabmeat, drained

    1 clove garlic, crushed

    3 ounces (85 g) cream cheese, softened, cut into chunks

Combine everything in your slow cooker and stir together. Cover the slow cooker, set it to low, and let it cook for 1 hour. Remove the lid and stir to blend in the now-melted cream cheese. Re-cover and cook for another hour.

Serve with celery, pepper, and cucumber dippers.

Yield: 8 servings, each with: 372 calories, 37 g fat, 13 g protein, 1 g carbohydrate, trace dietary fiber, 1 g usable carbs. (Analysis is exclusive of vegetables.)

Artichoke-Spinach-Ranch Dip

Artichoke dip, spinach dip, and ranch dip are all so popular, combining them seemed destined for greatness!

1 can (14 ounces, or 390 g) artichoke hearts, drained and chopped

1 package (10 ounces, or 280 g) frozen chopped spinach, thawed and drained

1 cup (225 g) mayonnaise

1 cup (230 g) sour cream

1 packet (1 ounce, or 28 g) ranch-style dressing mix

2 cups (160 g) shredded Parmesan cheese

1 clove garlic, crushed

Spray your slow cooker with nonstick spray. Mix everything together in your slow cooker. Cover, set it to low, and let it cook for 3 to 4 hours. Keep the dip hot in the slow cooker to serve.

Note: Serve dip with cut-up vegetables or low-carb crackers.

Yield: 12 servings, each with: 247 calories, 23 g fat, 7 g protein, 4 g carbohydrate, 1 g dietary fiber, 3 g usable carbs. (Analysis is exclusive of vegetables and crackers.)

Buffalo Wing Dip

I wanted to come up with a hot dip that had all the flavors of Buffalo wings. This is how it came out, and it's awesome!

> 1 pound (455 g) cream cheese at room temperature
>
> 4 ounces (115 g) crumbled blue cheese
>
> 4 scallions, minced
>
> 2 garlic cloves, crushed
>
> 1 teaspoon Worcestershire sauce
>
> 1 cup (225 g) cooked chicken, minced
>
> ½ cup (120 ml) Buffalo wing sauce

Turn on the slow cooker set to low and put the cream cheese in it. Dump in the blue cheese, too.

Mince your scallions fine—I used my food processor. Add them to the cheeses and crush in the garlic. Add the Worcestershire, too.

Mince your chicken quite fine. I used two skinned chicken leg and thigh quarters that I simply covered with water in my slow cooker and let cook on high for 3 to 4 hours. (I did this earlier in the day.) I stripped the meat off the bone and used my kitchen shears to snip across the grain, so it naturally came apart into little bits. If you don't want to work that hard, you could use canned chunk chicken, I bet—just drain it and mash it up good. Anyway, stir your teeny bits of chicken into the cheese mixture, which should be getting soft by now. Make sure it's all well blended and then put the top on the pot and let the whole thing cook for 3 to 4 hours.

An hour before your party, pour the buffalo wing sauce—I used *Wing Time* brand— evenly over the cheese mixture and re-cover the pot. Let it cook for that last hour and then serve with celery sticks for dipping.

Yield: This will serve a whole party, call it 15 people. Each will get: 164 calories, 14 g fat, 7 g protein, 2 g carbohydrate, 5 g usable carbs. (Analysis is exclusive of celery.)

Chicken Liver Pâté

If you like chicken livers, you'll like this, but you won't if you don't. I adore them myself and practically lived on pâté on fiber crackers for a few days after making this. You could also stuff this into celery stalks.

1/2 cup (80 g) finely chopped onion

1 clove garlic, crushed

1 cup (70 g) sliced mushrooms

3 tablespoons (45 g) butter

1 pound (455 g) chicken livers

2 tablespoons (28 ml) heavy cream

2 tablespoons (28 ml) brandy

1 bay leaf, crumbled

1/2 teaspoon dried thyme

1/2 teaspoon dried marjoram

1 tablespoon (4 g) chopped fresh parsley

3/4 teaspoon salt or Vege-Sal

1/2 teaspoon pepper

In a big, heavy skillet, start the onion, garlic, and mushrooms sautéing in the butter over low heat. While that's happening, halve the chicken livers where they naturally divide into two lobes. When the mushrooms have softened and changed color, add the livers and sauté, stirring occasionally, until they're sealed all over and the color of the surface has changed but they are not cooked through. Transfer the mixture to a food processor with the S-blade in place.

Add the cream, brandy, bay leaf, thyme, marjoram, parsley, salt or Vege-Sal, and pepper. Run the food processor until the mixture is finely pureed.

Spray a 3- or 4-cup (700 or 950 ml) glass casserole dish with nonstick cooking spray. Pour the mixture from the food processor into the casserole dish. Place the casserole dish in your slow cooker. Carefully pour water around the casserole dish to within 1 inch (2.5 cm) of the rim. Cover the slow cooker, set it to low, and let it cook for 8 hours or until the mixture is well set. Turn off the slow cooker and let the water cool until you can remove the casserole dish without risk of scalding your fingers. Remove the casserole dish and chill the pâté overnight before serving.

You can simply scoop this from the casserole dish with a knife and spread it on fiber crackers if you like, but it's fancier to turn it out, slice it, and serve it on a bed of greens.

Yield: 8 servings, each with: 138 calories, 8 g fat, 11 g protein, 4 g carbohydrate, trace dietary fiber, 4 g usable carbs.

Roasted Nuts and Seeds

I was astounded by how great a job my slow cooker did of roasting nuts! I got a little carried away, I confess. But then, I really like nuts! Make these often and keep them on hand, and you'll find yourself missing both chips and candy a whole lot less. This is one job where the size of the slow cooker matters. Use a 3-quart (2.8 liters) or, if you have a 5½-quart (5 liters) cooker, double the recipe.

Dana's Snack Mix, Slow Cooker–Style

This is similar to a snack mix that appears in *500 Low-Carb Recipes*, and it's addictive. Thank goodness it's also healthy! You'll likely find shelled pumpkin seeds and raw, shelled sunflower seeds at your health food store. You can also find the pumpkin seeds in Latino groceries, labeled "pepitas."

4 tablespoons (55 g) butter, melted

3 tablespoons (45 ml) Worcestershire sauce

1½ teaspoons garlic powder

2½ teaspoons seasoned salt

2 teaspoons onion powder

2 cups (276 g) raw pumpkin seeds, shelled

1 cup (145 g) raw sunflower seeds, shelled

1 cup (145 g) raw almonds

1 cup (100 g) raw pecans

1 cup (120 g) raw walnut pieces

1 cup (140 g) raw cashews

1 cup (145 g) dry-roasted peanuts

If you've got a little time, you can just put the butter in the slow cooker, turn it to low, and wait for it to melt. Otherwise, melt it on the stove or in the microwave and then transfer it to the slow cooker pot. Add the Worcestershire sauce, garlic powder, seasoned salt, and onion powder. Stir it all together. Add the nuts and seeds. Stir well until all the nuts are evenly coated. Cover the slow cooker, set it to low, and let it cook for 5 to 6 hours, stirring once or twice if you're around.

Uncover the pot, stir the nut and seed mix up, and cook for another 45 to 60 minutes to dry the nuts and seeds. Let them cool before storing them in an airtight container.

Yield: 24 servings of 1/3 cup, each with: 279 calories, 25 g fat, 9 g protein, 9 g carbohydrate, 3 g dietary fiber, 6 g usable carbs.

Blue Cheese Dressing Walnuts

I originally wanted to make these with powdered blue cheese dressing mix, only to find that there is no such thing, at least not in my grocery stores. So I tried using liquid dressing instead. It didn't end up tasting a lot like blue cheese, but it did end up tasting really good.

> 4 cups (400 g) walnuts
> 1/2 cup (115 g) blue cheese salad dressing
> 1 teaspoon garlic salt

Combine the walnuts and dressing in your slow cooker. Stir until the nuts are evenly coated with the dressing. Cover the slow cooker, set it to low, and let it cook for 3 hours, stirring once halfway through.

Stir in the garlic salt just before serving.

Yield: 16 servings, each with: 228 calories, 22 g fat, 8 g protein, 4 g carbohydrate, 2 g dietary fiber, 2 g usable carbs.

Cajun-Spiced Pecans

You can used purchased Cajun seasoning for this or make your own from the recipe on page 339.

> 1 pound (455 g) pecan halves
> 2 tablespoons (28 g) butter, melted
> 3 tablespoons (27 g) Cajun seasoning

Place the pecans in your slow cooker. Stir in the butter to coat the pecans. Add the Cajun seasoning and stir again to coat. Cover the slow cooker, set it to low, and let it cook for 3 hours, stirring once halfway through if you are around.

Yield: 16 servings, each with: 118 calories, 12 g fat, 1 g protein, 4 g carbohydrate, 1 g dietary fiber, 3 g usable carbs.

Candied Pecans

These are a great treat to leave around in pretty little dishes at a holiday party.

> 1 pound (455 g) pecan halves
> 1/2 cup (112 g) butter, melted
> 1/2 cup (12 g) Splenda
> 11/2 teaspoons ground cinnamon
> 1/4 teaspoon ground ginger
> 1/4 teaspoon ground allspice

Put the pecans in your slow cooker and stir in the melted butter, coating the pecans thoroughly. Sprinkle the Splenda, cinnamon, ginger, and allspice over the pecans and stir again to coat.

Cover the slow cooker, set it to high, let it cook for 30 minutes. Then uncover, turn it to low, and let it cook for 1 1/2 to 2 hours, stirring once or twice.

Yield: 8 servings, each with: 304 calories, 32 g fat, 2 g protein, 6 g carbohydrate, 3 g dietary fiber, 3 g usable carbs.

Kickin' Pecans

This isn't enough cayenne to be really hot, just enough to add a little kick. Hence the name.

> 3 cups (300 g) pecan halves
>
> 1 egg white
>
> 1 teaspoon cinnamon
>
> 1/2 teaspoon salt
>
> 1/4 teaspoon cayenne, or more to taste
>
> 1 cup (25 g) Splenda

Put the pecans in your slow cooker. Add the egg white and stir until the pecans are evenly coated.

In a bowl, stir together the cinnamon, salt, cayenne, and Splenda. Pour the mixture over the pecans and stir until they're evenly coated. Cover the slow cooker, set it to low, and let it cook for 3 hours, stirring every hour or so.

If the nuts aren't dry by the end of the 3 hours, uncover the slow cooker, stir, and cook for another 30 minutes until dry. Store in an airtight container.

Yield: 9 servings, each with: 242 calories, 24 g fat, 3 g protein, 7 g carbohydrate, 3 g dietary fiber, 4 g usable carbs.

Curried Pecans

These are astonishingly good. I may make them in quantity and give them away for Christmas this year!

> 3 tablespoons (45 g) butter
>
> 1/4 teaspoon blackstrap molasses
>
> 1 1/2 teaspoons curry powder
>
> 1/4 teaspoon salt
>
> 1/4 teaspoon ground cumin
>
> 12 ounces (340 g) pecan halves
>
> 2 tablespoons (3 g) Splenda

In a big, heavy skillet, melt the butter over medium-low heat. Stir in the molasses, curry powder, salt, and cumin and cook for just a minute or two.

Add the pecans and stir until they're evenly coated with the butter and seasonings. Then transfer them to your slow cooker. Sprinkle the Splenda over the pecans, stirring as you sprinkle, so you coat them evenly. Cover the slow cooker, set it to low, and let it cook for 2 to 3 hours, stirring once or twice during the cooking time.

Yield: 9 servings, each with: 169 calories, 17 g fat, 2 g protein, 4 g carbohydrate, 2 g dietary fiber, 2 g usable carbs.

Smokin' Chili Peanuts

Oh, my goodness. These are hot and crunchy and just too darned good. But they're not for the faint of heart.

> 1/4 cup (55 g) butter, melted
>
> 2 tablespoons (16 g) chili powder
>
> 1 tablespoon (15 ml) liquid smoke flavoring
>
> 1 jar (24 ounces, or 680 g) salted, dry-roasted peanuts

In your slow cooker, combine the butter, chili powder, and liquid smoke flavoring. Stir them together well. Add the peanuts and stir them until they're evenly coated with the butter and the seasonings. Cover the slow cooker, set it to low, and let it cook for 2 to 2 1/2 hours.

Remove the lid, stir, and let cook for another 30 minutes or until the peanuts are dry. Store them in the original jar!

Yield: 24 servings, each with: 185 calories, 16 g fat, 7 g protein, 6 g carbohydrate, 2 g dietary fiber, 4 g usable carbs.

Chili Garlic Peanuts

These Spanish-influenced peanuts make the perfect nibble with drinks.

> 2 tablespoons (28 g) bacon grease
>
> 3 cups raw (435 g) Spanish peanuts
>
> 2 teaspoons ancho chili powder
>
> 1/4 teaspoon cayenne
>
> 10 cloves garlic, crushed
>
> 1 teaspoon salt
>
> 1 tablespoon (15 ml) lime juice

Melt the bacon grease and dump it into your slow cooker (or put it in and turn the slow cooker on for a while). Then add the peanuts and stir to coat.

Now add the ancho chili powder, cayenne, and all that yummy garlic. Stir it all up well. Cover, set to low, and let cook for 45 to 60 minutes. Go stir, re-cover, and give them another 45 to 60 minutes. Then try one for doneness. If they're still underdone, give them another half hour, but if they're pretty done, go on to your next step.

When they're roasty and crunchy, stir in the salt and lime juice, making sure all the peanuts are coated. Leave the lid off and give them another 15 minutes. Stir and let them go a final fifteen minutes—you're just drying that lime juice.

Eat them warm or store in a snap-top container.

Yield: 12 servings, each with: 232 calories, 20 g fat, 10 g protein, 7 g carbohydrate, 3 g dietary fiber, 4 g usable carbs.

Asian Peanuts

1 tablespoon (15 g) coconut oil

24 ounces (680 g) raw peanuts

1/4 cup (60 ml) soy sauce

1 tablespoon (15 g) erythritol or xylitol

Put the coconut oil in the slow cooker and turn it on to low. Let the coconut oil melt. (If you're feeling impatient, you could just zap the coconut oil for a minute in your microwave before putting it in the pot.)

Dump in the peanuts and stir to coat with the oil.

Now add the soy sauce and erythritol, sprinkling each in as you stir. Keep stirring until everything's evenly coated. Cover the pot and let the peanuts roast for 3 to 4 hours, uncovering and stirring every hour or so.

Then uncover the pot and cook for another 40 to 60 minutes, stirring every 15 to 20 minutes, until the peanuts are dry. Cool and store in a snap-top container.

Yield: 24 servings of 1 ounce (28 g), each with: 167 calories, 15 g fat, 7 g protein, 5 g carbohydrate, 2 g dietary fiber, 3 g usable carbs.

Sweet and Salty Peanuts

Sweet and salty is a fantastic combination!

> 2 tablespoons (28 g) coconut oil
>
> 3 cups (435 g) raw peanuts
>
> 1/4 cup (60 g) erythritol or xylitol
>
> 1 teaspoon salt

Melt the coconut oil and pour into the slow cooker. Alternatively, put it in, switch the cooker on to high, and cover while the coconut oil melts.

Then add the peanuts and stir until they're evenly coated. Sprinkle the erythritol over the peanuts and again stir until everything is evenly coated.

Cover the pot and set to high if it isn't on yet. Set a timer for 1 hour. When it beeps, stir the peanuts well, making sure to scoop all the ones on the bottom and sides into the mass—this helps promote even cooking. Re-cover the pot and give them another hour.

Sprinkle with the salt and stir well again. Re-cover and let them cook for another 30 minutes to an hour until the nuts are crunchy and done through. Let them cool and store in a tightly lidded container.

Yield: 12 servings, each with: 227 calories, 20 g fat, 9 g protein, 6 g carbohydrate, 3 g dietary fiber, 3 g usable carbs.

Butter-Spice Almonds

3 cups (435 g) almonds

2 tablespoons (28 g) butter, melted

2 teaspoons vanilla extract

2 teaspoons butter-flavored extract

1/2 cup (12 g) Splenda

1 teaspoon ground cinnamon

1/4 teaspoon salt

Put the almonds in your slow cooker.

In a bowl, stir together the butter, vanilla extract, and butter-flavored extract until well combined. Pour the mixture over the almonds and stir to coat. Add the Splenda, cinnamon, and salt and stir to coat again. Cover the slow cooker, set it to low, and let it cook for 4 to 5 hours, stirring once or twice.

When the time's up, uncover the slow cooker, stir the almonds again, and let them cook for another 30 to 45 minutes. Store in an airtight container.

Yield: 6 servings, each with: 457 calories, 41 g fat, 14 g protein, 15 g carbohydrate, 8 g dietary fiber, 7 g usable carbs.

Buttery Vanilla Almonds

4 tablespoons (55 g) butter

2 teaspoons vanilla

3 tablespoons (45 g) erythritol or xylitol

¼ teaspoon salt

3 cups (435 g) almonds

Turn on the slow cooker and throw in the butter to melt. (Alternatively, melt the butter in your microwave and pour it in.) When the butter is melted, add the vanilla, erythritol, and salt and stir the whole thing until it's well-blended.

Now dump in the almonds and stir until they're all evenly coated. Set the slow cooker to low, cover, and set a timer for 1 hour. When the timer beeps, stir the almonds well, making sure to scoop them up from the bottom and off the sides. Re-cover and reset the timer for another hour. Repeat until your almonds have cooked 3 to 4 hours. Then cool and store in a tightly lidded container.

Yield: 12 servings, each with: 245 calories, 22 g fat, 7 g protein, 7 g carbohydrate, 4 g dietary fiber, 3 g usable carbs.

Maple-Glazed Walnuts

    3 cups (300 g) walnuts

    1 1/2 teaspoons ground cinnamon

    1 tablespoon (14 g) butter, melted

    1/4 teaspoon salt

    2 teaspoons vanilla extract

    1/3 cup (107 g) sugar-free pancake syrup

    1/3 cup (8 g) Splenda

Put the walnuts in your slow cooker.

In a bowl, mix together the cinnamon, butter, salt, vanilla extract, pancake syrup, and 1/4 cup (6 g) of the Splenda. Pour the mixture over the nuts and stir to coat. Cover the slow cooker, set it to low, and let it cook for 2 to 3 hours, stirring every hour or so.

Then uncover the slow cooker and cook, stirring every 20 minutes, until the nuts are almost dry. Stir in the remaining 2 tablespoons (3 g) Splenda, cook for another 20 minutes, and then remove from the slow cooker and cool. Store in an airtight container.

Yield: 9 servings, each with: 268 calories, 25 g fat, 10 g protein, 6 g carbohydrate, 2 g dietary fiber, 4 g usable carbs. (Analysis does not include the polyols in the sugar-free pancake syrup.)

Spiced Walnuts

Spicy and sweet, these walnuts are nothing short of addictive. They'd make a nice little nibble to pass around after supper, instead of a dessert.

2 tablespoons (28 g) coconut oil

1 teaspoon ground ginger

1 teaspoon curry powder

1/2 teaspoon cayenne

1/4 teaspoon onion powder

1/4 teaspoon garlic powder

1/2 teaspoon salt

1/4 cup (60 g) erythritol or xylitol

3 cups (300 g) shelled walnuts

Melt the coconut oil and pour it into the slow cooker (or throw it in solid, turn on the pot, and let it sit until it melts).

In the meantime, mix together all the seasonings and the erythritol.

When the oil is melted, dump the walnuts in the pot. Stir until they're evenly coated with the oil. Now sprinkle in the seasoning blend as you stir; keep stirring until they're evenly coated. Cover the pot, set for high, and set a timer for 1 hour.

When the timer beeps, stir the nuts, re-cover the pot, and set the timer for another hour. When it beeps again, check for doneness.

When they're crunchy and toasty, cool them and store in snap-top containers.

Yield: 12 servings, each with: 182 calories, 18 g fat, 4 g protein, 5 g carbohydrate, 1 g dietary fiber, 4 g usable carbs.

chapter two

Slow Cooker Eggs

Why should you cook eggs in your slow cooker? The answer is because sometimes you want a brunch dish that you can put in to cook and forget about while you do other things—and that will stay warm while people serve themselves. And it's also because eggs ain't just for breakfast anymore.

By the way, all of these recipes except the *Tuna Egg Casserole* can be halved if you're only serving four or five people. In that case, give them 1 hour on high and 2 to 3 on low.

Maria's Eggs Florentine

Our tester, Maria, came up with this recipe herself.

> 2 cups (225 g) shredded cheddar cheese, divided
>
> 1 package (10 ounces, or 280 g) frozen chopped spinach, thawed and drained
>
> 1 can (8 ounces, or 225 g) mushrooms, drained
>
> 1/4 cup (25 g) chopped onion
>
> 6 eggs, beaten
>
> 1 cup (235 ml) heavy cream
>
> 1 teaspoon black pepper
>
> 1/2 teaspoon Italian seasoning
>
> 1/2 teaspoon garlic powder

Spray your slow cooker with nonstick cooking spray. Spread 1 cup (115 grams) of the cheese on the bottom of the slow cooker. Layer the spinach, mushrooms, and onion.

In a bowl, combine the egg, cream, pepper, Italian seasoning, and garlic powder. Pour the mixture into the slow cooker. Top with the remaining 1 cup (115 grams) cheese. Cover the slow cooker, set it to high, and let it cook for 2 hours or until the center is set.

Yield: 4 servings, each with: 568 calories, 48 g fat, 27 g protein, 10 g carbohydrate, 4 g dietary fiber, 6 g usable carbs.

⌷ Artichoke Egg Casserole

Look at this! It's has artichokes, sun-dried tomatoes, bacon, and cheese!
You know you want it!

    12 eggs

    2 cups (450 g) creamed cottage cheese

    2 cans (14 ounces, or 390 g each) artichoke hearts, drained and chopped

    2 bunches scallions, sliced, including the crisp part of the green

    12 sun-dried tomato halves, chopped

    12 slices bacon, cooked crisp and crumbled

    3 cups (345 g) shredded Italian cheese blend

    4 teaspoons (4 g) dried basil

    4 cloves garlic, crushed

Coat your slow cooker with nonstick cooking spray. Turn on to high while you mix
this up. Let it heat.

This is simple. You just throw everything in a mixing bowl and whisk it up. Pour it
into the heated slow cooker and cover. Let it cook for 2 hours on high and then turn it
down to low and give it another 3 hours. That's all there is to it!

Yield: 8 servings, each with: 266 calories, 13 g fat, 23 g protein, 15 g carbohydrate, 2 g
dietary fiber, 13 g usable carbs.

Tuna Egg Casserole

This is sort of a cross between traditional tuna casserole and a quiche.

> 8 ounces (225 g) sliced mushrooms
>
> 1/2 onion, chopped
>
> 2 tablespoons (28 g) butter
>
> 6 eggs
>
> 1 cup (225 g) creamed cottage cheese
>
> 1/2 teaspoon salt or Vege-Sal
>
> 1/4 teaspoon pepper
>
> 1 can (12 ounces, or 340 g) tuna in water
>
> 1 cup (130 g) frozen peas
>
> 4 ounces (115 g) shredded Cheddar cheese

In your big, heavy skillet, over medium heat, start the mushrooms and onions sautéing in the butter. Use the edge of your spatula to chop the mushrooms into smaller bits as you stir.

Add the eggs and cottage cheese, plus the salt and pepper, and whisk them together.

Go stir your mushrooms and onions!

Open and drain your tuna and dump it in the egg mixture. Add the peas, too.

When your mushrooms are soft and your onion translucent, dump them in the slow cooker. Dump the egg and cheese mixture over it and stir it together. Now sprinkle the cheese over the top.

Cover the slow cooker, set to high, and give it an hour. Then turn it down to low, give it another 2 to 3 hours, and serve.

Yield: 5 servings, each with: 371 calories, 20 g fat, 37 g protein, 9 g carbohydrate, 2 g dietary fiber, 7 g usable carbs.

Note: Chunk light tuna is not only cheaper than white, but it's far less likely to be contaminated with mercury.

Broccoli-Bacon-Colby Quiche

This crustless quiche is wonderful, but feel free to make any quiche recipe you've got, minus the crust, in the same way. For this recipe, I use broccoli cuts that are bigger than chopped broccoli but smaller than florets, and I think they're ideal.

> 2 cups (312 g) frozen broccoli florets, thawed and coarsely chopped, or a bag of broccoli cuts
>
> 2 cups (225 g) shredded Colby cheese
>
> 6 slices cooked bacon
>
> 4 eggs
>
> 2 cups (475 ml) Carb Countdown dairy beverage
>
> 1 teaspoon salt or Vege-Sal
>
> 1 teaspoon dry mustard
>
> 2 teaspoons prepared horseradish
>
> 1/4 teaspoon pepper

Spray a 1 1/2-quart (1.4 L) glass casserole dish with nonstick cooking spray.

Put the broccoli in the bottom of the casserole dish. Spread the cheese evenly on top of the broccoli and crumble the bacon evenly over the cheese.

In a bowl, whisk together the eggs, Carb Countdown, salt or Vege-Sal, dry mustard, horseradish, and pepper and pour it over the broccoli in the casserole dish.

Place the casserole dish in your slow cooker and carefully pour water around the casserole dish to within 1 inch (2.5 cm) of the rim. Cover the slow cooker, set it to low, and let it cook for 4 hours.

Then turn off the slow cooker, uncover it, and let the water cool until you can remove the casserole dish without risk of scalding your fingers. Serve hot or at room temperature.

Yield: 6 servings, each with: 292 calories, 21 g fat, 20 g protein, 6 g carbohydrate, 2 g dietary fiber, 4 g usable carbs.

Chili Egg Puff Slow Cooker Style

Chili Egg Puff showed up in *500 Low Carb Recipes*; it is a brunch dish that causes nostalgic drooling when mentioned to those who have tried it. And if you buy pre-shredded cheese, it takes about three minutes to put together—maybe five if you have to shred your cheese yourself. So I figured I needed to slow-cooker-ize it.

    12 eggs

    2 cups (450 g) creamed cottage cheese

    2 cans (4 ounces, or 115 g each) diced green chiles

    1 teaspoon salt

    1/2 teaspoon pepper

    16 ounces (455 g) shredded Monterey Jack cheese

Coat your slow cooker with nonstick cooking spray. Turn it on to high and let it heat while you whisk everything else together. Pour into the slow cooker, cover, and let it cook on high for a couple of hours. Turn down to low and let it cook another 3 hours.

Yield: 8 servings, each with: 363 calories, 25 g fat, 30 g protein, 4 g carbohydrate, trace dietary fiber, 4 g usable carbs.

Crab Puff

I made this for a friend and her family when she was ill. They all thought it was the best "quiche" they'd ever had.

> 2 leeks
>
> 2 tablespoons (28 g) butter
>
> 2 cups (450 g) creamed cottage cheese
>
> 12 eggs
>
> 1 tablespoon (9 g) dry mustard
>
> 1 teaspoon salt or Vege-Sal
>
> 1/2 teaspoon pepper
>
> 1 teaspoon Tabasco sauce or to taste
>
> 1/2 cup (50 g) grated Parmesan cheese
>
> 1 can (12 ounces, or 340 g) crabmeat, drained
>
> 2 cups (230 g) shredded Monterey Jack cheese

Trim the leaves and the root off your leeks and split them the long way. Rinse them well, getting in between the layers where the dirt tends to lurk. Then lay them on your cutting board and slice them thinly into half-rounds.

Over medium-low heat, melt the butter in your big, heavy skillet and start sautéing the leeks.

In the meantime, measure the cottage cheese into a big mixing bowl and crack in the eggs. Add the mustard, salt, pepper, Tabasco, and Parmesan and whisk until it's well-blended.

Don't forget to stir your leeks from time to time!

When the leeks are softened, add them to the mixing bowl along with the crab and stir them both in well.

Coat your slow cooker with nonstick cooking spray and pour in half the egg and cheese mixture. Sprinkle half of the Monterey Jack evenly over this, add the rest of the egg mixture, and top with the rest of the cheese. Cover the pot and set to high.

I gave mine 2 hours on high and then turned it down to low and gave it another two, but you could turn it down after one hour and let it go 4 hours on low.

Yield: 8 servings, each with: 319 calories, 21 g fat, 26 g protein, 7 g carbohydrate, trace dietary fiber, 7 g usable carbs.

Slow Cooker Poultry

Here you will find roughly a billion ways to fix chicken and some ideas for turkey, too! You'll notice that many (but not all) of these recipes call for the poultry to be skinless. This is because the skin usually doesn't end up very tasty or interesting when moist-cooked as it is in a slow cooker.

I've often specified light meat or dark meat—breasts versus thighs. This is just what appealed to me. Feel free to use whichever you like best or what's on sale. Often it's cheapest to buy a whole cut-up chicken and strip the skin off yourself at home. That's fine, too—just remove any obvious globs of fat so your sauce doesn't end up greasy.

Chicken Burritos

Wow. This is easy, delicious, low-carb, low-calorie, and reheats easily.
What more do you want from a recipe?

2½ pounds (1.1 kg) boneless, skinless chicken thighs

5 cloves garlic, crushed

2 tablespoons (16 g) chili powder

2 tablespoons (28 ml) olive oil

2 tablespoons (28 ml) lime juice

1 teaspoon salt

1 large jalapeño, minced, or 2 teaspoons canned jalapeños

12 low-carb tortillas, 6-inch

1 cup (72 g) shredded lettuce

1 cup (120 g) shredded cheddar cheese

2/3 cup (154 g) light sour cream

3/4 cup (195 g) salsa

1/2 cup (8 g) chopped fresh cilantro (optional)

Place the chicken in your slow cooker.

In a bowl, mix the garlic, chili powder, oil, lime juice, salt, and jalapeño together. Pour over the chicken and stir to coat. Cover the slow cooker, set it to low, and let it cook for 10 hours. (Or cook on high for 5 hours.)

When the time's up, stir the mixture with a fork to reduce the chicken to a big pot of tasty chicken shreds. Fill each tortilla with 1/3 cup (79 g) chicken and top with lettuce, cheese, 1 tablespoon (15 g) sour cream, a generous tablespoon (16 g) salsa, and a sprinkling of cilantro if desired. Wrap and devour!

This is a great meal for a family that has some low-carbers and some non–low-carbers, just give them regular or (preferably) whole wheat flour tortillas. The chicken keeps well in the fridge and reheats quickly in the microwave for a fast snack. (I find that 45 seconds on 70 percent power is about right for a 1/3-cup (85 g) serving.)

Yield: 12 servings, each with: 225 calories, 13 g fat, 22 g protein, 14 g carbohydrate, 9 g dietary fiber, 5 g usable carbs.

Seriously Simple Chicken Chili

The name says it all!

> 2 pounds (900 g) boneless, skinless chicken breasts
>
> 1 jar (16 ounces, or 455 g) prepared salsa
>
> 1 tablespoon (8 g) chili powder
>
> 1 teaspoon chicken bouillon concentrate
>
> 3 ounces (85 g) shredded Monterey Jack cheese
>
> 6 tablespoons (90 g) light sour cream

Put the chicken in your slow cooker.

In a bowl, stir together the salsa, chili powder, and bouillon, making sure the bouillon's dissolved. Pour the mixture over the chicken. Cover the slow cooker, set it to low, and let it cook for 7 to 8 hours.

When the time's up, shred the chicken with a fork. Serve topped with the cheese and sour cream.

Yield: 6 servings, each with: 263 calories, 9 g fat, 39 g protein, 6 g carbohydrate, 2 g dietary fiber, 4 g usable carbs.

Chicken Chili Verde

This repeat from *15-Minute Low-Carb Recipes* is marvelous, and it's a really nice change from the traditional beef chili.

1¹/2 pounds (680 g) boneless, skinless chicken breasts

1¹/2 cups (384 g) prepared salsa verde

¹/2 medium onion, chopped

1 bay leaf

¹/2 teaspoon pepper

1 teaspoon ground cumin

1 teaspoon minced garlic or 2 cloves garlic, crushed

1 to 2 tablespoons (9 to 18 g) jarred, sliced jalapeño (I use 2 tablespoons (18 g), and it makes the chili pretty hot.)

2 teaspoons chicken bouillon concentrate

Guar or xanthan (optional)

Sour cream

Shredded Monterey Jack cheese

Chopped fresh cilantro

Place the chicken in your slow cooker and add the salsa verde, onion, bay leaf, pepper, cumin, garlic, jalapeños, and bouillon on top. Cover the slow cooker, set it to low, and let it cook for 9 to 10 hours.

When the time's up, shred the chicken with a fork. Stir it up, thicken the chili a little with the guar or xanthan if you think it needs it, and serve with sour cream, cheese, and cilantro on top.

Yield: 5 servings, each with: 190 calories, 2 g fat, 32 g protein, 7 g carbohydrate, trace dietary fiber, 7 g usable carbs. (Analysis does not include garnishes.)

Mean Old Rooster Chili

The name is no joke. We keep chickens, and I had a rooster who was a nasty, aggressive thing. We got tired of it and turned him into food. He was too old to be roasted or grilled, so I stewed him up and made him into this chili, a form in which he was far more agreeable. I know you're unlikely to have a mean old rooster around that needs dispatching, so I've started with the cooked chicken meat—or turkey, which will do fine, too. But if you happen to have a mean old rooster around, you know what to do!

2 pounds (900 g) cooked chicken or turkey meat

1 medium onion, chopped

2 medium Granny Smith apples, diced

2 cups (475 ml) chicken or turkey broth

1 garlic clove, crushed

1 tablespoon cumin

2 tablespoons (16 g) chili powder

1 teaspoon chicken bouillon concentrate

2 cans (15 ounces, or 425 g each) Eden Organic black soy beans

3/4 cup (175 ml) heavy cream

Dice up your chicken or turkey and throw it in the slow cooker.

Peel and chop your onion and core and chop your apples (don't bother peeling them). Throw them in the slow cooker, too. Add everything else but the cream. Cover the pot, set to low, and cook for 5 to 6 hours.

A little before suppertime, stir in the cream, re-cover, and let it heat another 15 to 30 minutes; then serve.

Yield: 8 servings, each with: 395 calories, 18 g fat, 45 g protein, 13 g carbohydrate, 6 g dietary fiber, 7 g usable carbs.

Dana's Kim's Kings Ranch Chicken

This is a great Southwestern-style casserole that serves a crowd. It started with an apparently popular dish (of which I had not heard) called King's Ranch Chicken. It included stuff like canned cream of mushroom soup and tortillas. It was also not a slow cooker dish. My friend Kim Workman Palmer posted her decarbed version on *Facebook*, and I took that and slow-cooker-ized it. By the way, I originally left out the canned tomatoes with chilies by mistake, and it was still mighty tasty. And it was a tad lower carb, too. But the tomatoes are canonical and awfully good.

1 red bell pepper

1 green bell pepper

1/2 medium onion

1/2 cup (120 ml) chicken broth

1 can (4 ounces, or 115 g) mushroom pieces

1 can (14 ounces, or 390 g) tomatoes with green chiles

2 1/2 cups (350 g) diced cooked chicken or turkey

1 tablespoon (15 ml) lime juice

1 tablespoon (8 g) chili powder

1 teaspoon salt

1 1/2 teaspoons paprika

3/4 teaspoon onion powder

1 clove garlic, crushed

1/4 teaspoon cayenne

1/4 teaspoon cumin

1 teaspoon chicken bouillon concentrate

3 ounces (85 g) cream cheese

1/2 cup (120 ml) heavy cream

2 egg yolks

8 ounces (225 g) shredded Mexican 4-cheese blend

Core and seed the peppers. With the S-blade in place, cut them in chunks and put them in your food processor. Peel your half onion and throw it in, too. Pulse to chop fairly fine. Let them sit while you go to the next step.

Put the chicken broth, mushrooms, and tomatoes with chiles—don't drain either the mushrooms or tomatoes first—in a sauce pan and start them heating over a medium burner.

Cut up your cooked chicken. I just snip mine up with my kitchen shears right into a big mixing bowl. Drizzle in the lime juice and toss. Sprinkle everything from the chili powder through the cumin over the chicken and toss to coat evenly.

Okay, back to your chicken broth and veggies. Whisk in the chicken bouillon concentrate and the cream cheese and keep whisking until the cheese melts in and the bouillon is dissolved. Now whisk in the cream.

Separate the eggs and do something else with the whites. (I fed mine to my dogs.) Put the yolks in a cereal bowl and whisk them up. Now add a ladleful—about 1/2 cup (115 g)—of the sauce into the yolk and whisk them together well. Then whisk this mixture back into the main batch of sauce and keep whisking until it thickens. Whisk in a little guar or xanthan, too, if needed, to get a texture a little thinner than commercial condensed mushroom soup.

Okay, you are now ready to assemble your casserole! Spray the slow cooker with nonstick spray. Spread half the chicken in the bottom. Grab that bowl off the food processor and drain off any liquid that has collected in the bottom. Now put half the pepper/onion mixture over the chicken. Spoon half the sauce over that and then sprinkle in half the cheese. Repeat the layers with the rest of the ingredients.

Cover the pot, set to low, and cook for 5 to 6 hours.

Yield: 8 servings, each with: 398 calories, 31 g fat, 23 g protein, 7 g carbohydrate, 1 g dietary fiber, 6 g usable carbs.

Chicken Cacciatore

Here's a slow cooker version of an old favorite. It's easy, too, what I call a dump-and-go recipe.

>   6 skinless chicken leg and side quarters (about 3 lbs, or 1.4 kg)
>
>   2 cups (500 g) no-sugar-added spaghetti sauce (I use Hunt's.)
>
>   1 can (8 ounces, or 225 g) whole mushrooms, drained
>
>   2 teaspoons dried oregano
>
>   1/2 cup (80 g) chopped onion
>
>   1 green bell pepper, diced
>
>   2 cloves garlic, crushed
>
>   1/4 cup (60 ml) dry red wine
>
>   Guar or xanthan (optional)

Simply put everything except the guar or xanthan in your slow cooker and stir it up to combine. Cover the slow cooker, set it to low, and let it cook for 7 hours.

When the time's up, remove the chicken with tongs and put it in a big serving bowl. Thicken the sauce up a little with the guar or xanthan if it needs it and ladle the sauce over the chicken.

If you like, you can serve this over *Cauli-Rice* (page 343), spaghetti squash, or even low-carb pasta, but I'd probably eat it as is.

Yield: 6 servings, each with: 293 calories, 8 g fat, 42 g protein, 11 g carbohydrate, 4 g dietary fiber, 7 g usable carbs.

Italian Chicken and Vegetables

1/2 head cabbage, cut in wedges

1 medium onion, sliced

8 ounces (225 g) sliced mushrooms

2 pounds (900 g) skinless chicken breasts

2 pounds (900 g) skinless chicken thighs

2 cups (500 g) no-sugar-added spaghetti sauce (I use Hunt's.)

Guar or xanthan (optional)

Grated Parmesan cheese

Put the cabbage, onion, and mushrooms in your slow cooker. Place the chicken on top of the vegetables. Pour the spaghetti sauce over the top.

Cover the slow cooker, set it to low, and let it cook for 6 hours. Thicken the sauce with guar or xanthan if needed and serve with Parmesan cheese.

Yield: 6 servings, each with: 254 calories, 5 g fat, 46 g protein, 4 g carbohydrate, 1 g dietary fiber, 3 g usable carbs.

Chicken Paprikash

This is pure Hungarian decadence! Feel free to use full-fat sour cream in this sumptuous gravy if you prefer. Or you could use plain yogurt, just drain off any watery whey first.

    1/2 cup (80 g) chopped onion

    1 tablespoon (14 g) butter

    1 tablespoon (15 ml) oil

    3 pounds (1.4 kg) chicken thighs

    1/2 cup (120 ml) chicken broth

    1/4 cup (60 ml) dry white wine

    1 1/2 tablespoons (24 g) tomato paste

    1 teaspoon chicken bouillon concentrate

    1 1/2 tablespoons (11 g) paprika

    1/2 teaspoon caraway seeds

    1/4 teaspoon pepper

    1/2 cup (115 g) light sour cream

    Guar or xanthan (optional)

In a big, heavy skillet, sauté the onion in the butter and oil over medium-low heat until it's just golden. Transfer it to your slow cooker. Add the chicken to the skillet, turn the heat up to medium, and brown the chicken all over. Transfer it to the slow cooker, too.

Pour off the fat from the skillet and pour in the broth and wine. Stir it around to dissolve the tasty brown stuff stuck to the skillet and then stir in the tomato paste and bouillon. When those are dissolved, pour the liquid over the chicken.

Sprinkle the paprika, caraway seeds, and pepper over the chicken. Cover the slow cooker, set it to low, and let it cook for 6 hours.

When the time's up, remove the chicken with tongs or a slotted spoon and put it on a platter. Whisk the sour cream into the liquid in the slow cooker and thicken it further with guar or xanthan if desired. Serve the sauce with the chicken.

Don't forget to serve this with *Fauxtatoes* (see recipe page 343) to ladle this beautiful gravy onto!

Yield: 5 servings, each with: 537 calories, 39 g fat, 39 g protein, 5 g carbohydrate, 1 g dietary fiber, 4 g usable carbs.

Chicken Stroganoff

Chicken and noodles with creamy sauce—you talk about comfort food! Feel free to make this with boneless, skinless chicken thighs or breasts instead. I prefer meat cooked on the bone, and I also think the bones enrich the sauce. They're cheaper, too.

8 ounces (225 g) sliced mushrooms

1 medium onion, sliced

4 cloves garlic, crushed

1 pound (455 g) chicken legs and thighs

1 1/2 cups (355 ml) chicken broth

2 teaspoons chicken bouillon concentrate

3 tablespoons (45 ml) Worcestershire sauce

2 packages tofu shirataki, fettucini width

1 cup (230 g) sour cream

Black pepper to taste

Guar or xanthan

Strip the skin from the chicken and save it for *Chicken Chips* (see recipe page 331).

Put the mushrooms, onions, and garlic in the slow cooker and lay the skinless legs and thighs on top.

Stir together the chicken broth, bouillon concentrate, and Worcestershire until the concentrate is dissolved and pour it over the whole thing. Cover and set to low. Cook for 6 hours.

Fish out the chicken with tongs or a slotted spoon and lay it on a plate. Give it 10 minutes to cool. In the meantime, re-cover the pot.

While your chicken is cooling, drain and rinse the shirataki and snip them a few times with your kitchen shears.

Okay, the chicken is now cool enough to handle. Strip the meat off the bones, which will be very easy. Use your kitchen shears to snip it back into the pot, in bite-sized bits. Stir in the sour cream and thicken to taste with your guar or xanthan.

Stir in the noodles and serve.

Yield: 3 servings, each with: 308 calories, 20 g fat, 17 g protein, 15 g carbohydrate, 2 g dietary fiber, 13 g usable carbs.

Curried Chicken with Coconut Milk

The day I first made this, my cleaning crew was here, and they couldn't stop talking about how great it smelled. It tastes even better! Find coconut milk in the Asian section of big grocery stores or at Asian markets. It comes in regular or light, and they generally have the same carb count, so choose whichever you prefer. But remember, coconut oil is really good for you.

3 pounds (1.4 kg) skinless chicken thighs

1/2 cup (80 g) chopped onion

2 cloves garlic, crushed

1 1/2 tablespoons (9 g) curry powder

1 cup (235 ml) coconut milk

1 teaspoon chicken bouillon concentrate

Guar or xanthan

Put the chicken in your slow cooker. Place the onion and garlic over it.

In a bowl, mix together the curry powder, coconut milk, and bouillon. Pour the mixture over the chicken and vegetables in the slow cooker. Cover the slow cooker, set it to low, and let it cook for 6 hours.

When the time's up, remove the chicken and put it on a platter. Thicken the sauce to a gravy consistency with guar or xanthan.

You'll want to serve this with *Cauli-Rice* (see recipe page 343) to soak up the extra curry sauce. It's too good to miss!

Yield: 5 servings, each with: 310 calories, 18 g fat, 32 g protein, 6 g carbohydrate, 2 g dietary fiber, 4 g usable carbs.

Chicken with Root Vegetables, Cabbage, and Herbs

I think of this as being a sort of French Country dish. Of course, I've never been to the French countryside, so what do I know? It's good, though, and you don't need another darned thing with it.

5 pounds (2.3 kg) chicken

1¹/₂ tablespoons (23 ml) olive oil

1¹/₂ tablespoons (21 g) butter

2 medium turnips, cut into ¹/₂-inch (13 mm) cubes

2 medium carrots, cut into ¹/₂-inch (13 mm) slices

1 medium onion, cut into ¹/₄-inch (6 mm) half-rounds

1 head cabbage

4 cloves garlic, crushed

¹/₂ teaspoon dried rosemary

¹/₂ teaspoon dried thyme

¹/₂ teaspoon dried basil

2 bay leaves, crumbled

In a big, heavy skillet, brown the chicken on both sides in the oil and butter over medium-high heat.

When the chicken is browned all over, remove it to a plate and reserve. Some extra fat will have accumulated in the skillet. Pour off all but a couple of tablespoons (28 ml) and then add the turnips, carrots, and onion. Sauté them, scraping the tasty brown bits off the bottom of the skillet as you stir, until they're getting a touch of gold, too.

Transfer the sautéed vegetables to your slow cooker.

Cut the cabbage into eighths and put it on top of the vegetables. Arrange the chicken on top of the cabbage. Sprinkle the garlic over the chicken and vegetables, making sure some ends up on the chicken and some down among the vegetables. Sprinkle the rosemary, thyme, basil, and bay leaves into the slow cooker, making sure some gets down into the vegetables. Season with salt and pepper. Cover the slow cooker, set it to low, and let it cook for 6 to 7 hours.

Yield: 8 servings, each with: 510 calories, 37 g fat, 36 g protein, 6 g carbohydrate, 2 g dietary fiber, 4 g usable carbs.

Slow Cooker Brewery Chicken and Vegetables

There are plenty of vegetables in here, so you don't need a thing with it, except maybe some bread for the carb-eaters in the family. And the gravy comes out a beautiful color!

8 ounces (225 g) turnips (two turnips roughly the size of tennis balls), peeled and cut into chunks

2 stalks celery, sliced

1 medium carrot, sliced

1/2 medium onion, sliced

1 tablespoon (18 g) chicken bouillon concentrate

2 1/2 to 3 pounds (1.1 to 1.4 kg) cut-up chicken (I use leg and thigh quarters, cut apart at the joints.)

12 ounces (355 ml) light beer

1 can (14 1/2 ounces, or 410 g) tomatoes with green chiles

Guar or xanthan (optional)

Put the turnips, celery, carrot, onion, bouillon, and chicken in your slow cooker. Pour the beer and the tomatoes over the lot. Cover the slow cooker, set it to low, and let it cook for 8 to 9 hours.

When the time's up, remove the chicken with tongs and place it on a serving platter. Then, using a slotted spoon, scoop out the vegetables. Put 1 1/2 cups (340 g) of them in a blender and pile the rest on and around the chicken on the platter. Scoop out 1 1/2 to 2 cups (355 to 475 ml) of the liquid left in the slow cooker and put it in the blender with the vegetables. Puree the veggies and broth and thicken the mixture a little more with the guar or xanthan, if it seems necessary. Add salt and pepper to taste and serve as a sauce with the chicken and vegetables.

Yield: 5 servings, each with: 415 calories, 26 g fat, 30 g protein, 10 g carbohydrate, 2 g dietary fiber, 8 g usable carbs.

Citrus Spice Chicken

This dish has a sunshiny citrus flavor! It's another dump-and-go recipe.

- 1/3 cup (80 ml) lemon juice
- 2 tablespoons (3 g) Splenda
- 1/2 teaspoon orange extract
- 1/2 cup (120 g) *Dana's No-Sugar Ketchup* (see recipe page 332) or purchased low-carb ketchup
- 2 tablespoons (40 g) low-sugar orange marmalade
- 1/2 teaspoon ground cinnamon
- 1/2 teaspoon ground allspice
- 1/8 teaspoon ground cloves
- 1/4 teaspoon cayenne
- 3 pounds (1.4 kg) skinless chicken thighs

In a bowl, stir together the lemon juice, Splenda, orange extract, ketchup, marmalade, cinnamon, allspice, cloves, and cayenne.

Put the chicken in your slow cooker and pour the sauce over it. Cover the slow cooker, set it to low, and let it cook for 6 hours.

Serve with *Cauli-Rice* (see recipe page 343).

Yield: 5 servings, each with: 191 calories, 6 g fat, 31 g protein, 2 g carbohydrate, trace dietary fiber, 2 g usable carbs.

☐ Tuscan Chicken

This is fabulous Italian chicken!

> 4 pounds (1.8 kg) skinless chicken thighs
>
> 1 tablespoon (15 ml) olive oil
>
> 1/2 cup (80 g) chopped onion
>
> 1 red bell pepper, cut into strips
>
> 1 green bell pepper, cut into strips
>
> 1 can (15 ounces, or 425 g) black soybeans, drained
>
> 1 can (14 1/2 ounces, or 410 g) crushed tomatoes
>
> 1/2 cup (120 ml) dry white wine
>
> 1 teaspoon dried oregano
>
> 1 clove garlic, crushed
>
> 1 teaspoon chicken bouillon concentrate

In a big, heavy skillet, brown the chicken in the oil over medium-high heat.

Meanwhile, put the onion, peppers, and soybeans in your slow cooker. Place the chicken on top of the vegetables and beans.

In a bowl, stir together the tomatoes, wine, oregano, garlic, and bouillon. Pour the mixture over the chicken. Cover the slow cooker, set it to low, and let it cook for 6 to 7 hours. Add salt and pepper to taste.

Yield: 8 servings, each with: 258 calories, 9 g fat, 31 g protein, 10 g carbohydrate, 5 g dietary fiber, 5 g usable carbs.

To serve, scoop up some of the dried beef and sauce with each bacon-wrapped piece of chicken.

Yield: 6 servings, each with: 472 calories, 32 g fat, 41 g protein, 4 g carbohydrate, trace dietary fiber, 4 g usable carbs.

Slow Cooker Chicken Mole

Chicken mole is the national dish of Mexico, and I'm crazy about it. On my honeymoon in Mexico, I bought a container of chicken mole at the deli at the local grocery store and kept it in the hotel room fridge to heat up in the microwave! Here's a slow cooker version.

1 can (14¹/2 ounces, or 410 g) tomatoes with green chiles

¹/2 cup (80 g) chopped onion

¹/4 cup (28 g) slivered almonds, toasted

3 cloves garlic, crushed

3 tablespoons (18 g) unsweetened cocoa powder

2 tablespoons (18 g) raisins

1 tablespoon (8 g) sesame seeds

1 tablespoon (1.5 g) Splenda

¹/4 teaspoon ground cinnamon

¹/4 teaspoon ground nutmeg

¹/4 teaspoon ground coriander

¹/4 teaspoon salt

3 pounds (1.4 kg) skinless chicken thighs

Guar or xanthan

2 tablespoons (14 g) slivered almonds, toasted

Put the tomatoes, onion, ¹/4 cup (28 g) almonds, garlic, cocoa powder, raisins, sesame seeds, Splenda, cinnamon, nutmeg, coriander, and salt in a blender or food processor and puree coarsely.

Place the chicken in your slow cooker. Pour the sauce over it. Cover the slow cooker, set it to low, and let it cook for 9 to 10 hours.

Remove the chicken from the slow cooker with tongs. Thicken the sauce to taste with guar or xanthan. Serve the sauce over the chicken. Top with the 2 tablespoons (14 g) almonds.

Yield: 8 servings, each with: 284 calories, 12 g fat, 37 g protein, 8 g carbohydrate, 2 g dietary fiber, 6 g usable carbs.

Mediterranean Chicken

This recipe, bursting with classic Mediterranean flavors, originally appeared in *500 More Low-Carb Recipes*.

> 8 ounces (225 g) sliced mushrooms
>
> 1 can (14½ ounces, or 410 g) tomatoes
>
> 1 can (6 ounces, or 170 g) artichoke hearts
>
> 2½ ounces (63 g) sliced black olives
>
> 3 pounds (1.4 kg) skinless chicken thighs
>
> 1 tablespoon (6 g) Italian seasoning
>
> 3/4 cup (175 ml) chicken broth
>
> 1 teaspoon chicken bouillon concentrate
>
> 1/4 cup (60 ml) dry white wine
>
> Guar or xanthan

Put the mushrooms, tomatoes, artichokes, and olives in your slow cooker. Place the chicken on top.

In a bowl, mix together the Italian seasoning, broth, bouillon, and wine. Pour the sauce over the chicken and vegetables. Cover the slow cooker, set it to low, and let it cook for 7 hours.

When the time's up, thicken the juices a bit with guar or xanthan.

Yield: 6 servings, each with: 215 calories, 7 g fat, 28 g protein, 8 g carbohydrate, 2 g dietary fiber, 6 g usable carbs.

Mediterranean Pepper and Olive Chicken

Years ago, I had a great dish of chicken braised with pepperoncini; I've been trying to replicate it ever since. I actually think this is better. I mean, how could added olives make it worse?

3 pounds (1.4 kg) chicken parts—legs, thighs, or breasts, whatever you like

2 tablespoons (28 ml) olive oil

1 small onion

12 jarred pepperoncini peppers

20 kalamata olives

1/4 cup (60 ml) chicken broth

2 tablespoons (28 ml) lemon juice

1 teaspoon chicken bouillon concentrate

2 cloves garlic, crushed

1 teaspoon oregano

Chopped fresh parsley, optional

Cut the chicken into serving pieces and skin. Save the skins for *Chicken Chips* (see recipe page 331)!

In your big, heavy skillet, over medium heat, start browning the chicken in the olive oil.

In the meantime, peel and chop your onion. Cut the stem ends off your pepperoncini and seed them, if you like. Pit your olives if you didn't buy them that way. (Just squish them with your thumb and flick out the pit.) Put all of this in the bottom of the slow cooker. When the chicken is golden, use tongs to place it on top of the vegetables.

Put the chicken broth, lemon juice, chicken bouillon concentrate, the crushed garlic, and the oregano in the skillet. Stir until the bouillon is dissolved, scraping up any tasty brown bits. Pour over the chicken, cover the pot, set to low, and cook for 6 hours. Serve the chicken with the peppers, onions, and olives and with the juices spooned over it.

Tofu shirataki spaghetti or angel hair would be nice with this.

Yield: 4 to 5 servings; Assuming 5, each will have: 302 calories, 16 g fat, 33 g protein, 6 g carbohydrate, 1 g dietary fiber, 5 g usable carbs.

Mu Shu Chicken

This took some figuring out. The high-carb recipe I started with called for a whole can of plums in syrup. That wasn't happening, and I discovered no one is canning plums in water anymore. I was in line at the grocery store, when the woman behind me put a box of prunes on the conveyor belt. Aha! This also makes good omelets, which saves you the carbs in the tortillas.

8 dried prunes

3 tablespoons (45 ml) lemon juice

3 tablespoons (45 ml) rice vinegar

1/8 teaspoon orange extract

1/4 teaspoon five-spice powder

1 tablespoon (8 g) grated ginger root

1 teaspoon dark sesame oil

1 clove garlic, crushed

1 tablespoon (1.5 g) Splenda, or other sugar-free sweetener to equal
   1 tablespoon (13 g) sugar

2 1/2 pounds (1.1 kg) boneless, skinless chicken breast or thighs (I like the thighs
   better.)

1 tablespoon (15 g) coconut oil

1 bag (14 ounces, or 390 g) coleslaw mix

1/4 onion, minced

2 tablespoons (28 ml) soy sauce

1 tablespoon (15 ml) dark sesame oil

8 large low-carb tortillas

Put the prunes in your slow cooker. Stir together everything from the lemon juice through the Splenda and pour it over the prunes. Place the chicken on top, cover the pot, set it for low, and let it cook 5 to 6 hours.

Okay, dinnertime has rolled around. Uncover your slow cooker and use tongs to pull out your chicken and put it on your cutting board. Let it cool while you go to the next step.

Melt your coconut oil in your big heavy skillet, over high heat, and stir-fry your cabbage and onion with the soy sauce and sesame oil until the cabbage is just wilted but still has some crunch.

Use your stick blender to blend the prunes up with all the liquid in the pot. (If you don't have a stick blender, throw it in your regular blender.) Thicken a touch with guar or xanthan if you think it needs it.

Now slice your chicken into shreds.

To serve, smear a little of the sauce on one of the tortillas and then add chicken and cabbage. Wrap and eat.

Yield: 8 servings, each with: 322 calories, 11 g fat, 33 g protein, 29 g carbohydrate, 16 g dietary fiber, 13 g usable carbs.

Orange Teriyaki Chicken

This has been officially rated "Very Easy, Very Good!"

> 1 bag (16 ounces, or 455 g) frozen Oriental vegetable mixture, unthawed
>
> 2 pounds (900 g) boneless, skinless chicken breasts, cubed
>
> 3/4 cup (175 ml) chicken broth
>
> 2 tablespoons (28 ml) *Low-Carb Teriyaki* Sauce (see recipe page 337) or purchased low-carb teriyaki sauce
>
> 1 teaspoon chicken bouillon concentrate
>
> 1 tablespoon (20 g) low-sugar orange marmalade
>
> 1/4 teaspoon orange extract
>
> 2 tablespoons (28 ml) lemon juice
>
> 1 teaspoon Splenda
>
> 1 teaspoon dry mustard
>
> 1/2 teaspoon ground ginger
>
> Guar or xanthan

Pour the vegetables into your slow cooker. Place the chicken on top.

In a bowl, combine the broth, teriyaki sauce, bouillon, marmalade, orange extract, lemon juice, Splenda, dry mustard, and ginger, stirring well. Pour the mixture over the chicken and veggies. Cover the slower cooker, set it to low, and let it cook for 4 to 5 hours.

Before serving, thicken the sauce a bit with guar or xanthan.

Serve over *Cauli-Rice* (see recipe page 343) if desired. Or for the carbivores, you can serve it over brown rice, lo mein noodles, or plain old spaghetti.

Yield: 6 servings, each with: 222 calories, 4 g fat, 36 g protein, 7 g carbohydrate, 2 g dietary fiber, 5 g usable carbs.

Thai Chicken Bowls

This was a big hit with Maria's family!

> 8 boneless, skinless, chicken thighs, cubed (a little over 2¼ lbs, or 1 kg)
>
> 2 cloves garlic, crushed
>
> 1/2 cup (80 g) chopped onion
>
> 2 stalks celery, sliced
>
> 2 teaspoons grated ginger root
>
> 1 teaspoon five-spice powder
>
> 1/2 teaspoon salt
>
> 1 tablespoon (15 ml) lemon juice
>
> 1 teaspoon hot sauce (optional)
>
> 28 ounces (805 ml) chicken broth
>
> 1 head cauliflower
>
> Guar or xanthan
>
> 6 tablespoons (36 g) sliced scallions
>
> 6 tablespoons (6 g) chopped cilantro

Place the chicken in your slow cooker. Top with the garlic, onion, celery, ginger, five-spice powder, salt, and lemon juice.

In a bowl, combine the hot sauce, if using, with the broth and pour it into the slow cooker. Cover the slow cooker, set it to low, and let it cook for 5 to 6 hours.

Okay, it's almost supper time. Run your cauliflower through the shredding blade of your food processor to make *Cauli-Rice*. Put your *Cauli-Rice* in a microwaveable casserole with a lid, add a couple of tablespoons (28 ml) of water, cover, and microwave on high for 6 minutes.

Thicken up the sauce in the slow cooker with a little guar or xanthan to about the texture of heavy cream.

Okay, the *Cauli-Rice* is done! Uncover it immediately, drain, and divide it into 6 bowls. Divide the chicken mixture, ladling it over the *Cauli-Rice*. Top with the scallions and cilantro.

Yield: 6 servings, each with: 138 calories, 4 g fat, 20 g protein, 4 g carbohydrate, 1 g dietary fiber, 3 g usable carbs.

Thai Hot Pot

This recipe takes a few more steps than some, but the results are worth it! If you can't get Southeast Asian fish sauce, you can substitute soy sauce.

1 1/2 pounds (680 g) boneless, skinless chicken thighs

1 medium carrot, sliced

1 medium onion, sliced

1 clove garlic, crushed

14 ounces (390 ml) coconut milk

1 tablespoon (8 g) grated ginger root

2 tablespoons (28 ml) fish sauce (nam pla or nuoc mam) or soy sauce

1 tablespoon (15 ml) lime juice

2 teaspoons Splenda

1/2 teaspoon hot sauce

1/3 cup (87 g) natural peanut butter

1 pound (455 g) shrimp, shelled

1 cup (75 g) fresh snow pea pods, cut into 1/2-inch (13 mm) pieces

Guar or xanthan

6 cups (720 g) *Cauli-Rice* (see recipe page 343)

1/3 cup (48 g) chopped peanuts

Put the chicken in your slow cooker and add the carrot, onion, and garlic.

In a blender, combine the coconut milk, ginger, fish sauce or soy sauce, lime juice, Splenda, hot sauce, and peanut butter and blend until smooth. Pour the sauce over the chicken and vegetables, using a rubber scraper to make sure you get all of it! Cover the slow cooker, set it to low, and let it cook for 8 hours.

Stir in the shrimp and snow peas, re-cover the slow cooker, and turn it up to high. Cook for 10 minutes or until the shrimp are pink through.

Thicken the sauce slightly with guar or xanthan. Serve over the *Cauli-Rice* (see recipe page 343) or brown rice for the carb-eaters. Top each serving with the peanuts.

Yield: 6 servings, each with: 480 calories, 32 g fat, 33 g protein, 19 g carbohydrate, 7 g dietary fiber, 12 g usable carbs.

Chicken in Thai Coconut Curry Sauce

This is a little like Panang chicken. Feel free to increase or decrease the heat to taste. If the family has differing heat tolerance, put a bottle of Sriracha hot sauce on the table!

3 Thai bird peppers (little hot red peppers; mine were dried)

8 ounces (225 g) sliced mushrooms

2 pounds (900 g) boneless, skinless chicken breast

1 can (13½ ounces, or 380 ml) coconut milk

1 cup (235 ml) chicken broth

1 teaspoon chicken bouillon concentrate

1 tablespoon (15 ml) lemon juice

3 tablespoons (45 ml) lime juice

1 tablespoon (15 g) thai red curry paste

1 tablespoon (8 g) grated ginger root

2 tablespoons (28 ml) fish sauce

Put the bird peppers on the bottom of your slow cooker and dump your sliced mushrooms on top of them. Cut the chicken into 6 servings and place on top of the mushrooms.

Now mix everything else together until the bouillon concentrate and the curry paste are dissolved. Pour over the chicken and mushrooms, cover the pot, set to low, and cook for 4 to 5 hours. Thicken the sauce a little with your guar or xanthan shaker and then serve.

I'd serve this with shirataki or *Cauli-Rice* (see recipe page 343) to sop up the super yummy sauce.

Yield: 6 servings, each with: 320 calories, 16 g fat, 38 g protein, 9 g carbohydrate, 2 g dietary fiber, 7 g usable carbs.

Thai-ish Chicken and Noodles

Don't let the need to make the *Not-Quite-Asian Sweet Chili Sauce* put you off; it's super-easy. Really, the whole thing is easy. And it's good. If you prefer, the traditional (non-tofu) shirataki noodles would be as good here as the tofu shirataki.

1 batch *Not-Quite-Asian Sweet Chili Sauce* (see recipe page 234.)

3 tablespoons (48 g) natural peanut butter

3 garlic cloves

1 cup (235 ml) chicken broth

1 teaspoon chicken bouillon concentrate

2 pounds (900 g) boneless, skinless chicken breast or thighs

1 package shirataki noodles, spaghetti width

1 cup (70 g) bagged coleslaw mix

1 cup (104 g) bean sprouts

Chopped fresh cilantro, optional

Chopped peanuts, optional

Make your *Not-Quite-Asian Sweet Chili Sauce*, adding the peanut butter, extra garlic, chicken broth, and bouillon concentrate before you run the blender.

Dice your chicken and throw it in the slow cooker. Pour the sauce over it, put the lid on, set it to low, and give it a good 2 to 3 hours.

Stir in the coleslaw mix and sprouts. Drain, rinse, and snip the shirataki noodles and stir them in, too. Put the lid back on and give it another 20 minutes or so—you don't want the bean sprouts to get unappealingly limp.

Serve with cilantro and peanuts on top. Or not—it's up to you.

Yield: 6 servings, each with: 282 calories, 8 g fat, 38 g protein, 9 g carbohydrate, 2 g dietary fiber, 7 g usable carbs. (Analysis does not include the polyols in the *Not-Quite-Asian Sweet Chili Sauce*.)

Southwestern Barbecue

This is incredibly popular, for something so easy!

> ½ cup (123 g) tomato sauce
>
> 1 tablespoon (1.5 g) Splenda
>
> 1½ tablespoons (14 g) canned, sliced jalapeños
>
> 2 tablespoons (28 ml) lime juice
>
> ⅛ teaspoon blackstrap molasses
>
> 1 teaspoon ground cumin
>
> ¼ teaspoon red pepper flakes
>
> 4 pounds (1.8 kg) skinless chicken thighs

Combine everything except for the chicken in your slow cooker and stir well. Place the chicken in the sauce, meaty side down. Cover the slow cooker, set it to low, and let it cook for 6 hours.

Serve the chicken with the sauce spooned over it.

Yield: 6 servings, each with: 215 calories, 7 g fat, 34 g protein, 2 g carbohydrate, trace dietary fiber, 2 g usable carbs.

Chicken and Dumplings

This takes some work, but boy, is it comfort food. You could make this with leftover turkey instead if you prefer. If you do that, put the cubed, cooked turkey in about 5 to 6 hours into the initial cooking time.

> 2 medium carrots, sliced
>
> 1 medium onion, chunked
>
> 2 medium turnips, cut into 1/2-inch (13 mm) cubes
>
> 1 1/2 cups (186 g) frozen green beans, cross-cut
>
> 8 ounces (225 g) sliced mushrooms
>
> 1 1/2 pounds (680 g) boneless, skinless chicken thighs, cut into 1-inch (2.5 cm) cubes
>
> 1 1/2 cups (355 ml) chicken broth
>
> 1 teaspoon poultry seasoning
>
> 3 teaspoons (18 g) chicken bouillon concentrate
>
> 1/2 cup (120 ml) heavy cream
>
> Guar or xanthan
>
> *Dumplings* (see recipe on next page)

In your slow cooker, combine the carrots, onion, turnips, green beans, mushrooms, and chicken.

In a bowl, mix together the broth, poultry seasoning, and bouillon. Pour the mixture over the chicken and vegetables. Cover the slow cooker, set it to low, and let it cook for 6 to 7 hours.

When the time's up, stir in the cream and thicken the gravy to a nice consistency with guar or xanthan. Add salt and pepper to taste. Re-cover the slow cooker and turn it to high.

While the slow cooker is heating up (it'll take at least 30 minutes), make your *Dumplings*, stopping before you add the liquid. Wait until the gravy in the slow cooker is boiling. Then stir into the dry ingredients the buttermilk and drop the biscuit dough by spoonfuls over the surface of the chicken and gravy. Re-cover the slow cooker and let it cook for another 25 to 30 minutes.

Yield: 8 servings, each with: 417 calories, 25 g fat, 36 g protein, 14 g carbohydrate, 4 g dietary fiber, 10 g usable carbs. (Analysis includes the *Dumplings*.)

Dumplings

Feel free to use this with other meat-and-gravy dishes if you like! (These instructions require gravy to boil the *Dumplings* in.)

> 3/4 cup (71 g) ground almonds, or "almond meal"
>
> 1/2 cup (80 g) rice protein powder (Get this at your health food store. If they don't have it, they can order it. I use NutriBiotic brand.)
>
> 1/4 cup (30 g) wheat gluten
>
> 2 tablespoons (28 g) butter
>
> 2 tablespoons (28 g) coconut oil
>
> 1/2 teaspoon salt
>
> 2 teaspoons baking powder
>
> 1/2 teaspoon baking soda
>
> 3/4 cup (175 ml) buttermilk

Put everything but the buttermilk into your food processor with the S-blade in place. Pulse the food processor to cut in the butter. (You want it evenly distributed in the dry ingredients.) Dump this mixture into a mixing bowl.

Check to make sure your gravy is boiling. (If it isn't, have a quick cup of tea until it is.) Now pour the buttermilk into the dry ingredients and stir it in with a few swift strokes. (Don't overmix; you just want to make sure everything's evenly damp.) This will make a soft dough. Drop by spoonfuls over the boiling gravy, cover the pot, and let it cook for 25 to 30 minutes.

Note: Grind 3/4 cup (70 g) almonds to cormeal-like consistency or use almond meal.

Yield: 12 servings, each with: 153 calories, 10 g fat, 14 g protein, 4 g carbohydrate, 1 g dietary fiber, 3 g usable carbs.

Chicken in Creamy Horseradish Sauce

Don't think that just because this has horseradish it's really strong. The sauce is mellow, subtle, and family-friendly.

4 pounds (900 g) cut-up chicken

1 tablespoon (14 g) butter

1 tablespoon (15 ml) olive oil

3/4 cup (175 ml) chicken broth

1½ teaspoons chicken bouillon concentrate

1 tablespoon (15 g) prepared horseradish

4 ounces (115 g) cream cheese, cut into chunks

¼ cup (60 ml) heavy cream

Guar or xanthan (optional)

In a big, heavy skillet, brown the chicken in the butter and oil over medium-high heat. Transfer the chicken to your slow cooker.

In a bowl, stir together the broth, bouillon, and horseradish. Pour the mixture over the chicken. Cover the slow cooker, set it to low, and let it cook for 6 hours.

When the time's up, remove the chicken with tongs and put it on a platter. Melt the cream cheese into the sauce in the slow cooker. Stir in the cream. Thicken the sauce with guar or xanthan if you think it needs it. Add salt and pepper to taste.

I think this would be good with *Fauxtatoes* (see recipe page 343) and green beans.

Yield: 8 servings, each with: 442 calories, 34 g fat, 30 g protein, 1 g carbohydrate, trace dietary fiber, 1 g usable carbs.

Chicken in Creamy Orange Sauce

4 pounds (1.8 kg) skinless chicken thighs

3 tablespoons (45 ml) oil

3 tablespoons (45 ml) brandy

1/2 cup (120 ml) white wine vinegar

1/2 cup (120 ml) lemon juice

1/2 teaspoon orange extract

1 teaspoon grated orange rind

1/3 cup (8 g) Splenda

8 scallions, sliced

6 ounces (170 g) light cream cheese, cut into chunks

Guar or xanthan (optional)

In a big, heavy skillet, brown the chicken in the oil over medium-high heat. Transfer the chicken to your slow cooker.

In a bowl, stir together the brandy, vinegar, lemon juice, orange extract, and Splenda. Pour the mixture over chicken. Cover the slow cooker, set it to low, and let it cook for 6 hours.

When the time's up, transfer the chicken to a platter. Add the scallions to the liquid in the slow cooker and then add the cream cheese and stir till it's melted. Thicken with guar or xanthan if you think it needs it. Add salt and pepper to taste. Serve the sauce over the chicken.

Cauli-Rice (see recipe page 343) in one form or another is the natural side dish with this. Add a big green salad, and there's supper!

Yield: 8 servings, each with: 359 calories, 20 g fat, 35 g protein, 5 g carbohydrate, trace dietary fiber, 5 g usable carbs.

"I've Got a Life" Chicken

This recipe from *15-Minute Low-Carb Recipes* is remarkably good. It's sweet, tangy, and fruity.

> 3 to 3¹/₂ pounds (1.4 to 1.6 kg) bone-in chicken parts (I use legs and thighs, but a whole cut-up chicken would work great.)
>
> 8 ounces (225 g) sliced mushrooms
>
> 3 tablespoons (45 ml) orange juice
>
> Grated zest of one orange
>
> 1 tablespoon (18 g) chicken bouillon concentrate
>
> ¹/₂ teaspoon pepper
>
> 8 ounces (225 g) canned tomato sauce
>
> 2 tablespoons (28 ml) soy sauce
>
> 2 tablespoons (3 g) Splenda
>
> ¹/₂ teaspoon blackstrap molasses
>
> 2 teaspoons minced garlic or 4 cloves garlic, crushed
>
> 1 teaspoon dried thyme
>
> Guar or xanthan

Remove the skin and any big lumps of fat from the chicken and place it in your slow cooker. (You can save time by buying chicken with the skin already removed, but it's more expensive.) Place the mushrooms on top.

In a bowl, mix together the orange juice, orange zest, bouillon, pepper, tomato sauce, soy sauce, Splenda, molasses, garlic, and thyme. Pour the mixture on top of the chicken and mushrooms. Cover the slow cooker, set it to low, and let it cook for 5 to 6 hours.

When the time's up, remove the chicken and put it on a platter. Use the guar or xanthan to thicken up the sauce in the slow cooker and serve the sauce with the chicken.

Yield: 6 servings, each with: 424 calories, 27 g fat, 35 g protein, 7 g carbohydrate, 1 g dietary fiber, 6 g usable carbs. (This analysis assumes that you eat all of the gravy.)

Slow Cooker Chicken Guadeloupe

This isn't authentically anything, but it borrows its flavors from the Creole cooking of the Caribbean.

> 1 cut-up broiler-fryer chicken, about 3½ pounds (1.5 kg), or whatever chicken parts you prefer
>
> ½ medium onion, chopped
>
> 2 teaspoons ground allspice
>
> 1 teaspoon dried thyme
>
> ¼ cup (60 ml) lemon juice
>
> 1 can (14½ ounces, or 410 g) tomatoes with green chiles
>
> 1 shot (3 tablespoons, or 45 ml) dark rum
>
> Guar or xanthan

Place the chicken, onion, allspice, thyme, lemon juice, tomatoes, and rum in your slow cooker. Cover the slow cooker, set it to low, and let it cook for 5 to 6 hours.

Remove the chicken carefully—it'll be sliding from the bone! Thicken up the sauce with guar or xanthan. Add salt and pepper to taste and serve the sauce over the chicken.

Yield: 5 servings, each with: 541 calories, 36 g fat, 41 g protein, 7 g carbohydrate, 1 g dietary fiber, 6 g usable carbs.

Yassa

This chicken stew comes from Senegal. Traditionally it is quite hot, so feel free to increase the cayenne if you like!

> 3 large onions, thinly sliced
>
> 6 cloves garlic, crushed
>
> 1/2 cup (120 ml) lemon juice
>
> 1 1/2 teaspoons salt
>
> 1/2 teaspoon cayenne, or more to taste
>
> 6 pounds (2.7 kg) chicken, cut up
>
> 1/4 cup (60 ml) oil
>
> 8 cups (960 g) *Cauli-Rice* (see recipe page 343)

In your slow cooker, combine the onions, garlic, lemon juice, salt, and cayenne. Add the chicken and toss so that all the chicken comes in contact with the seasonings. Cover your slow cooker and refrigerate overnight. (It's a good idea to stir this a few times if you think of it, though I don't expect you to get up in the middle of the night to do it!)

Using tongs, remove the chicken from the marinade. Pat it dry with paper towels and set it aside. Transfer the marinade to your slow cooker.

In a big, heavy skillet, heat the oil over medium-high heat. Place the chicken skin side down and cook it until the skin is browned. (You'll need to do this in batches unless your skillet is a lot bigger than mine!) Don't bother browning the other side of the chicken.

Transfer the chicken back to the slow cooker with the marinade. Cover the slow cooker, set it to low, and let it cook for 5 to 6 hours.

Remove the chicken from the slow cooker with tongs. Put the chicken on a platter, cover it with foil, and put it in a warm place.

Ladle the onions and liquid out of the slow cooker into the skillet and turn the heat to high. Boil this hard, stirring often, until most of the liquid has evaporated. (You want the volume reduced by more than half.) Serve the chicken, onions, and sauce over the *Cauli-Rice*.

Yield: 8 servings, each with: 638 calories, 46 g fat, 45 g protein, 11 g carbohydrate, 3 g dietary fiber, 8 g usable carbs.

Sort-of-Ethiopian Chicken Stew

The slow cooker method is hardly authentic, but the flavors come from an Ethiopian recipe—except that the Ethiopians would use a lot more cayenne! Increase it if you like really hot food.

1 cut-up broiler-fryer, about 3 pounds (1.4 kg)

1 medium onion, chopped

1 teaspoon cayenne

1 teaspoon paprika

1/2 teaspoon pepper

1/2 teaspoon grated ginger root

2 tablespoons (28 ml) lemon juice

1/2 cup (120 ml) water

Guar or xanthan

Place the chicken, onion, cayenne, paprika, pepper, ginger, lemon juice, and water in your slow cooker. Cover the slow cooker, set it to low, and let it cook for 5 to 6 hours.

If you'd like to make this really stewlike, you can pick the meat off the bones when it's done (which will be very easy), thicken the gravy with guar or xanthan, and then stir the chicken back into the liquid. Or you can just serve the gravy over the chicken. Take your pick.

Yield: 5 servings, each with: 437 calories, 31 g fat, 34 g protein, 3 g carbohydrate, 1 g dietary fiber, 2 g usable carbs.

African Chicken, Peanut, and Spinach Stew

This may be my favorite recipe in this chapter. It's an incredibly satisfying one-dish meal.

2 pounds (900 g) boneless, skinless chicken thighs

2 tablespoons (28 g) coconut oil

3 garlic cloves, crushed

3 tablespoons (24 g) grated ginger root

1 medium onion, chopped

1½ cups (355 ml) chicken broth

1 teaspoon chicken bouillon concentrate

2½ tablespoons (36 ml) soy sauce

1 tablespoon (15 ml) rice vinegar

1½ teaspoons dark sesame oil

½ teaspoon chili paste

3 tablespoons (48 g) natural peanut butter

10 ounces (280 g) frozen chopped spinach, thawed

Cut the chicken into ½-inch (13 mm) cubes and in your big, heavy skillet, start them browning in the coconut oil. While that's happening, crush your garlic, grate your ginger, and chop your onion.

When the chicken has a touch of color, transfer it to the slow cooker. Add the garlic, ginger, and onion.

Dissolve the chicken bouillon concentrate in the broth and add to the pot along with the soy sauce, vinegar, sesame oil, and chili garlic paste. Give it all a stir. Plunk the peanut butter on top, cover the pot, set to low, and let it cook for a good 5 to 6 hours.

About 30 minutes before serving, drain the thawed spinach well—I pick mine up with clean hands and squeeze it dry. Stir it into the pot, re-cover, and let the whole thing cook for another half an hour; then serve in bowls, with soup spoons.

Yield: 5 servings, each with: 352 calories, 21 g fat, 32 g protein, 9 g carbohydrate, 3 g dietary fiber, 6 g usable carbs.

Cranberry-Peach Turkey Roast

This fruity sauce really wakes up the turkey roast!

> 3 pounds (1.4 kg) turkey roast
>
> 2 tablespoons (28 ml) oil
>
> 1/2 cup (80 g) chopped onion
>
> 1 cup (120 g) cranberries
>
> 1/4 cup (6 g) Splenda
>
> 3 tablespoons (33 g) spicy mustard
>
> 1/4 teaspoon red pepper flakes
>
> 1 peach, peeled and chopped

If your turkey roast is a Butterball like mine, it will be a boneless affair of light and dark meat rolled into an oval roast, enclosed in a net sack. Leave it in the net for cooking so it doesn't fall apart.

In a big heavy skillet, heat the oil and brown the turkey on all sides. Transfer the turkey to the slow cooker.

In a blender or food processor with the S-blade in place, combine the onion, cranberries, Splenda, mustard, red pepper, and peach. Run it until you have a coarse puree. Pour the mixture over the turkey. Cover the slow cooker, set it to low, and let it cook for 6 to 7 hours.

Remove the turkey to a platter, stir up the sauce, and ladle it into a sauce boat to serve with the turkey. You can remove the net from the turkey before serving, if you like, but I find it easier just to use a good sharp knife to slice clear through the netting and let diners remove their own.

Yield: 8 servings, each with: 255 calories, 8 g fat, 31 g protein, 4 g carbohydrate, 1 g dietary fiber, 3 g usable carbs.

Ranch-E-Cue Wings

This is so simple!

> 2 pounds (900 g) turkey wings
>
> 3 tablespoons (45 ml) olive oil
>
> 1/2 cup (120 ml) chicken broth
>
> 3 teaspoons (15 g) ranch-style dressing mix
>
> 1/2 cup (120 g) *Dana's "Kansas City" Barbecue Sauce* (see recipe page 335) or purchased low-carb barbecue sauce

Cut the turkey wings at the joints, discarding the pointy wing tips.

In a big, heavy skillet, heat the oil and brown the turkey all over. Transfer the turkey to your slow cooker.

In a bowl, mix together the broth, dressing mix, and barbecue sauce. Pour the mixture over the wings. Cover the slow cooker, set it to low, and let it cook for 6 to 7 hours.

Yield: 4 servings, each with: 246 calories, 17 g fat, 18 g protein, 5 g carbohydrate, 0 g dietary fiber, 5 g usable carbs.

Turkey Loaf with Thai Flavors

Ground turkey is cheap, low-carb, and low-calorie—and by itself just plain boring. So jazz it up by adding some Thai flavors.

> 2 pounds (900 g) ground turkey
>
> 1 medium onion, chopped
>
> 1 can (4 1/2 ounces, or 130 g) mushroom slices, drained
>
> 4 cloves garlic, crushed
>
> 2 tablespoons (28 ml) lemon juice
>
> 4 tablespoon (60 ml) lime juice, divided
>
> 4 teaspoons (20 g) chili paste
>
> 3 tablespoons (24 g) grated ginger root
>
> 1 1/2 tablespoons (23 ml) fish sauce

1¹/₂ tablespoons (23 ml) soy sauce

1¹/₂ teaspoons pepper

¹/₂ cup (60 g) pork rind crumbs (Run some pork rinds through your food processor.)

¹/₂ cup (8 g) chopped fresh cilantro

¹/₂ cup (115 g) mayonnaise

Place the turkey in a big mixing bowl.

Place the onion, mushrooms, and garlic in a food processor. Pulse until everything is chopped medium-fine. Add it to the turkey.

Add the lemon juice, 2 tablespoons (28 ml) of the lime juice, the chili paste, ginger, fish sauce, soy sauce, pepper, pork rind crumbs, and cilantro to the bowl. Mix it around with clean hands until it is well blended.

Spray a rack or a collapsible-basket-type steamer with nonstick cooking spray and place it in your slow cooker. Add a cup (235 ml) of water under the rack. If the holes in the rack are pretty large, cover it with a sheet of foil and pierce it all over with a fork. Take two 18-inch (45 cm) squares of foil, fold them into strips about 2 iches (5 cm) wide, and criss-cross them across the rack or steamer, running the ends up the sides of the slow cooker. (You're making a sling to help lift the meat loaf out of the slow cooker.) Place the meat mixture on the rack or steamer and form it into an evenly-domed loaf. Cover the slow cooker, set it to low, and let it cook for 6 hours.

When the time's up, use the strips of foil to gently lift the loaf out of the slow cooker and place it on a platter.

In a bowl, mix together the mayonnaise and the remaining 2 tablespoons (28 ml) lime juice. Cut the loaf into wedges and serve it with the lime mayonnaise.

Yield: 8 servings, each with: 327 calories, 24 g fat, 25 g protein, 5 g carbohydrate, 1 g dietary fiber, 4 g usable carbs.

Mediterranean Turkey Loaf

Ground turkey is nutritious and often inexpensive, but it can be a little bland. Here's a way to liven it up a bit. This recipe serves a crowd, too. Make a big salad with vinaigrette, and there's supper.

2 pounds (900 g) ground turkey

1 cup (120 g) pork rind crumbs

1 medium onion, chopped

4 cloves garlic, crushed

2 teaspoons salt or Vege-Sal

1/2 teaspoon black pepper

1 egg

1/2 cup (75 g) crumbled feta cheese

2 tablespoons (12 g) Italian seasoning

1 cup (245 g) no-sugar-added spaghetti sauce, optional

You know the deal: Dump the turkey, pork rind crumbs, chopped onion, crushed garlic, salt and pepper, feta, Italian seasoning, and tomato paste in a big mixing bowl. Use clean hands to smoosh it all together really well.

Take two pieces of heavy-duty foil, long enough to reach down into your slow cooker, across the bottom, and back up the other side, and fold each into a strip about 2 inches (5 cm) wide. Put your basket steamer in the slow cooker and criss-cross the foil strips across it, going around the stem in the middle.

Dump the meat in the slow cooker and form it into a nice, even loaf on the steamer. Cover the slow cooker, set to low, and let the whole thing cook for 6 to 7 hours.

Use the foil strips to lift the meat loaf out onto a platter and serve. If you want, warm the no-sugar-added spaghetti sauce and top each serving with a couple of tablespoons (28 g).

Yield: 8 servings, each with: 284 calories, 15 g fat, 29 g protein, 8 g carbohydrate, 2 g dietary fiber, 6 g usable carbs.

Simple Turkey Drumsticks

You can't really fit a whole turkey in a slow cooker, but drumsticks fit nicely, and I love them. The serving size on these is huge, because carving a turkey drumstick into multiple servings is tough. We wound up with leftovers, but that's hardly a tragedy.

2½ pounds (1.1 kg) turkey legs—2 drumsticks

½ teaspoon salt or Vege-Sal

½ teaspoon garlic powder

½ teaspoon seasoned salt

½ teaspoon paprika

¼ teaspoon pepper

¼ cup (60 ml) chicken broth

Mix together all the seasonings and sprinkle them liberally over the drumsticks, covering all surfaces. Lay the drumsticks flat on the floor of your slow cooker. (This takes a large size slow cooker. My big one fits two drumsticks, flat.) Pour in the broth. Cover the pot, set to low, and cook for 5 hours.

Yield: 2 servings, each with: 689 calories, 32 g fat, 93 g protein, 1 g carbohydrate, trace dietary fiber, 1 g usable carbs.

Braised Turkey Wings with Mushrooms

Turkey wings are my favorite cut of turkey for the slow cooker. They fit in easily, they come in good individual serving sizes, and oh yeah, they taste great.

3¼ pounds (1.5 kg) turkey wings

¼ cup (60 ml) olive oil

½ cup (120 ml) chicken broth

1 teaspoon chicken bouillon concentrate

1 teaspoon poultry seasoning

1 tablespoon (16 g) tomato paste

1 cup (70 g) sliced mushrooms

½ medium onion, sliced

½ cup (115 g) sour cream

In a big, heavy skillet, brown the turkey all over in the oil over medium-high heat. Transfer the turkey to your slow cooker.

In a bowl, stir together the broth, bouillon, poultry seasoning, and tomato paste. Pour the mixture over the turkey. Add the mushrooms and onion. Cover the slow cooker, set it to low, and let it cook for 6 to 7 hours.

When the time's up, remove the turkey from the slow cooker with tongs. Whisk the sour cream into the sauce and serve the sauce over the turkey.

Yield: 3 servings, each with: 555 calories, 40 g fat, 41 g protein, 6 g carbohydrate, 1 g dietary fiber, 5 g usable carbs.

Turkey with Mushroom Sauce

3 pounds (1.4 kg) boneless, skinless turkey breast (in one big hunk,
    not thin cutlets)

2 tablespoons (28 g) butter

¼ cup (15 g) chopped fresh parsley

2 teaspoons dried tarragon

½ teaspoon salt or Vege-Sal

¼ teaspoon pepper

1 cup (70 g) sliced mushrooms

½ cup (120 ml) dry white wine

1 teaspoon chicken bouillon concentrate

Guar or xanthan (optional)

In a big, heavy skillet, sauté the turkey in the butter until it's golden all over. Transfer the turkey to your slow cooker.

Sprinkle the parsley, tarragon, salt or Vege-Sal, and pepper over the turkey. Place the mushrooms on top.

In a bowl, mix the wine and bouillon together until the bouillon dissolves. Pour it over the turkey. Cover the slow cooker, set it to low, and let it cook for 7 to 8 hours.

When the time's up, remove the turkey and put it on a platter. Transfer about half of the mushrooms to a blender and add the liquid from the slow cooker. Blend until the mushrooms are pureed. Scoop the rest of the mushrooms into the dish you plan to use to serve the sauce, add the liquid, and thicken further with guar or xanthan, if needed.

Yield: 8 servings, each with: 281 calories, 14 g fat, 34 g protein, 1 g carbohydrate, trace dietary fiber, 1 g usable carbs.

Chicken with Raspberry-Chipotle Sauce

Oh, my, is this wonderful. My only regret about this recipe is that the Raspberry-Chipotle Sauce loses its brilliant ruby color during the long, slow cooking. But the flavor definitely remains. Consider using this simple sauce uncooked as a condiment on roasted poultry or pork. If you can't find raspberry syrup at a local coffee joint, you can order it online.

3 pounds (1.4 kg) chicken

6 teaspoons (12 g) adobo seasoning

2 tablespoons (28 ml) oil

1 cup (125 g) raspberries

1/4 cup (60 g) raspberry-flavored sugar-free coffee flavoring syrup
  (Da Vinci makes one.)

1 chipotle chile canned in adobo sauce

1 tablespoon (15 ml) white wine vinegar

1/4 cup (4 g) chopped fresh cilantro (optional)

Sprinkle the chicken all over with the adobo seasoning.

In a big, heavy skillet, heat the oil over medium-high heat and then brown the chicken all over. Transfer the chicken to your slow cooker.

In a blender or food processor with the S-blade in place, combine the raspberries, raspberry-flavored coffee syrup, chipotle, and vinegar. Process till smooth. Pour the mixture evenly over the chicken. Cover the slow cooker, set it to low, and let it cook for 6 hours.

Stir the sauce before serving it over the chicken. Sprinkle a little cilantro over each piece of chicken, if desired.

Yield: 5 servings, each with: 492 calories, 36 g fat, 35 g protein, 5 g carbohydrate, 2 g dietary fiber, 3 g usable carbs.

Chicken Vindaloo

I made this at a local campground over Memorial Day Weekend, and it was a huge hit with fellow campers. It's exotic and wonderful.

>   6 pounds (2.7 kg) boneless, skinless chicken thighs
>
>   1 medium onion, chopped
>
>   5 cloves garlic, crushed
>
>   1/4 cup (32 g) grated ginger root
>
>   4 teaspoons (8 g) Garam Masala (see recipe page 340) or purchased garam masala
>
>   1 teaspoon ground turmeric
>
>   1/4 cup (60 ml) lime juice
>
>   1/4 cup (60 ml) rice vinegar
>
>   1/2 cup (120 ml) chicken broth
>
>   1 teaspoon salt

Put the chicken, onion, and garlic in your slow cooker.

In a bowl, stir together the ginger, garam masala, turmeric, lime juice, vinegar, broth, and salt. Pour the mixture over the chicken. Cover the slow cooker, set it to low, and let it cook for 6 to 7 hours.

Serve with *Slow Cooker Chutney* (see recipe page 307).

Yield: 12 servings, each with: 295 calories, 10 g fat, 46 g protein, 2 g carbohydrate, trace dietary fiber, 2 g usable carbs.

Chicken Stew

This dish is a nice change from the usual beef stew. It's light, flavorful, and your whole meal in one pot.

> 2 tablespoons (28 ml) olive oil
>
> 1¹/₂ pounds (680 g) boneless, skinless chicken thighs, cut into 1-inch (2.5 cm) cubes
>
> 8 ounces (225 g) sliced mushrooms
>
> 1 medium onion, sliced
>
> 3 cups (360 g) zucchini slices
>
> 4 cloves garlic, crushed
>
> 1 can (14 ounces, or 390 g) tomato wedges or diced tomatoes
>
> 3/4 cup (175 ml) chicken broth
>
> 1 teaspoon chicken bouillon concentrate
>
> 1 tablespoon (4 g) poultry seasoning
>
> Guar or xanthan

In a big, heavy skillet, heat 1 tablespoon (15 g) of the oil. Brown the chicken until it is golden all over. Transfer the chicken to your slow cooker.

Heat the remaining 1 tablespoon (15 g) of oil in the skillet and sauté the mushrooms, onion, and zucchini until the mushrooms change color and the onions are translucent. Transfer them to the slow cooker, too. Add the garlic and tomatoes to the slow cooker.

Put the broth and bouillon in the skillet and stir them around to dissolve any flavorful bits sticking to the skillet. Pour into the slow cooker. Sprinkle the poultry seasoning over the mixture. Cover the slow cooker, set it to low, and let it cook for 4 to 5 hours.

When the time's up, thicken the liquid in the slow cooker with guar or xanthan.

Yield: 6 servings, each with: 159 calories, 8 g fat, 11 g protein, 12 g carbohydrate, 2 g dietary fiber, 10 g usable carbs.

Chicken with Root Vegetables in Parmesan Cream

3 slices bacon

3 pounds (1.3 kg) chicken pieces—thighs, legs, or breasts, whatever you like

3 cloves garlic, crushed

2 turnips, peeled and sliced thin

1/4 large rutabaga, peeled and sliced thin

1/2 medium onion, peeled and sliced thin

4 cloves garlic, crushed

1 tablespoon dried sage

1/2 cup (120 ml) chicken broth

1 teaspoon chicken bouillon concentrate

2/3 cup (160 ml) heavy cream

1 cup (100 g) grated Parmesan cheese

In your big, heavy skillet, cook the bacon crisp. Remove from the pan and reserve. Skin the chicken—keep the skin for *Chicken Chips* (see recipe page 331)—and brown the chicken a bit in the bacon grease.

In the meantime, peel and slice your turnip, rutabaga, and onion. Put them in the slow cooker, stir them up a little, and place the chicken on top.

Mix together the garlic, sage, chicken broth, and chicken bouillon concentrate, stirring until the bouillon dissolves. Pour over the chicken, put on the lid, set to low, and let it cook for a good 6 to 7 hours.

When dinnertime comes, use a slotted spoon to transfer the chicken and vegetables to a platter and keep it in a warm place. Whisk the cream and Parmesan cheese into the sauce in the slow cooker. Re-cover the pot and let it heat for another 15 minutes. Then serve the chicken and vegetables with the sauce.

Yield: 6 servings, each with: 531 calories, 39 g fat, 37 g protein, 7 g carbohydrate, 1 g dietary fiber, 6 g usable carbs.

Lemon Chicken

3 pounds (1.4 kilogram) skinless chicken thighs

2 tablespoons (28 g) butter

1 teaspoon dried oregano

1/2 teaspoon seasoned salt

1/4 teaspoon pepper

1/4 cup (60 ml) chicken broth

3 tablespoons (45 ml) lemon juice

2 cloves garlic, crushed

2 tablespoons (8 g) chopped fresh parsley

1 teaspoon chicken bouillon concentrate

Guar or xanthan

In a big, heavy skillet, brown the chicken in the butter over medium-high heat.

In a bowl, mix together the oregano, seasoned salt, and pepper. When the chicken is golden, sprinkle the spice mixture over it. Transfer the chicken to your slow cooker.

Pour the broth and lemon juice in the skillet, stirring around to deglaze the pan. Add the garlic, parsley, and bouillon. Stir until the bouillon dissolves. Pour into the slow cooker.

Cover the slow cooker, set it to low, and let it cook for 4 to 5 hours. When the chicken is tender, remove it from the slow cooker. Thicken the sauce a bit with guar or xanthan. Serve the sauce with the chicken.

This dish goes well with *Cauli-Rice* (see recipe page 343).

Yield: 6 servings, each with: 200 calories, 9 g fat, 26 g protein, 2 g carbohydrate, 1 g dietary fiber, 1 g usable carbs.

Lemon-Herb Chicken

This is simple and classic.

3 pounds (1.4 kg) chicken parts—legs, thighs, or breasts, whatever you like

2 tablespoons (28 g) butter

1/2 medium onion, chopped

1/4 cup (60 ml) lemon juice

1/2 teaspoon chicken bouillon concentrate

1/4 cup (15 g) chopped fresh parsley

1 tablespoon (2 g) fresh thyme leaves

Cut the chicken into serving pieces and skin. Save the skins for *Chicken Chips* (see recipe page 331)!

In your big, heavy skillet, over medium heat, melt the butter and start the chicken browning.

In the meantime, chop the onion and throw it in the slow cooker. When the chicken is golden on both sides, use tongs to place the chicken on top of the onion.

Mix together the lemon juice and chicken bouillon concentrate until the bouillon dissolves. Pour over the chicken.

Chop the parsley and strip the thyme leaves from the stems. Scatter the herbs over the chicken. Cover the pot, set on low, and cook for 5 to 6 hours.

Serve chicken with the pan juices spooned over it. I like *Cauli-Rice* (see recipe page 343) with this to soak up the juices.

Yield: 4 to 5 servings; Assuming 4, each will have: 304 calories, 13 g fat, 41 g protein, 3 g carbohydrate, 1 g dietary fiber, 2 g usable carbs.

Chicken with Artichokes and Sun Dried Tomatoes

What a sunny flavor this dish has! And you don't need anything with it but a glass of wine.

> 2 pounds (900 g) boneless, skinless chicken breast or thighs, or both
>
> 2 tablespoons (28 ml) olive oil
>
> 2 cans (13½ ounces, or 380 g each) quartered artichoke hearts
>
> ½ cup (55 g) sun-dried tomatoes, oil packed
>
> ½ cup (90 g) roasted red peppers—cut in strips
>
> 2 cloves garlic, crushed
>
> ½ cup (120 ml) chicken broth
>
> 1 teaspoon chicken bouillon concentrate
>
> ¼ teaspoon pepper
>
> 3 tablespoons (45 ml) balsamic vinegar
>
> 3 tablespoons (27 g) capers, drained
>
> ¼ cup (10 g) minced fresh basil

Cut the chicken into 6 servings. In your big, heavy skillet, start it browning in the olive oil.

In the meantime, drain the artichokes and throw them in the slow cooker. Drain the tomatoes and chop them if they're in halves. (I buy them already in strips.) Drain and slice your roasted red peppers and add them as well. Crush the garlic and throw it in, too. Now, go flip your chicken!

Stir together the chicken broth, chicken bouillon concentrate, pepper, and balsamic vinegar until the bouillon dissolves.

When the chicken is just touched with gold on either side, lay it on the vegetables in the slow cooker. Pour the broth mixture over everything, put on the lid, set it to low, and let it cook for 5 to 6 hours.

To serve, place a serving of chicken on each plate and scoop some of the vegetables on top. Thicken the liquid in the pot just a touch with your guar or xanthan shaker and spoon that over, too. Now scatter a few capers and some basil over each plate and serve it forth.

This would be a perfect dish to serve over tofu shirataki angel hair!

Yield: 6 servings, each with: 296 calories, 10 g fat, 38 g protein, 12 g carbohydrate, 1 g dietary fiber, 11 g usable carbs.

Lemon~White Wine~Tarragon Chicken

This is similar to Chicken with Thyme and Artichokes (page 82), except, of course, that tarragon is very different from thyme and there are no artichokes.

> 3 pounds (1.4 kg) skinless chicken thighs
>
> 1/2 cup (120 ml) dry white wine
>
> 1/2 cup (120 milliliter) lemon juice
>
> 1 teaspoon Splenda
>
> 1 tablespoon (5 g) dried tarragon
>
> 1/2 teaspoon pepper
>
> 1 teaspoon chicken bouillon concentrate
>
> Guar or xanthan

Put the chicken in your slow cooker.

In a bowl, mix together the wine, lemon juice, Splenda, tarragon, pepper, and bouillon, stirring until the bouillon dissolves. Pour the mixture over the chicken. Cover the slow cooker, set it to low, and let it cook for 6 hours.

Remove the chicken to serving plates and thicken the remaining liquid with guar or xanthan to achieve the texture of cream.

Yield: 6 servings, each with: 176 calories, 5 g fat, 26 g protein, 3 g carbohydrate, trace dietary fiber, 3 g usable carbs.

Mom's 1960s Chicken, Redux

Back in the 1960s my mom would make a dish for company with chicken breasts, wrapped in bacon, laid on a layer of chipped beef, topped with a sauce made of sour cream and cream of mushroom soup. It tasted far more sophisticated than it sounds and never failed to draw raves from dinner party guests. This is my attempt to de-carb and slow-cooker-ize the same dish—without the carb-filled cream of mushroom soup.

2 1/4 ounces (62 g) dried beef slices (aka "chipped beef")

6 slices bacon

2 pounds (900 g) boneless, skinless chicken breasts

1 cup (70 g) sliced mushrooms

1 tablespoon (14 g) butter

1 cup (235 ml) heavy cream

1 teaspoon beef bouillon concentrate

1 pinch onion powder

1 pinch celery salt

1/4 teaspoon pepper

Guar or xanthan

1 cup (230 g) sour cream

Paprika

Line the bottom of your slow cooker with the dried beef.

Place the bacon in a glass pie plate or on a microwave bacon rack and microwave for 3 to 4 minutes on high. Drain the bacon and reserve. (What you're doing here is cooking some of the grease off of the bacon, without cooking it crisp.)

Cut the chicken into 6 servings. Wrap each piece of chicken in a slice of bacon and place it in the slow cooker on top of the dried beef.

In a big, heavy skillet, sauté the mushrooms in the butter until they're soft. Add the cream and bouillon and stir until the bouillon dissolves. Stir in the onion powder, celery salt, and pepper and then thicken with guar or xanthan until the mixture reaches a gravy consistency. Stir in the sour cream.

Spoon this mixture over the chicken breasts and sprinkle with a little paprika. Cover the slow cooker, set it to low, and let it cook for 5 to 6 hours.

Chicken with Apples and Rosemary

This happened because our darling friend Keith Johnson, the Organic Gardening God, showed up at the door with an incredibly fragrant branch of fresh rosemary.

> 2 pounds (900 g) cut up chicken—legs, thighs, or breasts, whatever you like
>
> 1 Granny Smith apple
>
> 1 onion
>
> 1 cup (235 ml) chicken broth
>
> 1/4 teaspoon pepper
>
> 1 teaspoon chicken bouillon concentrate
>
> 1 tablespoon (2 g) fresh rosemary leaves
>
> 1/2 cup (120 ml) heavy cream
>
> Guar or xanthan

Lay the chicken in your slow cooker. Slice the apple and onion both about 1/4-inch (6 mm) thick and lay them on top of the chicken.

Mix together the broth, pepper, and bouillon concentrate until the concentrate is dissolved and pour it over the whole thing. Scatter the rosemary needles evenly over everything.

Cover and cook on low for 5 to 6 hours.

When time is up, use a slotted spoon to fish the chicken, apples, and onions out and put them on a platter. Now whisk the cream into the juice in the pot and use your guar or xanthan shaker to thicken the whole thing to a heavy cream consistency. Serve the gravy with the chicken, apples, and onions.

Yield: 5 servings, each with: 385 calories, 28 g fat, 25 g protein, 7 g carbohydrate, 1 g dietary fiber, 6 g usable carbs.

Chicken with Thyme and Artichokes

This is sort of classic, yet very little work.

> 1¹/₂ pounds (680 g) boneless, skinless chicken thighs
>
> 2 tablespoons (28 ml) olive oil
>
> ¹/₂ cup (120 ml) dry white wine
>
> 1 tablespoon (15 ml) lemon juice
>
> 1 teaspoon chicken bouillon concentrate
>
> 2 teaspoons dried thyme
>
> 1 clove garlic, crushed
>
> ¹/₄ teaspoon pepper
>
> 1 can (13 ounces, or 365 g) artichoke hearts, drained
>
> Guar or xanthan

In a big, heavy skillet, brown the chicken in the oil over medium-high heat until golden on both sides. Transfer to your slow cooker.

In a bowl, stir together the wine, lemon juice, bouillon, thyme, garlic, and pepper. Pour the mixture over the chicken. Place the artichokes on top. Cover the slow cooker, set it to low, and let it cook for 6 hours.

Scoop out the chicken and artichokes with a slotted spoon. Thicken the liquid left in the pot with just enough guar or xanthan to make it the thickness of half-and-half.

Serve the chicken and artichokes, plus the sauce, over *Cauli-Rice* (see recipe page 343).

Yield: 4 servings, each with: 314 calories, 10 g fat, 42 g protein, 7 g carbohydrate, trace dietary fiber, 7 g usable carbs.

Tequila Lime Chicken

Please don't write me asking what to substitute for the tequila; the flavor is too distinctive. If you must, just leave it out and make Lime Chicken.

3/4 teaspoon salt or Vege-Sal

1/4 teaspoon pepper

1/4 teaspoon cayenne

1/2 teaspoon garlic powder

1/4 teaspoon onion powder

1/4 teaspoon thyme

3 pounds (1.4 kg) skinless chicken thighs

2 tablespoons (28 g) butter

1 tablespoon (15 ml) olive oil

4 cloves garlic

3 tablespoons (45 ml) lime juice

1 tablespoon (15 ml) tequila

1 teaspoon chicken bouillon concentrate

Mix together everything from the salt or Vege-Sal through the thyme.

If your chicken came with the skin on, skin it and save the skin for *Chicken Chips* (see recipe page 331). Sprinkle the seasoning mixture over all sides of your chicken.

Put your big, heavy skillet over medium heat and add the butter and olive oil. Let the butter melt and swirl the two together. Now add the chicken and let brown until it's golden on both sides. While it's cooking, crush or mince your garlic.

Transfer the chicken to your slow cooker with tongs and pour all the fat into the cooker on top of it. Put the pan back on the burner.

Throw the garlic in the pan and stir it around for minute. Then add the lime juice, tequila, and chicken bouillon concentrate. Stir everything around, scraping up all the nice browned bits and making sure the bouillon concentrate is dissolved. Then pour this mixture evenly over the chicken.

Cover the slow cooker, set to low, and let it cook for 5 hours. Then remove the chicken to a platter, thicken up the sauce, and serve it over the chicken.

Yield: 5 servings, each with: 265 calories, 13 g fat, 31 g protein, 2 g carbohydrate, trace dietary fiber, 2 g usable carbs.

Lay a big sheet of foil on your counter and pile all the vegetables in the middle. Sprinkle the salt and pepper over them. Crumble in the bacon. Dot with the butter. You could add a spoonful of the bacon grease, too, if you wanted.

Lay another sheet of foil on top. Roll up all the edges, making a tight packet. Drop it in your slow cooker on top of whatever is cooking. This will take 3 to 4 hours on low.

Yield: 3 to 4 servings; Assuming 4, each will have: 71 calories, 6 g fat, 2 g protein, 2 g carbohydrate, 1 g dietary fiber, 1 g usable carbs.

Cheesy Cauliflower Packet

> ¹/₄ large head cauliflower
> ¹/₄ green bell pepper
> ¹/₄ onion
> 1 tablespoon (14 g) butter
> ¹/₄ cup (30 g) shredded Cheddar cheese
> Salt and pepper

Cut the cauliflower into chunks no bigger than 1 inch (2.5 cm); smaller will cook faster. Dice the pepper and onion.

Lay a big sheet of foil on your counter and pile the vegetables in the middle. Dot with the butter, sprinkle on the cheese, and salt and pepper it. Lay another sheet of foil over it and roll up the edges, making a packet. Drop this into your slow cooker on top of whatever supper is cooking—two hours on low is about right.

Yield: 4 servings, each with: 67 calories, 5 g fat, 3 g protein, 3 g carbohydrate, 1 g dietary fiber, 2 g usable carbs.

🍲 Foil Packet Side Dishes

This is a nifty little technique: You wrap your vegetable side dish in a foil packet and then drop it in the slow cooker right on top of your main dish, whatever it may be. You get two dishes, with only the one slow cooker to wash.

However, since most vegetables cook more quickly than the main dishes do, you'll need to put them in later. That means these side dishes won't work for days when you're out from breakfast until supper. They're ideal, however, for those days when you're in and out of the house all day. Just make up the packet at the same time you put your main dish in to cook and stash it in the fridge. Then drop it in the slow cooker on one of those quick trips through the house, between picking up the dry cleaning and taking the kid to gymnastics.

I haven't tried it, but I'm betting using frozen vegetables would add a good hour to these cooking times, maybe more.

🍲 Hobo UnPotatoes Slow-Cooker Style

4 slices cooked bacon

1/4 large head cauliflower

1/4 medium chopped onion

1/4 cup (28 g) shredded carrot

1/3 cup (40 g) diced celery

1/4 teaspoon salt or Vege-Sal

1/4 teaspoon pepper

1 tablespoon (14 g) butter

If you didn't start with cooked bacon, you might microwave it. Five minutes on high would be about right in my microwave.

Cut your cauliflower into chunks no bigger than 1 inch (2.5 cm). Chop your onion, shred your carrot, and dice your celery—all that stuff.

Chive-and-Garlic Spinach Packet

This is the easiest creamed spinach you'll ever make.

> 2 ounces (55 g) frozen chopped spinach, thawed
>
> 1 clove garlic, crushed
>
> 1/4 cup (60 g) cream cheese with chives and onions
>
> 1 tablespoon (14 g) butter

Drain your spinach really well—I dump mine into a colander in the sink and then squeeze it out with clean hands.

Stir the crushed garlic into the spinach.

Take a big sheet of foil and lay it on your counter. Pile the spinach on top. Add the cream cheese, in clumps, instead of one big blob. Dot with the butter.

Lay another sheet of foil over the spinach and roll up the sides, making a tight packet. Drop on top of whatever you're cooking in the slow cooker and let it cook for 60 to 90 minutes.

Yield: 4 servings, each with: 80 calories, 7 g fat, 1 g protein, 2 g carbohydrate, trace dietary fiber, 2 g usable carbs.

Slow Cooker Chutney

This is the slow cooker version of my *Major Gray's Chutney* recipe from *500 More Low-Carb Recipes*. It's wonderful with anything curried.

> 2 pounds (900 g) sliced peaches
>
> 1/3 cup (33 g) ginger root slices
>
> 1 1/2 cups (38 g) Splenda
>
> 3 cloves garlic
>
> 1 teaspoon red pepper flakes
>
> 1 teaspoon cloves
>
> 1 1/2 cups (355 ml) cider vinegar
>
> Guar or xanthan

Combine everything but the guar or xanthan in your slow cooker. Cover the slow cooker, set it to low, and let it cook for 4 hours.

Take the lid off and let it cook for another hour to let it cook down. Thicken a bit more, if you like, and store in an airtight container in the fridge.

Yield: 32 servings (1 quart total), each with: 15 calories, trace fat, trace protein, 4 g carbohydrate, 1 g dietary fiber, 3 g usable carbs.

Slow Cooker Cranberry Sauce

I like to have cranberry sauce on hand for those occasions when I don't want to do much cooking. It adds interest to plain roasted chicken (or even store-bought rotisseried chicken.) It's easy to do and makes plenty!

24 ounces (680 g) cranberries

1 cup (235 ml) water

2 cups (50 g) Splenda

Simply combine everything in your slow cooker and give it a stir. Cover the slow cooker, set it to low, and let it cook for 3 hours.

This won't be as syrupy as commercial cranberry sauce because of the lack of sugar. If this bothers you, you can thicken your sauce with your trusty guar or xanthan shaker, but I generally leave mine as is. This makes quite a lot, so divide it between three or four snap-top containers and store it in the freezer. This way, you'll have cranberry sauce on hand whenever you bring home a rotisseried chicken!

Yield: Makes about 23/4 cups, or 22 servings of 2 tablespoons, each with: 15 calories, trace fat, trace protein, 4 g carbohydrate, 1 g dietary fiber, 3 g usable carbs.

Cranberry-Peach Chutney

This is seriously kicked-up from regular cranberry sauce! It's a natural with curried poultry, but try it with any simple poultry or pork dish.

12 ounces (340 g) cranberries

1 1/2 cups (255 g) diced peaches (I use unsweetened frozen peach slices, diced.)

1 clove garlic, minced

3 inches (7.5 cm) ginger root, sliced into paper-thin rounds

1 lime, sliced paper-thin

1 1/4 cups (31 g) Splenda

1 cinnamon stick

1 teaspoon mustard seed

1/4 teaspoon salt

1/4 teaspoon orange extract

1/4 teaspoon baking soda

Combine everything but the baking soda in your slow cooker. Cover the slow cooker, set it to low, and let it cook for 3 hours, stirring once halfway through.

When the time's up, stir in the baking soda and keep stirring till the fizzing subsides. Store in a tightly lidded container in the fridge. If you plan to keep it for long, freezing's a good idea.

Why use baking soda? Because by neutralizing some of the acid in the cranberries, it lets you get away with less Splenda—and fewer carbs.

Yield: Makes about 2 1/2 cups, or 20 servings of 2 tablespoons, each with: 31 calories, trace fat, trace protein, 8 g carbohydrate, 1 g dietary fiber, 7 g usable carbs.

Cranberry Chutney

This is a cranberry sauce with a kick! It's great with anything curried or just with chicken or pork.

> 12 ounces (340 g) fresh cranberries
>
> 2/3 cup (16 g) Splenda—or other sugar-free sweetener to equal 2/3 cup (133 g) sugar
>
> 1/2 cup (120 ml) water
>
> 1/2 cup (120 ml) cider vinegar
>
> 6 whole allspice berries
>
> 6 whole cloves
>
> 3 cinnamon sticks
>
> 3 garlic cloves, crushed
>
> 1/2 medium onion, diced
>
> Guar or xanthan

Simply combine everything but the guar or xanthan in your slow cooker. Cover, set to low, and let cook for 4 hours. Then let it cool, thicken to a syrupy consistency with your guar or xanthan shaker, and store in a snap-top container in the fridge. If you're not going to use it up in a week or two, consider two or three smaller containers in the freezer.

Yield: 12 servings, each with: 51 calories, 1 g fat, 1 g protein, 13 g carbohydrate, 5 g dietary fiber, 8 g usable carbs.

chapter eleven

Slow Cooker Desserts

There are desserts that adapt well to the slow cooker, and then there are desserts that don't. In this chapter, I've really played to the slow cooker's strengths. Custards actually cook better in a slow cooker than in the oven, which is why you'll find half a dozen of them here. Indeed, they're so easy in the slow cooker and so appealing and nutritious, you may find yourself making custard more often.

Your slow cooker also excels at baking cheesecake, though you may not know it yet. Give it a try!

Chocolate Fudge Custard

This really is dense and fudgy. It's intensely chocolatey, too.

>   1 cup (235 ml) Carb Countdown dairy beverage
>
>   3 ounces (85 g) unsweetened baking chocolate
>
>   2/3 cup (16 g) Splenda
>
>   1 cup (235 ml) heavy cream
>
>   1/2 teaspoon vanilla extract
>
>   1 pinch salt
>
>   6 eggs, beaten

In a saucepan, over the lowest possible heat (use a double boiler or heat diffuser if you have one), warm the Carb Countdown with the chocolate. When the chocolate melts, whisk the two together and then whisk in the Splenda.

Spray a 6-cup (1.4 L) glass casserole dish with nonstick cooking spray. Pour the cream into it and add the chocolate mixture. Whisk in the vanilla extract and salt. Now add the eggs, one by one, whisking each in well before adding the next one.

Put the casserole dish in your slow cooker and pour water around it up to 1 inch of the top rim. Cover the slow cooker, set it to low, and let it cook for 4 hours.

Then turn off the slow cooker, remove the lid, and let the water cool enough so it won't scald you before removing the casserole dish. Chill the custard well before serving.

Yield: 6 servings, each with: 299 calories, 28 g fat, 10 g protein, 6 g carbohydrate, 2 g dietary fiber, 4 g usable carbs.

Flan

This is my slow cooker version of *Maria's Flan* from *500 Low-Carb Recipes*. It's so rich!

    2 tablespoons (42 g) sugar-free imitation honey

    1 teaspoon blackstrap molasses

    1 cup (235 ml) Carb Countdown dairy beverage

    1 cup (235 ml) heavy cream

    6 eggs

    2/3 cup (16 g) Splenda

    1 teaspoon vanilla

    1 pinch nutmeg

    1 pinch salt

Spray a 6-cup (1.4 L) glass casserole dish with nonstick cooking spray. In a bowl, mix together the honey and the molasses. Pour the mixture in the bottom of the casserole dish.

In a mixing bowl, preferably one with a pouring lip, combine the Carb Countdown, cream, eggs, Splenda, vanilla, nutmeg, and salt. Whisk everything together well. Pour the mixture into the casserole dish.

Carefully lower the casserole dish into your slow cooker. Now pour water around the casserole dish to within 1 inch of the rim. Cover the slow cooker, set it to low, and let it cook for 3 to 31/2 hours.

Yield: 6 servings, each with: 229 calories, 20 g fat, 8 g protein, 3 g carbohydrate, trace dietary fiber, 3 g usable carbs. (Analysis does not include the polyols in the imitation honey.)

Southeast Asian Coconut Custard

I adapted this from a carby recipe in another slow cooker book. Maria, who tested it, says it's wonderful and also has a Latino feel to it. Look for shredded unsweetened coconut in Asian markets and health food stores.

1/4 cup (84 g) sugar-free imitation honey

1/2 teaspoon blackstrap molasses

1 1/2 teaspoons grated ginger root

1 tablespoon (15 ml) lime juice

1 can (14 ounces, or 390 ml) coconut milk

2/3 cup (16 g) Splenda

1/4 teaspoon ground cardamom

1 teaspoon grated ginger root

1/2 cup (120 ml) Carb Countdown dairy beverage

1/2 cup (120 ml) heavy cream

1/2 teaspoon vanilla extract

4 eggs

1/2 cup (40 g) shredded unsweetened coconut

Spray a 6-cup (1.4 L) glass casserole dish with nonstick cooking spray. Put the honey and molasses in the casserole dish. Cover the casserole dish with plastic wrap or a plate and microwave on high for 2 minutes. Add the 1 1/2 teaspoons ginger and lime juice and stir. Set aside.

In a mixing bowl, combine the coconut milk, Splenda, cardamom, 1 teaspoon ginger, Carb Countdown, cream, vanilla extract, and eggs. Whisk until well combined. Pour into the casserole dish. Cover the casserole dish with foil and secure it with a rubber band.

Put the casserole dish in your slow cooker and pour water around it to within 1 inch of the rim. Cover the slow cooker, set it to low, and let it cook for 3 to 4 hours.

Turn off the slow cooker, uncover, and let it cool till you can lift out the casserole dish without scalding your fingers. Chill overnight.

Before serving, stir the coconut in a dry skillet over medium heat until it's golden. Remove the custard from the fridge and run a knife carefully around the edge. Put a plate on top and carefully invert the custard onto the plate. Sprinkle the toasted coconut on top.

Yield: 8 servings, each with: 227 calories, 22 g fat, 5 g protein, 5 g carbohydrate, 2 g dietary fiber, 3 g usable carbs. (Analysis does not include the polyols in the imitation honey.)

Maple Custard

This is for all you maple fans out there, and I know you are legion!

> 1½ cups (355 ml) Carb Countdown dairy beverage
> ½ cup (120 ml) heavy cream
> ⅓ cup (107 ml) sugar-free pancake syrup
> ⅓ cup (8 g) Splenda
> 3 eggs
> 1 pinch salt
> 1 teaspoon vanilla extract
> ½ teaspoon maple extract

Simply whisk everything together and pour the mixture into a 6-cup (1.4 L) glass casserole dish you've sprayed with nonstick cooking spray. Put the casserole dish in your slow cooker and pour water around it to within 1 inch of the rim. Cover the slow cooker, set it to low, and let it cook for 4 hours.

When the time's up, turn off the slow cooker, remove the lid, and let it sit until the water is cool enough so that you can remove the casserole without risk of scalding. Chill well before serving.

Yield: 6 servings, each with: 135 calories, 12 g fat, 6 g protein, 2 g carbohydrate, 0 g dietary fiber, 2 g usable carbs. (Analysis does not include the polyols in the sugar-free pancake syrup.)

Maple-Pumpkin Custard

This is very much like the filling of a pumpkin pie, without the crust. The pecans add a little textural contrast.

> 1 can (15 ounces, or 425 g) canned pumpkin purée
>
> 1 cup (235 ml) Carb Countdown dairy beverage
>
> 1/2 cup (120 ml) heavy cream
>
> 1/3 cup (107 ml) sugar-free pancake syrup
>
> 1/3 cup (8 g) Splenda
>
> 1/2 teaspoon maple flavoring
>
> 3 eggs
>
> 1 pinch salt
>
> 1 tablespoon (6 g) pumpkin pie spice
>
> 1/3 cup (37 g) chopped pecans
>
> 1 1/2 teaspoons butter
>
> *Whipped Topping* (see recipe page 342)

In a mixing bowl, preferably one with a pouring lip, whisk together the pumpkin, Carb Countdown, cream, pancake syrup, Splenda, maple flavoring, eggs, salt, and pumpkin pie spice.

Spray a 6-cup (1.4 L) glass casserole dish with nonstick cooking spray. Pour the custard mixture into it. Place it in your slow cooker. Now carefully fill the space around the casserole with water up to 1 inch from the rim. Cover the slow cooker, set it to low, and let it cook for 3 to 4 hours.

Remove the lid, turn off the slow cooker, and let it cool till you can remove the casserole dish without scalding your fingers. Chill the custard for at least several hours.

Before serving, put the pecans and butter in a heavy skillet over medium heat and stir them for 5 minutes or so. Set aside. Also have the *Whipped Topping* made and standing by.

Serve the custard with a dollop of *Whipped Topping* and 1 tablespoon (7 g) of toasted pecans on each serving.

Yield: 6 servings, each with: 341 calories, 31 g fat, 7 g protein, 10 g carbohydrate, 3 g dietary fiber, 7 g usable carbs. (Analysis does not include the polyols in the sugar-free pancake syrup.)

Hot Cinnamon Mocha

Assemble this in your slow cooker before going skating, caroling, or to a football game and have a winter party waiting when you get home!

> ½ gallon (1.9 L) chocolate-flavored Carb Countdown dairy beverage
>
> 2 cinnamon sticks
>
> 3 tablespoons (18 g) instant coffee granules
>
> 1½ teaspoons vanilla extract

Combine everything in your slow cooker and give it a stir. Cover the slow cooker, set it to high, and let it cook for 3 hours. Turn the slow cooker to low and serve from the slow cooker.

If it's a grown-up party, put a bottle of *Mockahlua* on the side for spiking! (See recipe page 342.)

Yield: 10 servings, each with: 92 calories, 4 g fat, 10 g protein, 5 g carbohydrate, 2 g dietary fiber, 3 g usable carbs.

About Cheesecake

There were so many cheesecake recipes in *500 More Low-Carb Recipes* that I only did three for this book. However, cheesecake works very well in the slow cooker, so feel free to experiment with baking your favorite low-carb cheesecake recipes this way.

You'll notice I've called for light cream cheese (or Neufchâtel, which is, so far as I can tell, the same thing) and light sour cream in these recipes, instead of the full-fat versions. There's a reason for this: The light versions generally have no more carbohydrate than their full-fat counterparts, and they are, of course, lower calorie. I consider that a gain, and the cheesecakes come out very well. However, feel free to use the full-fat versions if you prefer.

(Since writing the above paragraph, my feelings have changed. I now deliberately aim for 75 percent of my calories to come from fat and prefer full fat cream cheese.)

Rhubarb Flummery

Because it's so sour, rhubarb is low-carb. This is a simple, old-fashioned dessert.

  1 pound (455 g) frozen rhubarb

  1/2 cup (12 g) Splenda

  1/2 cup (120 ml) water

  1/8 teaspoon orange extract

  Guar or xanthan

Place the rhubarb in your slow cooker and stir in the Splenda, water, and orange extract. Cover the slow cooker, set it to low, and let it cook for 5 to 6 hours.

When the time's up, the rhubarb will be very soft. Mash it with a fork to a rough pulp. Thicken the sauce to a soft pudding consistency with guar or xanthan and serve hot or cold.

This dessert is great with a little heavy cream or *Whipped Topping* (see recipe page 342).

Yield: 6 servings, each with: 16 calories, trace fat, trace protein, 4 g carbohydrate, 1 g dietary fiber, 3 g usable carbs.

Mochaccino Cheesecake

This cheesecake is extraordinary, as good as any dessert I ever had in a restaurant. This alone is a good enough reason to go buy a large, round slow cooker and an 8-inch (20 cm) springform to fit into it! It's also a good excuse to make some *Mockahlua* (see recipe page 342), but who needs an excuse to do that?

Crisp Chocolate Crust (see recipe on the next page)

16 ounces (455 g) light cream cheese or Neufchâtel cheese, softened

1 egg

1/4 cup (60 ml) heavy cream

1/2 cup (45 g) + 2 tablespoons (12 g) unsweetened cocoa powder

1/2 cup (12 g) Splenda

1/4 cup (60 ml) *Mockahlua* (see recipe page 342)

2 tablespoons (28 ml) brewed coffee

Using your electric mixer, beat together the cream cheese, egg, and cream until quite smooth. (You'll need to scrape down the sides of the bowl several times.) Now beat in the cocoa powder, Splenda, *Mockahlua*, and coffee. When it's all well blended and very smooth, pour into the crust. Cover the springform pan tightly with foil, squeezing it in around the rim.

Take a big sheet of foil, at least 18 inches (46 centimeters) long, and roll it into a loose cylinder. Bend it into a circle and place it in the bottom of your slow cooker. (You're making a rack to put the pan on.) Pour 1/4 inch of water in the bottom of the slow cooker and then put the pan on the donut of foil. Cover the slow cooker, set it to high, and let it cook for 3 to 4 hours.

Turn off the slow cooker, uncover, and let cool for at least 20 to 30 minutes before you try to remove the pan from the slow cooker. Chill well before serving.

It's nice to make the *Whipped Topping* (see recipe page 342), with a little *Mockahlua* in it, to serve on top of this, but it's hardly essential.

Yield: 12 servings, each with: 284 calories, 24 g fat, 11 g protein, 10 g carbohydrate, 4 g dietary fiber, 6 g usable carbs. (Analysis includes Crisp Chocolate Crust. You could cut this into eight, more generous servings if you'd like.)

Crisp Chocolate Crust

> 1¹/₂ cups (218 g) almonds
>
> ¹/₄ cup (6 g) Splenda
>
> 2 squares bitter chocolate, melted
>
> 3 tablespoons (45 g) butter, melted
>
> 2 tablespoons (20 g) vanilla whey protein powder

Preheat the oven to 325°F (170°C, or gas mark 3).

Using the S-blade of your food processor, grind the almonds until they're the texture of corn meal. Add the Splenda and pulse to combine. Pour in the chocolate and butter and run processor till evenly distributed. (You may need to stop the processor and run the tip of a knife blade around the outer edge to get everything to combine properly.) Then add the protein powder and pulse again to combine.

Turn the mixture into an 8-inch (20 cm) springform pan you've coated with nonstick cooking spray. Press firmly and evenly into place. Bake for 10 to 12 minutes in the preheated oven. Cool before filling.

Yield: 12 servings, each with: 164 calories, 15 g fat, 6 g protein, 5 g carbohydrate, 3 g dietary fiber, 2 g usable carbs.

New York–Style Cheesecake

You can top this with fruit if you like, but it's mighty good just as it is.

> *"Graham" Crust* (see recipe on the next page)
>
> 1 pound (455 g) light cream cheese or Neufchâtel cheese, softened
>
> ¹/₂ cup (115 g) light sour cream
>
> 2 eggs
>
> ¹/₂ cup (12 g) Splenda
>
> 2 teaspoons vanilla extract
>
> 1 pinch salt

Prepare the *"Graham" Crust* and let it cool.

Using your electric mixer, beat the cheese, sour cream, and eggs until they're very smooth. (You'll need to scrape down the sides of the bowl at least a few times.) Now

beat in the Splenda, vanilla extract, and salt. Pour into the waiting crust. Cover the pan tightly with foil, squeezing it in around the rim.

Take a big sheet of foil, at least 18 inches (45 cm) long, and roll it into a loose cylinder. Bend it into a circle and place it in the bottom of your slow cooker. (You're making a rack to put the pan on.) Pour 1/4 inch of water into your slow cooker and then put the pan on the donut of foil. Cover the slow cooker, set it to high, and let it cook for 3 to 4 hours.

Turn off the slow cooker, uncover, and let cool for at least 20 to 30 minutes before you try to remove the pan from the slow cooker. Chill well before serving.

Yield: 12 servings, each with: 241 calories, 21 g fat, 8 g protein, 6 g carbohydrate, 2 g dietary fiber, 4 g usable carbs. (You could cut this into eight, more generous servings if you'd like.)

"Graham" Crust

Wheat germ and wheat bran give this a "graham" flavor.

> 1¹/₄ cups (181 g) almonds
> 2 tablespoons (14 g) wheat germ
> 2 tablespoons (14 g) wheat bran
> 3 tablespoons (4.5 g) Splenda
> 1 pinch salt
> 6 tablespoons (85 g) butter, melted

Preheat the oven to 325°F (170°C, or gas mark 3).

Put the almonds in your food processor with the S-blade in place. Run it until they're ground to about the texture of corn meal. Add the wheat germ, wheat bran, Splenda, and salt and pulse to combine. Now turn on the processor and pour in the butter, running the processor until everything's well combined. (You may need to stop the processor and run a knife around the bottom edge to make sure all the dry ingredients come in contact with the butter.)

Turn this mixture out into an 8-inch (20 cm) springform pan you've sprayed with nonstick cooking spray. Press firmly into place. Bake for 10 to 12 minutes or until just turning gold around the edges. Cool before filling.

Yield: 12 servings, each with: 144 calories, 14 g fat, 3 g protein, 4 g carbohydrate, 2 g dietary fiber, 2 g usable carbs.

Peanut Butter Cheesecake

You can certainly eat this plain, but I'd likely top it with some sugar-free chocolate sauce. Hershey's makes one that's available in my grocery store, or you could order some from a low-carb e-tailer. Or you could make some from the recipe on page 341. Or for that matter, you could melt 6 to 8 ounces (170 to 225 grams) of your favorite sugar-free chocolate bars and swirl them into the peanut butter batter before baking. The possibilities are endless!

Crisp Chocolate Crust (see recipe page 322) or *"Graham" Crust*
   (see recipe page 323)
16 ounces (455 g) light cream cheese or Neufchâtel cheese, softened
1/2 cup (115 g) light sour cream
1 egg
3/4 cup (195 g) natural peanut butter (salted is better than no-salt-added, here)
2/3 cup (16 g) Splenda
1/2 teaspoons blackstrap molasses

Have your crust made and standing by.

Using your electric mixer, beat the cream cheese or Neufchâtel, sour cream, and egg until they're very smooth. (You'll want to scrape down the sides of the bowl several times.) Now beat in the peanut butter, Splenda, and molasses.

When the mixture is very smooth and well blended, pour it into the crust. Cover the pan tightly with foil, squeezing it in around the rim.

Take a big sheet of foil, at least 18 inches (45 cm) long, and roll it into a loose cylinder. Bend it into a circle and place it in the bottom of your slow cooker. (You're making a rack to put the pan on.) Pour 1/4 inch of water into the slow cooker and then put the pan on the donut of foil. Cover the slow cooker, set it to high, and let it cook for 3 to 4 hours.

Turn off the slow cooker, uncover, and let cool for at least 20 to 30 minutes before you try to remove the pan from the slow cooker. Chill well before serving.

Yield: 12 servings, each with: 364 calories, 32 g fat, 13 g protein, 10 g carbohydrate, 4 g dietary fiber, 6 g usable carbs. (Analysis includes Crisp Chocolate Crust. Analysis does not include any chocolate sauce or melted chocolate you might add! You could cut this into eight, more generous servings if you'd like.)

Chocolate Chocolate-Chip Pudding Cake

YUM! It's so gooey, chocolatey, and good! This is high enough in carbs that you'll want to save it for special occasions, but wow! Whipped cream or no-sugar-added vanilla ice cream would be good with this, but they're hardly essential. Serve hot or cold.

1/2 cup (56 g) almond meal

1/2 cup (80 g) vanilla whey protein powder

1 teaspoon guar or xanthan, divided

1/4 cup (23 g) plus 3 tablespoons (18 g) unsweetened cocoa powder

3/4 cup (180 g) erythritol or xylitol, divided

2 teaspoons baking powder

1/4 teaspoon salt

1/2 cup (120 ml) half and half

3 tablespoons (45 g) butter—melted

1/2 cup (88 g) no-sugar chocolate chips

1/2 cup (12 g) Splenda, divided

2 tablespoons (3 g) Splenda

1 cup (235 ml) hot water

Coat your slow cooker with nonstick cooking spray.

In a mixing bowl, combine the almond meal, vanilla whey protein, 1/2 teaspoon of guar or xanthan, 3 tablespoons (18 g) of cocoa powder, 1/4 cup (60 g) plus 2 tablespoons (30 g) of erythritol, 1/4 cup (6 g) plus 2 tablespoons (3 g) of Splenda, baking powder, and salt. Stir together.

Add the half and half and melted butter and whisk together well. Stir in the chocolate chips and scrape the batter into the slow cooker.

In another bowl, combine the remaining 1/4 cup (60 g) plus 2 tablespoons (30 g) erythritol, 1/4 cup (6 g) Splenda, 1/2 teaspoon guar or xanthan, and 1/4 cup (23 g) cocoa powder. Sprinkle this mixture over the batter in the slow cooker. Now pour the hot water evenly over that. Do not mix.

Cover and cook on high for 1 1/2 to 2 hours and then serve.

Yield: 6 servings, each with: 328 calories, 19 g fat, 22 g protein, 23 g carbohydrate, 12 g dietary fiber, 11 g usable carbs.

It was a great day for me when I figured out that my Bundt pan just exactly fit in my big slow cooker, hanging from the rim, and allowing the lid to fit on tightly. I really like baking in my slow cooker. Not only are the results excellent, but it uses less energy than my oven. In the summer, it will heat up the kitchen less. And on holidays, it frees up the oven for other things, like a turkey or a ham. But you will need a slow cooker that fits a Bundt pan.

About dried egg white powder: You can find this in cans in the baking aisle, but I recommend buying it through Amazon.com; you'll get it cheaper. It's pricey, but it improves the texture of nut meal-based baked goods quite a lot.

Chocolate Chip Cinnamon Zucchini Snack Cake

This is a moist and sturdy cake, perfect for snacking on right out of your hand.

2¼ cups (252 g) almond meal, divided

½ cup (115 g) dried egg white powder

2 teaspoons baking powder

2 teaspoons guar or xanthan

1 cup (160 g) vanilla whey protein powder

½ teaspoons baking soda

3/4 teaspoon salt

1½ teaspoons cinnamon

½ cup (120 g) erythritol or xylitol

½ cup (12 g) Splenda

3 eggs

2/3 cup (150 g) coconut oil, melted

2/3 cup (154 g) plain yogurt

1½ cups (180 g) shredded zucchini—about 1 small zucchini

1 cup (175 g) sugar-free chocolate chips

Heavily grease a Bundt pan and use 1/4 cup (28 g) of the almond meal to flour it.

In a mixing bowl, combine all the other dry ingredients and stir until they're evenly distributed.

In another bowl, whisk together the eggs, melted coconut oil, and yogurt. If you haven't shredded your zucchini, take care of that little matter now, before you combine the wet ingredients with the dry ones.

Okay, dump the egg/oil/yogurt mixture into the dry ingredients and whisk them together, making sure you leave no pockets of dry stuff at the bottom. Now whisk in the zucchini and finally the chocolate chips.

Scrape the batter into the prepared Bundt pan and place the pan in your slow cooker. Set it for high and let it cook for 3 hours or until it's pulling away from the sides of the pan and a wooden skewer inserted halfway between the walls of the pan comes out clean. Turn off the slow cooker and leave it uncovered until the pan cools enough for you to handle it. Then turn out on a wire rack to finish cooling.

Note: This, too, is not as sweet as commercial baked goods. Again, feel free to increase the sweetener if you like.

Yield: 16 servings, each with: 328 calories, 20 g fat, 24 g protein, 17 g carbohydrate, 8 g dietary fiber, 9 g usable carbs.

Pumpkin Bread

This has enough carbs that it's not Induction food, and it probably shouldn't be a staple. But it's a magnificent treat: sweet and spicy and moist. With as much protein per slice as 4 eggs, it'll keep you full for a long, long time. It would make a great breakfast for egg-resistant kids! Since there are only two in my household, I cut it into slices, put each in a zipper-lock bag, and freeze them, so I have a treat with my tea whenever I like.

2 1/4 cups (252 g) almond meal, divided

1 1/2 cups (240 g) vanilla whey protein powder

1/2 cup (115 g) egg white powder

2 teaspoons baking powder

2 teaspoons baking soda

2 teaspoons guar or xanthan

1 cup (240 g) erythritol or xylitol

1 cup (25 g) Splenda

1 1/2 teaspoons salt

1 1/2 teaspoon cinnamon

1 teaspoon nutmeg

1/2 teaspoon ground cloves

1/4 teaspoon ground ginger

1 cup (225 g) coconut oil, melted

4 eggs

1 can (15 ounces, or 425 g) pumpkin purée

2/3 cup (160 ml) water

1 cup (120 g) chopped walnuts

Heavily grease your Bundt pan. Use 1/4 cup (28 g) of the almond meal to flour the pan.

In a big mixing bowl, combine all the dry ingredients, from the remaining 2 cups (224 g) almond meal through the ginger. Stir everything together until it's all evenly distributed. Break up any big lumps of stuff.

In another bowl, whisk together the melted oil, eggs, pumpkin purée, and water. Dump this mixture into the dry ingredients and whisk it all together, making sure there are no pockets of dry stuff anywhere.

Now whisk in the walnuts.

Scrape the batter into the prepared Bundt pan. Place the pan in your slow cooker, cover, and turn it on to high. Cook for 2½ to 3 hours or until a wooden skewer inserted halfway between the walls of the pan comes out clean.

Uncover the slow cooker and turn it off. Let the pumpkin bread cool there until you can handle the pan without burning yourself. Then remove from the slow cooker and turn it out on a wire rack to finish cooling.

Note: This version is mildly sweet, because I don't like stuff overwhelmingly sweet. If you're still coming off of major sugar addiction, you can increase the erythritol and Splenda each by as much as ½ cup (120g and 12g).

Yield: 16 slices, each with: 360 calories, 24 g fat, 27 g protein, 13 g carbohydrate, 2 g dietary fiber, 11 g usable carbs.

Caramel Mocha Latte

This isn't a baked good, but it would be good with them! And I couldn't figure out where else to put it.

12 cups (2.8 L) brewed coffee

3 cups (700 ml) heavy cream

½ cup (120 g) sugar-free chocolate coffee flavoring syrup

½ cup (120 g) caramel sugar-free coffee flavoring syrup

Just combine everything in your slow cooker and keep it on low to serve.

Yield: 12 generous servings, each with: 210 calories, 22 g fat, 1 g protein, 3 g carbohydrate, 0 g dietary fiber, 3 g usable carbs.

chapter twelve

Just A Few Extras . . .

This is where I've tucked the recipes that you need to make other recipes but that aren't, themselves, slow cooker stuff. It just seemed easiest to put them all in one place, you know? Most of these have appeared in one or more of my previous cookbooks. And by the way, we didn't count these toward your grand total of 300 slow cooker recipes—that's why they're extras.

Chicken Chips

Every time I mention on Facebook that I've made these, someone asks for the recipe. It's so simple and so good! Just take the skin you've peeled off any chicken and any chunks of fat, too, and spread them on your broiler rack. Slide them into the oven at 350°F (180°C, or gas mark 4) and let them roast for 15 minutes or so until they're brown and crisp. Salt them and eat them like chips. That's all. You'll wish you could buy sacks of extra chicken skin!

My MasterCook doesn't have a nutritional listing for just chicken skin, but these have no carbs. They're a good source of gelatin, too, which is great for your joints, hair, nails, and skin.

Dana's No-Sugar Ketchup

This recipe has appeared in all my cookbooks because ketchup is an essential ingredient in so many recipes, but store-bought ketchup usually has so much sugar. Recently, commercially-made low-carb ketchup has been appearing in the grocery stores. If you can get this, do so because food processors can get ingredients the home cook cannot, so store-bought low-carb ketchup is lower in carbs than this. If you can't find low-carb ketchup, however, this is easy to make, tastes great, and is about half the carbs of regular ketchup. Be aware that recipes that list ketchup as an ingredient are analyzed for this homemade version, so if you use commercial low-carb ketchup, the carb counts will be a tad lower.

6 ounces (170 g) tomato paste

2/3 cup (160 ml) cider vinegar

1/3 cup (80 ml) water

1/3 cup (8 g) Splenda

2 tablespoons (20 g) minced onion

2 cloves garlic

1 teaspoon salt

1/8 teaspoon ground allspice

1/8 teaspoon ground cloves

1/8 teaspoon pepper

Put everything in your blender and run it until the onion disappears. Scrape it into a container with a tight lid and store it in the refrigerator.

Yield: Makes roughly 1 1/2 cups, or 12 servings of 2 tablespoons, each with: 15 calories, trace fat, 1 g protein, 5 g carbohydrate, 1 g fiber, 4 g usable carbs.

Barbecue Green Beans

These are fab!

> 4 cups (496 g) cross-cut frozen green beans, unthawed
>
> ¼ cup (40 g) chopped onion
>
> 4 slices cooked bacon, drained and crumbled
>
> ⅓ cup (85 g) low-carb barbecue sauce (see recipe page 335 or use purchased sauce)

Put the green beans in your slow cooker. Add the onion and bacon and then stir in the barbecue sauce. Cover the slow cooker, set it to high, and let it cook for 3 hours. (If you prefer, set it to low and let it cook for 5 to 6 hours.)

Yield: 6 servings, each with: 58 calories, 2 g fat, 3 g protein, 8 g carbohydrate, 2 g dietary fiber, 6 g usable carbs.

Southern Beans

Southerners will be shocked to know that I never tasted green beans slowly cooked with bacon until I moved to southern Indiana, but I liked them right off. Around our house, this recipe is jokingly referred to as The Sacred Masonic Vegetable because my husband's never been to a Masonic banquet that didn't feature beans cooked this way!

> 4 cups (496 g) frozen green beans, unthawed
>
> ⅓ cup (53 g) diced onion
>
> ¼ cup (30 g) diced celery
>
> 4 slices bacon, cooked and crumbled
>
> 1 tablespoon (15 g) bacon grease
>
> ½ cup (120 ml) water

Place the beans in the slow cooker and stir in everything else. Cover the slow cooker, set it to low, and let it cook for 4 hours.

Yield: 6 servings, each with: 75 calories, 4 g fat, 3 g protein, 7 g carbohydrate, 3 g dietary fiber, 4 g usable carbs.

chapter ten

Slow Cooker Sides

My guess is you use your slow cooker mostly for main dishes because that's the way it'll make your life the most convenient. Many of the main dishes in this book are complete meals, full of vegetables as well as protein, and they don't need a thing with them except a beverage. With the main dishes that do need a side, the easiest and most appealing thing is often a salad.

Yet there are good reasons to cook a side dish in your slow cooker. Some of them just plain take less work and watching this way, like the Southern Beans. Sometimes you want to make an interesting side to go with a plain meat roasting in the oven and want to be able to ignore it for an hour or two or three while you do something else. In both of these instances, the slow cooker is your very good friend.

Chipotle Turkey Legs

This dish has spicy, rich Southwestern flavor.

> 3 turkey drumsticks, about 2 pounds (900 g) total
>
> 1 1/2 teaspoons cumin
>
> 1 teaspoon chili powder
>
> 1 teaspoon dried, powdered sage
>
> 1 teaspoon minced garlic or 2 cloves garlic, crushed
>
> 1/2 teaspoon red pepper flakes
>
> 1/4 teaspoon turmeric
>
> 1 or 2 canned chipotle chiles in adobo sauce, plus a couple teaspoons of the sauce they come in
>
> 1 can (8 ounces, or 225 g) tomato sauce
>
> 1 tablespoon (15 ml) Worcestershire sauce
>
> Guar or xanthan
>
> 6 tablespoons (42 g) shredded queso quesadilla* or Monterey Jack cheese (optional)

Place the turkey in your slow cooker. (If you can fit more, feel free. My 3-quart (2.8 L) slow cooker will only hold 3.)

In a blender, combine the cumin, chili powder, sage, garlic, red pepper flakes, turmeric, chiles, tomato sauce, and Worcestershire sauce. Run it for a minute and then pour the mixture over the turkey. Cover the slow cooker, set it to low, and let it cook for 5 to 6 hours.

When the time's up, remove each turkey leg to a serving plate, thicken the sauce with guar or xanthan, and spoon the sauce over the turkey legs. If you like, sprinkle 2 tablespoons (14 g) of shredded cheese over each turkey leg and let it melt for a minute or two before serving.

*This is a mild, white Mexican cheese.

Yield: 3 servings, each with: 451 calories, 22 g fat, 54 g protein, 9 g carbohydrate, 2 g dietary fiber, 7 g usable carbs. (Analysis depends on the size of the turkey leg.)

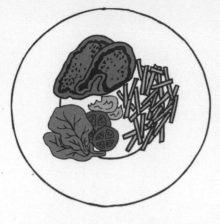

chapter four

Slow Cooker Beef

Are you tired of steaks and burgers? Use your slow cooker, and you'll be on your way to beef stews, pot roasts, chili, and other classic comfort foods—all waiting when you get home!

New England Boiled Dinner

This is our traditional St. Patrick's Day dinner, but it's a simple, satisfying one-pot meal on any chilly night. This is easy, but it takes a long time to cook. Do yourself a favor and assemble it ahead of time. If you have carb-eaters in the family, you can add a few little red boiling potatoes still in their jackets to this.

6 small turnips, peeled and quartered

2 large stalks celery, cut into chunks

2 medium onions, cut into chunks

3 pounds (1.4 kg) corned beef

1/2 head cabbage, cut into wedges

Spicy brown mustard

Horseradish

Butter

Place the turnips in your slow cooker along with the celery and the onions. Set the corned beef on top and add water to cover. There will be a seasoning packet with the corned beef—empty it into the slow cooker. Cover the slow cooker, set it to low, and let it cook for 10 to 12 hours. (You can cut the cooking time down to 6 to 8 hours if you set the slow cooker to high, but the low setting yields the most tender results.)

When the time's up, remove the corned beef from the slow cooker with a fork or tongs, put the lid back on the slow cooker to retain heat, put the beef on a platter, and keep it someplace warm. Place the cabbage in the slow cooker with the other vegetables. Re-cover the slow cooker, set it to high, and let it cook for 1/2 hour.

With a slotted spoon, remove all the vegetables and pile them around the corned beef on the platter. Serve with the mustard and horseradish as condiments for the beef and butter for the vegetables.

Yield: 8 servings, each with: 372 calories, 25 g fat, 26 g protein, 9 g carbohydrate, 2 g dietary fiber, 7 g usable carbs.

Maple-Glazed Corned Beef with Vegetables

This is a trifle less traditional than, but just as good as, the *New England Boiled Dinner* (see recipe on previous page). The pancake syrup and mustard, plus last-minute glazing under the broiler, give it a new aspect.

6 medium turnips, cut into chunks

2 medium carrots, cut into chunks

1 medium onion, quartered

5 pounds (2.3 kg) corned beef brisket

2 cups (475 ml) water

1 medium head cabbage, cut into wedges

3 tablespoons (60 g) sugar-free pancake syrup

1 tablespoon (11 g) brown mustard

Horseradish

Place the turnips, carrots, and onion in your slow cooker. Place the corned beef on top. Scatter the contents of the accompanying seasoning packet over everything and pour the water over the whole thing. Cover the slow cooker, set it to low, and let it cook for 9 to 10 hours, and a bit more won't hurt!

When the time's up, carefully remove the corned beef and put it on your broiler rack, fatty side up. Use a slotted spoon to skim out the vegetables, put them on a platter, cover, and keep in a warm place.

Place the cabbage in the slow cooker, set it to high, and let it cook for 15 to 20 minutes or until just tender. (Or you can pour the liquid from the pot into a saucepan and cook the cabbage in it on your stovetop, which is faster.)

While the cabbage is cooking, mix together the pancake syrup and the mustard. Spread the mixture over the corned beef, just the side that is up. When the cabbage is almost done, run the corned beef under your broiler for 2 to 3 minutes until glazed.

Transfer the cabbage to the platter with a slotted spoon. Slice the corned beef across the grain and serve immediately.

Serve this with horseradish and mustard.

Yield: 12 servings, each with: 416 calories, 28 g fat, 29 g protein, 10 g carbohydrate, 3 g dietary fiber, 7 g usable carbs. (Analysis does not include the polyols in the sugar-free pancake syrup.)

3-Minute Slow Cooker Pot Roast

This recipe, originally from *15-Minute Low-Carb Recipes*, is very 1965, but it's still incredibly easy, and it tastes great.

> 8 ounces (225 g) sliced mushrooms
>
> 2 to 3 pounds (0.9 to 1.4 kg) boneless chuck pot roast
>
> 1 envelope (1 ouncek, or 28 g) French onion soup mix
>
> 1/2 cup (120 ml) dry red wine
>
> Guar or xanthan

Place the mushrooms in the bottom of your slow cooker and add the beef on top of them.

In a bowl, mix together the onion soup mix and wine and pour it into the slow cooker. Cover the slow cooker, set it to low, and let it cook for 8 hours.

When the time's up, remove the beef (carefully—it will be very tender) and use the guar or xanthan to thicken the juices in the slow cooker. Serve this gravy with the pot roast.

Yield: 6 servings, each with: 358 calories, 24 g fat, 25 g protein, 6 g carbohydrate, 1 g dietary fiber, 5 g usable carbs. (This analysis assumes you use a 2-pound (900 g) roast and that you eat every drop of the gravy.)

Pot Roast Brisket

This is such a classic.

> 3 pounds (1.4 kg) brisket
>
> Salt and pepper
>
> 2 tablespoons (28 ml) olive oil
>
> 1 large onion
>
> 1 carrot
>
> 2 celery ribs
>
> 2 bay leaves
>
> 1 teaspoon beef bouillon concentrate

Salt and pepper the brisket all over. Put your big heavy skillet over high heat, add the olive oil, and start browning the brisket; you want it good and brown all over.

In the meantime, coat your slow cooker with nonstick cooking spray.

Chop the onion, peel and shred the carrot, and chunk your celery—keep any unwilted leaves; they add a wonderful flavor. Put all the veggies on the bottom of the slow cooker and add one of the bay leaves.

When the brisket is brown all over, use tongs to place it on the vegetables. Put the second bay leaf on top of it, cover the pot, and set it to low. Let it cook a good 7 hours.

When cooking time is up, use your tongs to fish out the brisket and put it on a platter. Remove the bay leaves and add the bouillon concentrate. Now use a stick blender to puree the vegetables into the liquid. This will also thicken your gravy, though you can thicken it a tad more with your guar or xanthan shaker if you like. Salt and pepper to taste.

Now slice your brisket across the grain and serve with the gravy. *Fauxtatoes* (see recipe page 343) are good with this. Roasted turnips would be good, too.

Yield: 6 to 8 servings; Assuming 6, each will have: 764 calories, 65 g fat, 39 g protein, 4 g carbohydrate, 1 g dietary fiber, 3 g usable carbs.

Slow Cooker Texas Brisket

In Texas, barbecue generally means beef brisket. This uses similar flavors, but it doesn't require all that slow smoking—or even going outside.

> 3 pounds (1.4 kg) beef brisket
>
> 2 tablespoons (28 g) bacon grease or (28 ml) olive oil
>
> 1/4 cup (65 g) low-carb barbecue sauce (*Dana's "Kansas City" Barbecue Sauce* [see recipe page 335], or alternatively, Stubb's barbecue sauce, available in grocery stores, is one of the lowest sugar commercial barbecue sauces I've found.)
>
> 1 tablespoon (15 ml) Worcestershire sauce
>
> 1 tablespoon (15 ml) liquid Barbecue Smoke®
>
> 2 cloves garlic, crushed
>
> 1/2 teaspoon celery salt
>
> 1/2 teaspoon lemon pepper
>
> 1/4 teaspoon salt or Vege-Sal
>
> 1/2 medium onion, chopped

In your big, heavy skillet, over high heat, start the brisket browning in the bacon grease. You want it well-browned all over.

In the meantime, mix together the barbecue sauce, Worcestershire sauce, liquid smoke, garlic, celery salt, lemon pepper, and salt.

Chop your half an onion. Coat your slow cooker with nonstick cooking spray and spread the onion over the bottom.

When the beef is well-browned all over, lay it on the onion. Pour the sauce all over it. Cover the slow cooker, set to low, and let it cook for a good 6 hours.

When it's done, fish it out, lay it on a platter, and slice it across the grain. Serve with the liquid from the pot spooned over it.

Yield: 6 servings, each with: 759 calories, 65 g fat, 39 g protein, 3 g carbohydrate, trace dietary fiber, 3 g usable carbs.

Balsamic Pot Roast

Balsamic vinegar and rosemary give this pot roast an Italian accent.

3½ pounds (1.6 kg) beef round, trimmed of fat

2 tablespoons (28 ml) olive oil

1 large onion, sliced

2 cloves garlic, crushed

1 cup (235 ml) beef broth

1 teaspoon beef bouillon concentrate

¼ cup (60 ml) balsamic vinegar

½ teaspoon dried rosemary, ground

1 cup (180 g) canned diced tomatoes

Guar or xanthan

In a big, heavy skillet, sear the beef in the oil until browned all over. Transfer the beef to your slow cooker. Scatter the onion and garlic around the beef.

In a bowl, stir together the broth, bouillon, vinegar, and rosemary. Pour the mixture over the beef. Pour the tomatoes on top. Season with pepper. Cover the slow cooker, set it to low, and let it cook for 8 hours.

When the time's up, remove the beef with tongs and place it on a serving platter. Scoop the onions out with a slotted spoon and pile them around the roast. Thicken the juice left in the slow cooker with guar or xanthan and serve it with the beef.

Yield: 8 servings, each with: 451 calories, 29 g fat, 42 g protein, 5 g carbohydrate, trace dietary fiber, 5 g usable carbs.

Reuben Hot Pot

I wanted to come up with something using the flavors of a Reuben sandwich. This came out even better than I hoped. It's really tasty and unusual.

> 28 ounces (785 g) sauerkraut
>
> 3 pounds (1.4 kg) corned beef brisket
>
> 1 cup (225 g) *Russian Dressing* (see recipe below.)
>
> 3 tablespoons (33 g) brown mustard

Drain and rinse your sauerkraut and dump half of it in the slow cooker. Slap your corned beef on top. Smear it with half the dressing and mustard and top with the rest of the sauerkraut. Put the rest of the dressing and mustard on top of that. Cover the pot, set to low, and let it cook for a good 7 to 8 hours. Serve with more mustard!

Yield: 8 servings, each with: 358 calories, 26 g fat, 26 g protein, 5 g carbohydrate, 3 g dietary fiber, 2 g usable carbs.

Russian Dressing

Russian dressing is an essential part of a Reuben sandwich, but the bottled stuff has quite a lot of sugar in it. This is easy to make, so long as you have the no-sugar ketchup in the house. You might like it on salads, too, or as a dip for vegetables.

> 1/2 cup (115 g) mayonnaise
>
> 6 tablespoons (90 g) *Dana's No-Sugar Ketchup* (see recipe page 332) or commercial no-sugar-added ketchup
>
> 4 sugar-free bread and butter pickle slices (These are available in big grocery stores; I get Mt. Olive brand or Kroger's house brand.)
>
> 2 tablespoons (28 ml) pickle juice
>
> 2 tablespoons (28 ml) white wine vinegar
>
> 1/4 teaspoon pepper

Throw everything in your food processor with the S-blade in place and pulse until the pickle is chopped but not pulverized. Alternatively, chop your pickles with a knife and then just stir everything together.

Yield: 8 servings, each with: 107 calories, 12 g fat, trace protein, 2 g carbohydrate, trace dietary fiber, 2 g usable carbs.

🍲 Bavarian Pot Roast

Given the Bavarian theme and all, I'm thinking *Fauxtatoes* (see recipe page 343) and cooked cabbage are the obvious side dishes with this.

> 1 large red onion, sliced 1-inch (2.5 cm) thick
>
> 2 tablespoons (3 g) Splenda
>
> 1/4 teaspoon blackstrap molasses
>
> 2 tablespoons (28 ml) cider vinegar
>
> 1 teaspoon salt
>
> 1 teaspoon beef bouillon concentrate
>
> 2 1/2 pounds (1.1 kg) beef round, trimmed of fat and cubed
>
> Guar or xanthan (optional)

Place the onion in your slow cooker.

In a bowl, mix together the Splenda, molasses, vinegar, salt, and bouillon. Pour the mixture over the onion. Place the beef on top. Cover the slow cooker, set it to low, and let it cook for 7 to 8 hours.

When the time's up, thicken the broth with guar or xanthan if desired.

Yield: 8 servings, each with: 297 calories, 18 g fat, 29 g protein, 2 g carbohydrate, trace dietary fiber, 2 g usable carbs.

Pot Roast with Beer and Mushrooms

Chuck roast is usually cheap, and it's very flavorful. Add mushrooms and onions, all that jazz, and it's a party in your mouth.

> 2 pounds (900 g) chuck roast
>
> 2 tablespoons (28 g) bacon grease
>
> 1 pound (455 g) sliced mushrooms (I used criminis.)
>
> 1 medium onion, sliced
>
> 3 carrots, peeled and sliced
>
> 4 cloves garlic
>
> 12 fluid ounces (355 ml) light beer
>
> 1 can (8 ounces, or 225 g) tomato sauce
>
> 3 tablespoons (45 ml) lemon juice
>
> 1 teaspoon beef bouillon concentrate

Put your big, heavy skillet over medium-high heat and start searing your chuck roast in the bacon grease. You want it nice and brown all over. While that's happening, go on to the next step.

Dump your sliced mushrooms (you bought them sliced, right?) in the slow cooker and add the onion, carrots, and garlic. Stir the veggies together a bit.

When the chuck is crusty and brown all over, throw it on top of the vegetables.

Now pour the beer, tomato sauce, lemon juice, and beef bouillon concentrate in the skillet. Stir it all around, scraping up all the nice brown bits and making sure the bouillon concentrate is dissolved. Pour this over the stuff in the slow cooker. Slap on the lid and set it to low.

Let it cook for 6 hours or so. Then fish out the roast, put it on a platter, and surround it with the veggies. Thicken up the sauce with your guar, xanthan, or glucomannan shaker and serve with the meat and vegetables.

Serve this with *Fauxtatoes* (see recipe page 343)—indeed, I like to spoon the *Fauxtatoes* onto each plate and then pile some vegetables on top and pour on the gravy.

Yield: 6 servings, each with: 431 calories, 28 g fat, 27 g protein, 14 g carbohydrate, 3 g dietary fiber, 11 g usable carbs. (Analysis is exclusive of *Fauxtatoes*.)

Peking Slow Cooker Pot Roast

This sounds nuts, but it tastes great! This recipe, originally from *500 Low-Carb Recipes*, takes starting ahead, but it's not a lot of work.

> 3 to 5 pounds (1.4 to 2.3 kg) beef roast (round, chuck, or rump)
>
> 5 or 6 cloves garlic, sliced thin
>
> 1 cup (235 ml) cider vinegar
>
> 1 cup (235 ml) water
>
> 1 small onion, thinly sliced
>
> 1 1/2 cups (355 ml) strong coffee (instant works fine)
>
> 1 teaspoon guar or xanthan

At least 24 to 36 hours before you want to actually cook your roast, stick holes in the beef with a thin-bladed knife and insert a garlic slice into each hole. Put the beef in a big bowl and pour the vinegar and the water over it. Put it in the refrigerator and let it sit there for a day or so, turning it over when you think of it so the whole thing marinates.

On the morning of the day you want to serve your roast, pour off the marinade and put the beef in your slow cooker. Place the onion on top of the beef. Pour the coffee over the beef and onion. Cover the slow cooker, set it to low, and let it cook for 8 hours for a smaller roast or up to 10 hours for a larger one.

When the time's up, remove the beef carefully from the cooker. (It will now be so tender it's likely to fall apart.) Scoop out 2 cups (475 milliliters) of the liquid and some of the onions and put them in a blender with the guar or xanthan. Blend for few seconds and then pour the mixture into a saucepan set over high heat. Boil this sauce hard for about 5 minutes to reduce it a bit. Add salt and pepper to the sauce to taste. (It's amazing the difference the salt and pepper make here; I didn't like the flavor of this sauce until I added the salt and pepper, and then I liked it a lot.) Slice the beef and serve it with this sauce.

Warning: Do not make this with a tender cut of beef! This recipe will tenderize the toughest cut; a tender one will practically dissolve. Use inexpensive, tough cuts, and prepare to be amazed at how fork-tender they get.

Yield: 12 servings, each with: 324 calories, 24 g fat, 24 g protein, 3 g carbohydrate, trace dietary fiber, 3 g usable carbs. (This analysis is for a 4-pound (1.8 kg) boneless roast.)

Sauerbrauten

This classic German pot roast takes advance planning, but it's not a lot of work, and it yields impressive results. Don't forget the *Fauxtatoes* (see recipe page 343) for that gravy!

4 pounds (1.8 kg) boneless beef round or chuck

1 cup (235 ml) cider vinegar

1 cup water

1/2 onion, sliced

2 bay leaves

1 teaspoon pepper

1/4 cup (6 g) Splenda

2 tablespoons (28 g) bacon grease or (28 ml) oil

1/4 teaspoon ground ginger

1 cup (230 g) light sour cream (Use full-fat sour cream if you prefer, but it's no lower carb.)

Guar or xanthan (optional)

Pierce the beef all over with a fork. In a deep, non-reactive bowl (stainless steel, glass, or enamel), combine the vinegar, water, onion, bay leaves, pepper, and Splenda. Place the beef in the marinade and put the bowl in the refrigerator. Marinate the beef for at least 3 days, and 5 or 6 days won't hurt. Turn it over at least once a day, so both sides marinate evenly.

When the time comes to cook your *Sauerbrauten*, remove the beef from the marinade and pat it dry with paper towels. Reserve the marinade.

In a big, heavy skillet, heat the bacon grease or oil and sear the beef all over. Transfer the beef to your slow cooker.

Scoop the onion and bay leaves out of the marinade with a slotted spoon and put them on top of the beef. Remove 1 cup (235 milliliters) of the marinade from the bowl and add the ginger to it. Pour this over the beef and discard the remaining marinade. Cover the slow cooker, set it to low, and let it cook for 7 to 8 hours.

When the time's up, remove the beef to a serving plate. Stir the sour cream into the liquid in the slow cooker and thicken it if you think it needs it with guar or xanthan. Add salt and pepper to taste and serve the sauce with the beef.

Yield: 10 servings, each with: 407 calories, 26 g fat, 38 g protein, 3 g carbohydrate, trace dietary fiber, 3 g usable carbs.

⬚ Chipotle Brisket

Our tester, who loved this recipe, halved it. You can feel free to do the same.

4 pounds (1.8 kg) beef brisket, cut into pieces if necessary to fit into your slow cooker

2 tablespoons (28 ml) olive oil

1 medium onion, thinly sliced

4 stalks celery, thinly sliced

4 cloves garlic, crushed

1 tablespoon (9 g) dry mustard

1 tablespoon (3 g) dried oregano

1 teaspoon ground cumin

2 teaspoons pepper

1 teaspoon salt or Vege-Sal

1 can (16 ounces, or 455 g) tomato sauce

1/2 cup (120 ml) beef broth

1 teaspoon beef bouillon concentrate

1/4 cup (60 ml) red wine vinegar

1/2 cup (12 g) Splenda

1/2 teaspoon blackstrap molasses

2 chipotle chiles canned in adobo sauce

2 bay leaves

Guar or xanthan

In a big, heavy skillet, brown the beef all over in the oil over medium-high heat. Transfer the beef to your slow cooker.

Add the onion and celery to the skillet and sauté until softened. Stir in the garlic, dry mustard, oregano, cumin, pepper, and salt or Vege-Sal and sauté for another minute or two. Transfer the mixture to the slow cooker, on top of the brisket.

In a blender or food processor, combine the tomato sauce, broth, bouillon, vinegar, Splenda, molasses, and chipotles and blend until smooth.

Put the bay leaves in the slow cooker, on top of the beef, and pour the sauce over the whole thing. Cover the slow cooker, set it to low, and let it cook for 12 hours.

When the time's up, remove the beef to a platter. Remove the bay leaves. Thicken the sauce to taste with guar or xanthan and serve the sauce over the beef.

Yield: 8 servings, each with: 779 calories, 64 g fat, 41 g protein, 8 g carbohydrate, 2 g dietary fiber, 6 g usable carbs.

Simple Salsa Beef

Here's one of those super-simple dump-and-go recipes. It's great for a day when you didn't get dinner in the slow cooker the night before!

> 3 turnips, peeled and cubed
>
> 1 pound (455 g) baby carrots
>
> 3 pounds (1.4 kg) beef arm pot roast
>
> 2 cups (520 g) salsa
>
> Guar or xanthan (optional)

Put the turnips and carrots in your slow cooker; then place the beef on top. Pour the salsa over the lot. Cover the slow cooker, set it to low, and let it cook for 8 to 10 hours.

When the time's up, remove the beef and pull it apart into shreds with two forks. Scoop the vegetables out onto serving plates with a slotted spoon. Pile the beef on top. If desired, thicken the sauce with a little guar or xanthan. Spoon the sauce over the vegetables and beef.

Yield: 8 servings, each with: 200 calories, 5 g fat, 26 g protein, 11 g carbohydrate, 3 g dietary fiber, 8 g usable carbs.

Beef and Broccoli

This doesn't come out exactly like stir-fry, but it's still Chinese-y-good, and it's a lot less last-minute trouble.

> 1 pound (455 g) beef round, cut into 1-inch (2.5 cm) cubes
>
> 1 can (4 ounces, or 115 g) sliced mushrooms, drained
>
> 1 medium onion, cut into wedges
>
> 1/2 cup (120 ml) beef broth
>
> 1 teaspoon beef bouillon concentrate
>
> 1 tablespoon (1.5 g) Splenda
>
> 1 teaspoon grated ginger root
>
> 1 tablespoon (15 ml) dry sherry
>
> 2 tablespoons (28 ml) soy sauce
>
> 1 clove garlic, crushed
>
> 1 teaspoon dark sesame oil
>
> 1 tablespoon (8 g) sesame seeds
>
> 2 cups (312 g) frozen broccoli florets
>
> Guar or xanthan

Combine the beef, mushrooms, onion, broth, bouillon, Splenda, ginger, sherry, soy sauce, garlic, and sesame oil in your slow cooker. Sprinkle the sesame seeds on top. Cover the slow cooker, set it to low, and let it cook for 8 to 10 hours.

When the time's up, add the broccoli to the slow cooker, re-cover the slow cooker, and let it cook for another 30 minutes. Thicken the juices a little with guar or xanthan.

Serve over *Cauli-Rice* (see recipe page 343) if desired.

Yield: 4 servings, each with: 314 calories, 17 g fat, 29 g protein, 10 g carbohydrate, 4 g dietary fiber, 6 g usable carbs.

Beef Carbonnade

Très French!

    2 pounds (900 g) beef round, cut into 1-inch (2.5 cm) cubes

    2 tablespoons (28 ml) olive oil

    1 large onion, sliced

    2 medium carrots, cut 1-inch (2.5 cm) thick

    2 turnips, cubed

    12 ounces (355 ml) light beer

    1/4 cup (60 ml) red wine vinegar

    3 tablespoons (4.5 g) Splenda

    1/4 teaspoon blackstrap molasses

    1 cup (235 ml) beef broth

    2 teaspoons beef bouillon concentrate

    3 cloves garlic, crushed

    2 teaspoons dried thyme

    2 teaspoons Worcestershire sauce

    1/2 teaspoon pepper

    2 bay leaves

    Guar or xanthan

In a big, heavy skillet, sear the beef all over in the oil. Place the beef in your slow cooker. Add the onion, carrots, and turnips and stir everything around a bit.

In a bowl, mix together the beer, vinegar, Splenda, molasses, broth, bouillon, garlic, thyme, Worcestershire sauce, and pepper. Pour the mixture into the slow cooker. Throw the bay leaves on top. Cover the slow cooker, set it to low, and let it cook for 8 hours.

When the time's up, remove the bay leaves and add guar or xanthan to thicken the sauce a bit.

You can serve this as is, or to be more traditional, serve it over *Fauxtatoes* (see recipe page 343).

Yield: 6 servings, each with: 411 calories, 24 g fat, 34 g protein, 10 g carbohydrate, 2 g dietary fiber, 8 g usable carbs.

Beef Stroganoff

This creamy gravy is fabulous!

> 2 pounds (900 g) beef round, cut into 1-inch (2.5 cm) cubes
>
> 1 large onion, chopped
>
> 1 can (8 ounces, or 225 g), sliced mushrooms, undrained
>
> 1 can (14 ounces, or 425 ml) beef broth
>
> 1 teaspoon beef bouillon concentrate
>
> 2 teaspoons Worcestershire sauce
>
> 1 teaspoon paprika
>
> 8 ounces (225 g) cream cheese (regular or light)
>
> 8 ounces (225 g) sour cream (regular or light)

Put the beef in your slow cooker. Put the onion on top and then dump in the mushrooms, liquid and all.

In a bowl, mix the beef broth with the bouillon, Worcestershire sauce, and paprika. Pour the mixture into the slow cooker. Cover the slow cooker, set it to low, and let it cook for 8 to 10 hours.

When the time's up, cut the cream cheese into cubes and stir it into the mixture in the slow cooker until melted. Stir in the sour cream.

Serve over *Fauxtatoes* (see recipe page 343) or *Cauli-Rice* (see recipe page 343), if desired. Actually, because noodles are traditional with *Beef Stroganoff*, this would be a good place to serve low-carb pasta, if you have a brand you like.

Note: This can be made with plain yogurt in place of both the cream cheese and sour cream. After getting everything together in the slow cooker and starting the cooking, place a strainer in a bowl. Line the strainer with a clean coffee filter and pour two 8-ounce (225 g) containers of plain yogurt into it. Set the strainer and bowl in the refrigerator and let the yogurt drain all day. Whisk the resulting yogurt cheese into your Stroganoff in place of cream cheese and sour cream.

Yield: 8 servings, each with: 413 calories, 31 g fat, 28 g protein, 5 g carbohydrate, 1 g dietary fiber, 4 g usable carbs.

Beef with Asian Mushroom Sauce

Once you have the *Hoisin Sauce* on hand, this is very quick to put together. The *Hoisin Sauce* is a snap, and it keeps well in the fridge.

4 ounces (115 g) sliced mushrooms

4 pounds (1.8 kg) beef tip roast

1/4 cup (60 ml) *Hoisin Sauce* (see recipe page 337)

2 cloves garlic, minced

1/2 teaspoon salt

1/4 cup (60 ml) beef broth

Guar or xanthan

6 tablespoons (36 g) sliced scallions

Put the mushrooms in your slow cooker and place the beef on top. Spread the *Hoisin Sauce* over the beef, scatter the garlic and salt over it, and pour in the broth around it. Cover the slow cooker, set it to low, and let it cook for 9 hours.

When the time's up, remove the beef from the slow cooker and put it on a platter. Add guar or xanthan to thicken up the sauce a bit and then pour the sauce into a sauce boat. Slice the beef and serve it with the sauce, topped with the scallions.

Yield: 6 servings, each with: 658 calories, 43 g fat, 61 g protein, 4 g carbohydrate, 1 g dietary fiber, 3 g usable carbs.

Asian Slow Cooker Short Ribs

Look for black bean sauce in Asian markets or in the international aisle of a big grocery store. You'll only use a little at a time, but it keeps a long time in the fridge, and it adds authenticity to Asian dishes.

6 pounds (2.7 kg) beef short ribs

3 tablespoons (45 ml) oil

1 stalk celery, chopped

1/4 cup (37 g) shredded carrot

1/2 cup (80 g) chopped onion

2 tablespoons (16 g) grated ginger root

6 teaspoons (30 g) Chinese black bean sauce

3 teaspoons (16 g) chili garlic paste

3 cloves garlic, crushed

1/4 cup (60 ml) soy sauce

1 cup (235 ml) dry red wine

2 cups (475 ml) beef broth

1 teaspoon five-spice powder

1 tablespoon (1.5 g) Splenda

Guar or xanthan

In a big, heavy skillet, brown the ribs all over in the oil. Transfer the ribs to your slow cooker.

Add the celery, carrot, and onion to the skillet and sauté over medium-high heat until they soften and start to brown. Stir in the ginger, black bean sauce, chili garlic paste, and garlic and sauté for another couple of minutes. Now stir in the soy sauce, wine, broth, five-spice powder, and Splenda. Pour the mixture over the ribs. Cover the slow cooker, set it to low, and let it cook for 6 to 7 hours.

When the time's up, transfer the ribs to a platter and scoop the vegetables into a blender with a slotted spoon. Add 2 cups (475 ml) of the liquid and run the blender till the vegetables are pureed. Thicken the sauce to a heavy cream consistency with guar or xanthan and serve the sauce with the ribs.

Yield: 12 servings, each with: 948 calories, 86 g fat, 35 g protein, 3 g carbohydrate, trace dietary fiber, 3 g usable carbs.

Good Low-Carb Slow Cooked Short Ribs

This was one of the first recipes I adapted from Peg Bracken's *I Hate To Cook Book*, aka The World's Funniest Cookbook (and also one of the most useful). It was higher carb, and it wasn't originally a slow cooker recipe, but it adapted well to both!

> 1 can (8 ounces, or 225 g) tomato sauce
>
> 3/4 cup (175 ml) water
>
> 2 tablespoons (28 ml) wine or cider vinegar
>
> 4 tablespoons (60 ml) soy sauce
>
> 2 teaspoons Splenda
>
> 3 to 4 pounds (1.4 to 1.8 kg) beef short ribs
>
> 1 large onion, sliced
>
> Guar or xanthan (optional)

In a bowl, mix together the tomato sauce, water, vinegar, soy sauce, and Splenda.

Put the ribs in your slow cooker. Place the onion on top of the ribs. Pour the sauce over the onion and ribs. Cover the slow cooker, set it to low, and let it cook for 8 to 9 hours. (Because it's more convenient to use frozen ribs, that's what I assumed you were using for this recipe. If you put the ribs in thawed, cut about 1 hour off the cooking time.)

When the time's up, thicken the sauce with guar or xanthan if you prefer. (This recipe gives you tremendously tasty ribs in a thin but flavorful sauce—it's more like a broth. You can thicken it a bit with guar or xanthan, but I rather like it as it is.)

Yield: 7 servings, each with: 559 calories, 31 g fat, 61 g protein, 5 g carbohydrate, 1 g dietary fiber, 4 g usable carbs. (This analysis is for 3 pounds (1.4 kg) of ribs. The total carbs will vary with how much of the sauce you eat because most of the carbs are in there. Furthermore, that calorie count assumes that you eat all of the fat that cooks off of the ribs—which I wouldn't suggest.)

Short Ribs with Mushrooms

Short ribs can be pricey, but man, are they good!

2 pounds (900 g) beef short ribs

8 ounces (225 g) crimini mushrooms (Buy them sliced if you can.)

1/2 onion

2 cloves garlic

1 cup (235 ml) beef broth

1 teaspoon beef bouillon concentrate

1/4 teaspoon dried thyme

2 tablespoons (28 ml) dry white wine

2 tablespoons (28 ml) dry sherry

1 bay leaf

1/2 teaspoon pepper

1 teaspoon tomato paste

Guar or Xanthan

Lay the short ribs on your broiler rack and slide them under a high flame, about 4 to 5 inches (10 to 13 cm) from the heat. Set your timer for 8 minutes.

Meanwhile, slice the mushrooms if you didn't buy them sliced and put them in the slow cooker. Slice your half onion, crush the garlic, and throw them in with the mushrooms. Stir everything together to distribute evenly.

Somewhere in here, the timer will go off. Use tongs to turn the ribs and broil the other side for another 8 minutes.

Okay, the ribs are browned. Put a bay leaf on top of the mushrooms and onions and the ribs on top of that.

Mix together everything else and pour it over the ribs and mushrooms. Cover the pot, set to low, and cook for 5 to 6 hours.

When it's done, fish the short ribs out with your tongs. Remove the bay leaf and then use your guar or xanthan shaker to thicken up the liquid in the pot to heavy cream consistency. Ladle the sauce, mushrooms, and onions over each serving.

We ate this as is, but it would be wonderful over either *Fauxtatoes* (see recipe page 343) or shirataki fettucini.

Yield: 6 servings, each with: 348 calories, 18 g fat, 38 g protein, 4 g carbohydrate, 1 g dietary fiber, 3 g usable carbs.

Short Ribs with Wine and Mushrooms

Short ribs are very flavorful, and this is a simple way to make the most of them.

> 4 pounds (1.8 kg) beef short ribs
>
> 2 bay leaves
>
> 1 tablespoon (15 ml) Worcestershire sauce
>
> 1 tablespoon (18 g) beef bouillon concentrate
>
> 1/2 cup (120 ml) dry red wine
>
> 1 can (8 ounces, or 225 g) mushrooms, drained
>
> Guar or xanthan

Place the ribs in your slow cooker. Add the bay leaves, Worcestershire sauce, and bouillon. Pour the wine over everything. Place the mushrooms on top. Cover the slow cooker, set it to low, and let it cook for 8 to 10 hours.

When the time's up, use a slotted spoon to scoop out the ribs and mushrooms and put them on a platter. There may be a fair amount of grease on the liquid in the pot; it's best to skim it off. Thicken the sauce to taste with guar or xanthan.

Fauxtatoes (see recipe page 343) are the ideal side with this, so you have something to eat all that gravy on!

Yield: 10 servings, each with: 388 calories, 22 g fat, 42 g protein, 1 g carbohydrate, trace dietary fiber, 1 g usable carbs.

Insanely Good Slow~Cooker Barbecued Beef Ribs

These really are insanely good. And they are so easy, too. I only find beef ribs at my grocer's now and then, and I always grab a couple of slabs to stick in the freezer.

> 3¹/2 pounds (1.6 kg) beef ribs
>
> 2 tablespoons (14 g) paprika
>
> 1¹/2 teaspoons pepper
>
> ¹/2 teaspoon salt, Vege-Sal, or hickory smoked salt
>
> 1 tablespoon (1.5 g) Splenda or other sugar-free sweetener to equal
>
> 1 tablespoon (13 g) sugar
>
> 1 teaspoon chili powder
>
> 1 teaspoon garlic powder
>
> 1 teaspoon onion powder
>
> ¹/4 teaspoon cayenne pepper

These are super-easy and so good! Whack your slab of ribs into as many sections as it takes for them to fit in your slow cooker—I just cut mine in half.

Lay the ribs on your broiler rack, set your broiler to high, and slide the ribs underneath, about 4 to 5 inches (10 to 13 cm) from the heat. Give them about 7 to 8 minutes per side until they're browned.

While the ribs are browning, mix together everything else. When the ribs are done browning, pull them out and sprinkle this mixture liberally all over them, both sides.

Throw the ribs in the slow cooker—you can put one section on top of the other, that's fine. Cover, set to low, and cook for 5 to 6 hours. Serve with any leftover seasoning mixture and a big roll of paper towels.

Yield: 8 servings, each with: 632 calories, 54 g fat, 33 g protein, 2 g carbohydrate, 1 g dietary fiber, 1 g usable carbs.

Short Rib Stew

3 pounds (1.4 kg) beef short ribs

2 tablespoons (28 ml) olive oil

1 medium onion, chopped

8 ounces (225 g) sliced mushrooms

1 1/2 cups (355 ml) beef broth

1/2 teaspoon pepper

1/2 teaspoon dried marjoram

1/2 teaspoon caraway seeds

1 tablespoon (15 ml) lemon juice

2 tablespoons (28 ml) red wine vinegar

1 teaspoon beef bouillon concentrate

In a big, heavy skillet, brown the ribs all over in the oil over medium-high heat. Transfer the ribs to your slow cooker. In the skillet, over medium-low heat, sauté the onion and mushrooms until they're just softened. Transfer them to the slow cooker, too.

In a bowl, mix together the broth, pepper, marjoram, caraway seeds, lemon juice, vinegar, and bouillon. Pour the mixture over the ribs. Cover the slow cooker, set it to low, and let it cook for 7 to 8 hours.

You can thicken the pot liquid if you like, but I rather like this as is, especially with *Fauxtatoes* (see recipe page 343).

Yield: 6 servings, each with: 955 calories, 87 g fat, 36 g protein, 5 g carbohydrate, 1 g dietary fiber, 4 g usable carbs.

Chuck with Avocado Aioli

This was a big hit with our tester's family!

3 pounds (1.4 kg) boneless beef chuck roast

1 tablespoon (15 ml) olive oil

1 medium onion, finely chopped

1/2 cup (120 ml) water

1 teaspoon beef bouillon concentrate

3 tablespoons (45 ml) Worcestershire sauce

1 teaspoon dried oregano

1 clove garlic, crushed

Avocado Aioli (See recipe on next page.)

Season the beef with salt and pepper.

In a big, heavy skillet, sear the beef all over in the oil. Transfer the beef to your slow cooker. Add the onion.

In a bowl, combine the water and bouillon. Pour it over the beef. Add the Worcestershire sauce, oregano, and garlic. Cover the slow cooker, set it to low, and let it cook for 8 hours.

Serve with the *Avocado Aioli*.

Yield: 8 servings, each with: 381 calories, 28 g fat, 27 g protein, 3 g carbohydrate, trace dietary fiber, 3 g usable carbs.

Avocado Aioli

You don't have to reserve this for use with the *Chuck with Avocado Avioli* (see recipe on previous page). Serve it as a dip with vegetables, too. California avocados are the little, black, rough-skinned ones, and they're lower in carbs than the big, green, smooth-skinned Florida avocados.

> 2 ripe California avocados
>
> ¼ cup (60 g) mayonnaise
>
> 1 tablespoon (15 ml) lime juice
>
> 1 to 2 cloves garlic, crushed
>
> ¼ teaspoon salt

Scoop the avocado flesh into a blender or food processor. Add the mayonnaise, lime juice, garlic, and salt and process until smooth.

Yield: 8 servings, each with: 127 calories, 13 g fat, 1 g protein, 3 g carbohydrate, 2 g dietary fiber, 1 g usable carbs.

Cube Steaks in Gravy

This is a great down-home, stick-to-the-ribs type of dish.

> 1 tablespoon (15 ml) olive oil
>
> 1¹/₂ pounds (680 g) cube steaks
>
> 1 medium onion, sliced
>
> 8 ounces (225 g) sliced mushrooms
>
> 3 cups (700 ml) beef broth
>
> 1 tablespoon (18 g) beef bouillon concentrate
>
> Guar or xanthan

In a big, heavy skillet, heat the oil and brown the steaks on both sides.

Put the onion and mushrooms in your slow cooker.

In a bowl, stir the broth and bouillon and pour the mixture over the veggies. Place the steaks on top. Cover the slow cooker, set it to low, and let it cook for 6 to 7 hours.

When the time's up, remove the steaks and thicken the sauce with guar or xanthan to your liking.

Serve with *Fauxtatoes* (see recipe page 343).

Yield: 6 servings, each with: 297 calories, 17 g fat, 29 g protein, 5 g carbohydrate, 1 g dietary fiber, 4 g usable carbs.

Easy Italian Beef

This is way easy but full of flavor!

> 2 tablespoons (28 ml) olive oil
>
> 2 pounds (900 g) beef chuck, trimmed of fat
>
> 1/2 cup (120 ml) beef broth
>
> 1 tablespoon (18 g) beef bouillon concentrate
>
> 1 package (0.7 ounces, or 19 g) Italian salad dressing mix

In a big, heavy skillet, heat the oil over medium-high heat and brown the beef on both sides. Transfer the beef to your slow cooker.

In a bowl, combine the broth, bouillon, and salad dressing mix. Pour the mixture over the beef. Cover the slow cooker, set it to low, and let it cook for 6 to 8 hours.

Yield: 4 servings, each with: 543 calories, 42 g fat, 37 g protein, 1 g carbohydrate, 0 g dietary fiber, 1 g usable carbs.

Roman Stew

Instead of using the usual Italian seasonings, this was adapted from a historic Roman stew recipe using spices from the Far East. It's unusual and wonderful.

3 pounds (1.4 kg) beef stew meat, cut into 1-inch (2.5 cm) cubes

3 tablespoons (45 ml) olive oil

4 cloves garlic

2 cups (200 g) sliced celery

1 teaspoon salt or Vege-Sal

1/4 teaspoon ground cinnamon

1/4 teaspoon ground cloves

1/4 teaspoon pepper

1/8 teaspoon ground allspice

1/8 teaspoon ground nutmeg

1 can (14 1/2 ounces, or 410 g) diced tomatoes, undrained

1/2 cup (120 ml) dry red wine

Guar or xanthan (optional)

In a big, heavy skillet, brown the beef in the oil over medium-high heat, in a few batches. Transfer the beef to your slow cooker. Add the garlic and celery to the slow cooker and then sprinkle the salt or Vege-Sal, cinnamon, cloves, pepper, allspice, and nutmeg over the beef and vegetables. Pour the tomatoes and the wine over the beef and vegetables. Cover the slow cooker, set it to low, and let it cook for 7 to 8 hours.

You can thicken the pot juices a little if you like with guar or xanthan, but it's not really necessary.

Yield: 8 servings, each with: 369 calories, 17 g fat, 44 g protein, 5 g carbohydrate, 1 g dietary fiber, 4 g usable carbs.

Mexican Stew

This Tex-Mex dinner is a simple family-pleaser.

  2 pounds (900 g) beef stew meat, cut into 1-inch (2.5 cm) cubes

  1 can (14 1/2 ounces, or 410 g) tomatoes with green chiles

  1/2 cup (80 g) sliced onion

  1 teaspoon chili powder

  1 envelope (1 1/4 ounces, or 35 g) taco seasoning mix

  1 can (15 ounces, or 425 g) black soybeans

  1/2 cup (115 g) sour cream

Put the beef, tomatoes, onion, and chili powder in your slow cooker. Cover the slow cooker, set it to low, and let it cook for 8 to 9 hours.

Stir in the taco seasoning and soybeans. Re-cover the slow cooker, turn it to high, and let it cook for another 20 minutes. Place a dollop of sour cream on each serving.

This makes 6 generous servings, and it could even serve 8.

Yield: 6 servings, each with: 399 calories, 18 g fat, 46 g protein, 12 g carbohydrate, 5 g dietary fiber, 7 g usable carbs.

Beef and Zucchini Stew

Don't try adding the zukes at the beginning, or they'll cook to a mush! Put out some vegetables and dip for the ravening hoards, and sip a glass of wine while you're waiting that last hour.

> 2 pounds (900 g) boneless beef chuck, trimmed of fat and cubed
>
> 1 medium onion, sliced
>
> 1 large red bell pepper, cut into 1-inch squares
>
> 1 large green bell pepper, cut into 1-inch squares
>
> 1 cup (245 g) no-sugar-added spaghetti sauce (I suggest Hunt's.)
>
> 1/2 cup (120 ml) beef broth
>
> 1/2 teaspoon beef bouillon concentrate
>
> 1 1/2 pounds (680 g) zucchini, cut into 1/2-inch (13 mm) slices
>
> Guar or xanthan (optional)

In your slow cooker, combine the beef with the onion and peppers.

In a bowl, stir together the spaghetti sauce, broth, and bouillon. Pour the mixture over the beef and vegetables and stir. Cover the slow cooker, set it to low, and let it cook for 9 hours.

Turn the slow cooker to high, stir in the zucchini, re-cover, and let it cook for 1 more hour.

When the time's up, thicken the sauce with guar or xanthan if needed.

Yield: 6 servings, each with: 367 calories, 24 g fat, 27 g protein, 10 g carbohydrate, 3 g dietary fiber, 7 g usable carbs.

Comfort Food Casserole

This is one of those meal-in-a-bowl sorts of things that just seem—well, comforting, somehow. I've found that slow cooking really brings out the best in turnips. They end up remarkably like potatoes.

1½ pounds (680 g) ground round

1 tablespoon (15 ml) oil

1 medium onion, chopped

4 cloves garlic, crushed

4 stalks celery, diced

1 cup (235 ml) beef broth

1 teaspoon beef bouillon concentrate

½ teaspoon salt or Vege-Sal

1 teaspoon pepper

2 teaspoons dried oregano

1 teaspoon dry mustard

2 tablespoons (32 g) tomato paste

4 ounces (115 g) cream cheese

3 turnips, cubed

3/4 cup (86 g) shredded cheddar cheese

In a big, heavy skillet, brown and crumble the beef over medium-high heat. Pour off the fat and transfer the beef to your slow cooker.

Add the oil to the skillet and reduce the heat to medium-low. Add the onion, garlic, and celery and sauté until they're just softened. Add the broth, bouillon, salt or Vege-Sal, pepper, oregano, dry mustard, and tomato paste and stir. Now add the cream cheese, using the edge of a spatula to cut the cream cheese into chunks. Let this mixture simmer, stirring occasionally, until the cream cheese is melted.

Meanwhile add the turnips to the slow cooker.

When the cream cheese has melted into the sauce, pour the sauce into the slow cooker. Stir until the ground beef and turnips are coated. Cover the slow cooker, set it to low, and let it cook for 6 hours. Serve with cheddar cheese on top.

Yield: 6 servings, each with: 549 calories, 40 g fat, 35 g protein, 12 g carbohydrate, 3 g dietary fiber, 9 g usable carbs.

Hamburger and Turnip Layered Casserole

This started out as a high-carb slow cooker casserole with potatoes and canned mushroom soup. This is a little more work, but it's a lot fewer carbs.

    1½ pounds (680 g) ground chuck

    1 medium onion

    2 medium turnips

    4 slices cooked bacon

    4 ounces (115 g) shredded Cheddar cheese

    1 can (4 ounces, or 115 g) diced green chilies

    4 ounces (115 g) jarred roasted red peppers

    1 can (4 ounces, or 115 g) mushrooms

    1¼ cups (285 ml) half and half

    1 teaspoon onion powder

    1 tablespoon (18 g) beef bouillon concentrate

    ½ teaspoon pepper

In your big, heavy skillet, start browning and crumbling your beef. While that's happening, chop your onion. When a little grease has cooked out of the beef, throw in the onion, too, and continue cooking until the pink is gone.

If you haven't cooked your bacon, lay it on a microwave bacon rack or in a Pyrex pie plate and give it 4 to 5 minutes on high or until done crisp.

Peel your turnips, cut them in half, and slice those halves thin. If you didn't buy your cheese shredded, shred it. Open and drain your green chiles and drain and chop your roasted red peppers.

Now drain the liquid from the mushrooms into a measuring cup with the half and half, onion powder, beef bouillion concentrate, and pepper. Mix it up until the bouillon dissolves. Now add enough guar or xanthan to give the liquid a cream sauce consistency—somewhere between heavy cream and canned cream of mushroom soup. Stir in the mushrooms. This is your sauce.

Okay, it's time to layer. Here's how it goes: Beef mixture, peppers (both kinds), cheese, turnips, and then sauce. Repeat until you run out of ingredients. Try to end with sauce, though it's not a tragedy if you don't.

Cover the slow cooker, set it to low, and cook for 6 to 7 hours. That's all.

Yield: 6 servings, each with: 499 calories, 38 g fat, 29 g protein, 10 g carbohydrate, 2 g dietary fiber, 8 g usable carbs.

Noodleless Spinach Lasagna

This is a great choice when you need to feed a crowd after being out all afternoon.

 2 pounds (900 g) ground chuck

 ¹/₂ medium onion, chopped

 2 tablespoons (6 g) oregano

 5 cloves garlic

 26 ounces (735 g) no-sugar-added spaghetti sauce

 ¹/₂ teaspoon beef bouillon concentrate

 ¹/₄ teaspoon red pepper flakes

 24 ounces (680 g) creamed cottage cheese, small curd

 8 ounces (225 g) whipped cream cheese with chives and onions

 20 ounces (560 g) frozen chopped spinach, thawed

 8 ounces (225 g) shredded mozzarella cheese

 ¹/₄ cup (25 g) grated Parmesan cheese

In your big, heavy skillet, over medium heat, start browning the meat while you chop the onion. Throw the onion in there and continue browning and crumbling the meat, adding the oregano and two cloves of the garlic, crushed. When the pink is gone from the meat, tilt the pan, spoon off the fat, and then stir in the spaghetti sauce, beef bouillon concentrate, and red pepper flakes. Turn the burner to low and let this simmer while you go on to the next step.

Mix the cottage cheese and chive cream cheese together, along with the remaining garlic, crushed. Blend this all very well.

Drain your spinach—I dump mine into a colander in the sink and then use clean hands to squeeze it out very well.

It's time to assemble your lasagna! In your slow cooker pot, layer everything like this: Meat sauce, cottage cheese mixture, spinach, and then mozzarella. Make three sets of layers and finish with the end of the sauce. Sprinkle the Parmesan on top. Cover, set to low, and cook for 4 to 5 hours.

Yield: 10 servings, each with: 514 calories, 36 g fat, 35 g protein, 13 g carbohydrate, 4 g dietary fiber, 9 g usable carbs.

Eric's Goop Suey

This started with a high-carb recipe for something called American Chop Suey. I played around with it, whacked out a bunch of carbs, and came up with this. It didn't seem anything like chop suey to me, so I was going to call it All-American Glop. Then Eric, aka That Nice Boy I Married, said it reminded him of his very favorite childhood dish, a thing he'd simply called goop. A *Facebook* fan named Rita Taylor suggested splitting the difference and naming it *Eric's Goop Suey*. So I did.

1¹/₂ pounds (680 g) ground chuck

1 medium onion, chopped

1 large green bell pepper, chopped

2 cloves garlic, crushed

1 teaspoon paprika

1¹/₂ teaspoons salt

¹/₂ teaspoon pepper

1 cup (115 g) shredded Cheddar cheese

2 tablespoons (32 g) tomato paste

1 can (14 ounces, or 390 g) diced tomatoes

2 ounces (55 g) cream cheese

2 packages tofu shirataki fettuccini

In your big, heavy skillet, over medium heat, start browning and crumbling the ground beef while you chop the onion and green pepper. Throw them in, too, and keep cooking and breaking up the meat until all the pink is gone. Spoon off most of the fat that's cooked out and then dump the meat and veggies in your slow cooker.

Add the garlic, paprika, salt, pepper, shredded Cheddar, tomato paste, and canned tomatoes, undrained. Stir it all up. Plunk the cream cheese on top, cover the pot, set to low, and let it cook 5 to 7 hours.

When suppertime comes around, snip open your shirataki and dump them into a strainer in the sink. Snip across them a few times with your kitchen shears and then put them in a microwaveable bowl and give them 2 minutes on high. Drain again and then give them another two minutes on high. Drain one more time, stir into the mixture in the slow cooker, and serve with extra grated cheese on top if desired.

Yield: 5 servings, each with: 535 calories, 40 g fat, 32 g protein, 11 g carbohydrate, 1 g dietary fiber, 10 g usable carbs.

Firehouse Chili

Here's a crowd-pleaser! I served this on a rainy afternoon at our local campground and made a lot of friends! You could halve this, but you'd be left with a half a can of soybeans, and you know you'll eat it up, so why bother?

2 pounds (900 g) ground chuck

1¹/₂ cups (240 g) chopped onion

4 cloves garlic, crushed

3 tablespoons (24 g) chili powder

3 teaspoons (7 g) paprika

4 teaspoons (10 g) ground cumin

¹/₄ cup (60 g) *Dana's No Sugar Ketchup* (see recipe page 332) or purchased low-carb ketchup

2 tablespoons (32 g) tomato paste

1 can (14¹/₂ ounces, or 410 g) diced tomatoes

12 ounces (355 ml) light beer

1 teaspoon Splenda

2¹/₂ teaspoons (15 g) salt

1 can (15 ounces, or 425 g) black soybeans

In a big, heavy skillet, brown and crumble the beef over medium-high heat. Drain it and place it in your slow cooker. Add the onion, garlic, chili powder, paprika, cumin, ketchup, tomato paste, tomatoes, beer, Splenda, salt, and soybeans. Stir everything up. Cover the slow cooker, set it to low, and let it cook for 8 hours.

This is good with shredded cheese and sour cream. What chili isn't? But it also stands on its own very well.

Yield: 10 servings, each with: 329 calories, 21 g fat, 21 g protein, 12 g carbohydrate, 4 g dietary fiber, 8 g usable carbs.

Texas Red

Using no tomatoes or beans not only makes this classically Texan, but it also makes it lower carb than most chilis. And it's good and hot!

- 2 pounds (900 g) beef chuck
- 3 tablespoons (45 g) bacon grease or as needed
- 1 medium onion
- 3 tablespoons (27 g) canned sliced jalapeño peppers, or a couple of fresh jalepeño peppers
- 4 cloves garlic, crushed
- 2 tablespoons (16 g) ancho chili powder
- 2 tablespoons (16 g) chili powder (any one of the popular blends sold simply as chili powder)
- 2 teaspoons cumin
- 2 teaspoons oregano
- 1 teaspoon pepper
- 1/2 teaspoon cayenne
- 1/2 cup (120 ml) beef broth
- 1 teaspoon beef bouillon concentrate

Cut your beef into 1/2-inch (13 mm) cubes—this is easier if it's half frozen. Put your big, heavy skillet over high heat, add some of the bacon grease, and start browning your beef cubes. Unless your skillet is bigger than mine, you'll need to do them in batches—I had three batches. Just don't crowd them too much. Add more bacon grease to the skillet as needed. As they're browned, transfer the beef cubes to the slow cooker.

While your beef cubes are browning, dice your onion fairly small and throw it in the slow cooker, too. Chop up those jalapeño slices a bit or seed and chop fresh jalapeños, throw them in, and crush in your garlic. Now wash your hands really well with soap and water, or you'll be sorry the next time you touch your eyes or nose!

Measure in the ancho chili powder, standard chili powder, cumin, oregano, pepper, and cayenne. Stir it all up.

Once all the beef is in the slow cooker, dump the broth in the skillet along with the bouillon concentrate. Stir to deglaze the skillet and dissolve the bouillon concentrate. Pour this over the beef mixture and give it all one more stir. Slap the lid on, set it to low, and let it cook for 8 hours or on high for 4 hours.

Serve with shredded cheese and sour cream—and a paper napkin to blow your nose on!

Yield: 5 servings, each with: 494 calories, 38 g fat, 31 g protein, 8 g carbohydrate, 3 g dietary fiber, 5 g usable carbs.

Free Venison Chili

This is *Free Venison Chili* because I got piles and piles of deer bones for free from a local deer processor this autumn. Most of it I fed to my dogs, but I got enough good meat off some of those bones to make this chili. If you don't have any free venison, I see no reason not to use beef chuck, round, or rump. (I have no clue what part of the deer I used.)

2 pounds (900 g) venison, cut in 1-inch (2.5 cm) cubes

2 celery ribs

2 cans (14½ ounces, or 410 g each) tomatoes with green chiles

1 medium onion, chopped

4 garlic cloves, crushed

1 cup (235 ml) light beer

2 teaspoons dried oregano

1 teaspoon ground cumin

1 teaspoon pepper

1 teaspoon salt or Vege-Sal

½ teaspoon thyme

½ teaspoon paprika

½ teaspoon coriander

½ teaspoon celery salt

2 tablespoons (16 g) chili powder

2 bay leaves

2 teaspoons sugar-free pancake syrup

4 teaspoons (24 g) cocoa powder

2 teaspoons (3 g) Splenda or equivalent quantity of another sugar-free sweetener

This couldn't be more simple! Throw everything in your slow cooker and stir to combine well. Cover the pot, set on low, and let it cook all day—8 hours is good, and more won't hurt. Remove the bay leaves and serve with the usual shredded Cheddar cheese and sour cream.

Yield: 6 servings, each with: 244 calories, 5 g fat, 37 g protein, 12 g carbohydrate, 3 g dietary fiber, 6 g usable carbs. (Analysis does not include the polyols in the sugar-free pancake syrup.)

Carne all'Ungherese

The original recipe, from which I adapted this, said it was an Italian version of a Hungarian stew. Whatever it is, it's good!

> 1/4 cup (60 ml) olive oil
>
> 1 1/2 pounds (680 g) beef stew meat, cut into 1-inch (2.5 cm) cubes
>
> 1 medium onion, chopped
>
> 1 green pepper, cut into strips
>
> 2 cloves garlic, crushed
>
> 1 cup (235 ml) beef broth
>
> 1 teaspoon beef bouillon concentrate
>
> 1 teaspoon dried marjoram
>
> 1 tablespoon (16 g) tomato paste
>
> 1 tablespoon (7 g) paprika
>
> 1 tablespoon (28 ml) lemon juice
>
> 1/2 cup (115 g) plain yogurt

In a big, heavy skillet, heat a tablespoon or two (15 to 28 ml) of the oil over medium-high heat. Start browning the stew meat. It will take two or three batches; add more oil as you need it. Transfer each batch of browned meat to your slow cooker as it's done.

When all the meat is browned, put the last of the oil in the skillet, reduce the heat to medium-low, and add the onion. Sauté the onion until it's just softening and add it to the slow cooker. Add the green pepper to the slow cooker.

In a bowl, mix together the garlic, broth, bouillon, marjoram, tomato paste, paprika, and lemon juice, stirring until the bouillon and tomato paste are dissolved. Pour the mixture over the meat and onions. Cover the slow cooker, set it to low, and let it cook for 6 to 7 hours.

When the time's up, stir in the yogurt.

Serve over *Fauxtatoes* (see recipe page 343).

Yield: 5 servings, each with: 382 calories, 22 g fat, 38 g protein, 7 g carbohydrate, 1 g dietary fiber, 6 g usable carbs. (Analysis does not include *Fauxtatoes*.)

Swiss Steak

Here's a no-work version of this old-time favorite.

> 1 large onion, sliced
>
> 3 pounds (1.4 kg) beef round
>
> 1 tablespoon (18 g) beef bouillon concentrate
>
> 8 ounces (235 ml) vegetable juice (such as V8)
>
> 2 stalks celery, sliced
>
> Guar or xanthan (optional)

Place the onion in your slow cooker. Place the beef on top.

In a bowl, stir the bouillon into the vegetable juice. Pour the mixture over the beef. Scatter the celery on top. Cover the slow cooker, set it to low, and let it cook for 8 to 10 hours.

When the time's up, thicken the juices with guar or xanthan if desired.

Serve over puréed cauliflower.

Yield: 8 servings, each with: 360 calories, 22 g fat, 35 g protein, 3 g carbohydrate, 1 g dietary fiber, 2 g usable carbs.

Oxtails Pontchartrain

This has a lot of New Orleans elements, including some serious heat, so I named it after Lake Pontchartrain. Oxtails are bony, but very flavorful, and they take very well to the slow cooker. If you haven't had oxtails, don't fear them; they're just muscle meat, like a steak or a roast. It's just that there's a high bone-to-meat ratio.

4 pounds (1.8 kg) beef oxtails

3 tablespoons (27 g) Cajun seasoning

2 tablespoons (28 ml) olive oil

3 large banana peppers, sliced

1 medium onion, sliced

1 medium carrot, shredded

2 stalks celery, sliced

1 clove garlic, crushed

1 cup (235 ml) dry red wine

1/4 cup (60 ml) brandy

1 1/2 teaspoons dried thyme

3 bay leaves

1 can (14 1/2 ounces, or 410 g) diced tomatoes

2 chipotle chiles canned in adobo sauce, chopped (You can use just one if you'd like to cut the heat a bit.)

Sprinkle the oxtails all over with the Cajun seasoning.

In a big, heavy skillet, heat the oil and brown the oxtails all over. Transfer the oxtails to your slow cooker.

Add the peppers, onion, carrot, celery, and garlic to the skillet and sauté them until they're just softened. Add them to the slow cooker, too, and mix them in with the oxtails.

Pour the wine and brandy in the skillet and stir it around. Stir in the thyme and add the bay leaves, tomatoes, and chipotles. Stir this all up and pour it over the oxtails and veggies. Cover the slow cooker, set it to low, and let it cook for 8 hours.

Yield: 6 servings each with: 935 calories, 48 g fat, 96 g protein, 13 g carbohydrate, 3 g dietary fiber, 10 g usable carbs.

Pepperoncini Beef

Pepperoncini are hot-but-not-scorching pickled Italian salad peppers. You'll find these in the same aisle as the olives and pickles. They make this beef very special.

2 to 3 pounds (0.9 to 1.4 kg) boneless chuck pot roast

1 cup (120 g) pepperoncini peppers, undrained

1/2 medium onion, chopped

Guar or xanthan

Place the beef in your slow cooker, pour the peppers on top, and strew the onion over that. Cover the slow cooker, set it to low, and let it cook for 8 hours.

When the time's up, remove the beef, put it on a platter, and use a slotted spoon to scoop out the peppers and pile them on top of the beef. Thicken the juices in the pot with the guar or xanthan. Add salt and pepper to taste and serve the sauce with the beef.

Yield: 6 servings, each with: 325 calories, 24 g fat, 24 g protein, 3 g carbohydrate, trace dietary fiber, 3 g usable carbs. (This analysis is for a 2-pound (900 g) roast.)

Beef in Beer

Here's a simple recipe from *500 Low-Carb Recipes*. The tea, the beer, and the long, slow cooking make this as tender as can be. I've changed this just a little. Originally, you dredged the beef in soy powder or low-carb bake mix, but I've decided that's inessential. And it's another step and a messy one at that.

> 2 to 3 tablespoons (28 to 45 ml) olive oil
>
> 2 pounds (900 g) boneless beef round roast
>
> 1 medium onion, sliced
>
> 1 can (8 ounces, or 225 g) tomato sauce
>
> 12 ounces (355 ml) light beer
>
> 1 teaspoon instant tea powder
>
> 1 can (4 ounces, or 115 g) mushrooms, drained
>
> 2 cloves garlic, crushed

Heat oil in a big, heavy skillet over medium-high heat and sear the beef until it's brown all over. Transfer the beef to your slow cooker.

In the oil left in the skillet, fry the onion for a few minutes and add that to the slow cooker, too.

Pour the tomato sauce and beer over the beef. Sprinkle the tea over it and add the mushrooms and garlic. Cover the slow cooker, set it to low, and let it cook for 8 to 9 hours.

This is good served with *Fauxtatoes* (recipe page 343).

Yield: 6 servings, each with: 374 calories, 24 g fat, 28 g protein, 7 g carbohydrate, 2 g dietary fiber, 5 g usable carbs.

Chili-Cocoa Pot Roast

This can be placed somewhere between barbecue and a chili, with pot roast thrown in as well! Chocolate and chiles are a classic combination in Mexican cookery, dating back to the Aztecs, at least.

2¹/₂ pounds (1.1 kg) rump roast

3 tablespoons (45 g) bacon grease or (45 ml) olive oil or (45 g) coconut oil

1 medium onion, chopped

3 garlic cloves, crushed

1 can (14.5 ounces, or 410 g) tomatoes with green chiles

1 can (8 ounces, or 225 g) tomato sauce

3 tablespoons (24 g) *Chili-Cocoa Rub* (see recipe page 159.)

1 tablespoon (6 g) cocoa powder

1 tablespoon (1.5 g) Splenda, or other sugar-free sweetener to equal

　1 tablespoon (13 g) sugar

1 teaspoon beef bouillon concentrate

In your big, heavy skillet, over high heat, start searing the rump roast in the grease. You want it browned well on all sides.

While that's happening, chop your onion and crush your garlic. Coat your slow cooker with nonstick cooking spray and throw the onion and garlic in there. Go turn your roast.

Mix together the tomatoes, tomato sauce, *Chili-Cocoa Rub*, cocoa powder, Splenda, and beef bouillon concentrate until the bouillion concentrate is dissolved.

When your roast is well seared all over, put it on top of the onions and garlic and pour the tomato mixture over it. Cover and cook on low for 6 hours.

Serve with the tomato mixture spooned over the meat. A dollop of sour cream on each serving is wonderful, but it's not essential. We also like sliced avocado and a green salad with this.

Yield: 6 servings, each with: 365 calories, 16 g fat, 44 g protein, 10 g carbohydrate, 2 g dietary fiber, 8 g usable carbs.

Chili-Cocoa Rub

Once you have this on hand, you'll find lots of uses for it.

1/4 cup (72 g) salt or Vege-Sal

2 tablespoons (3 g) Splenda

1 tablespoon (15 g) erythritol

2 teaspoons cocoa powder

3 tablespoons (27 g) garlic powder

1 tablespoon (7 g) onion powder

3 tablespoons (21 g) cumin

2 tablespoons (16 g) chili powder

2 tablespoons (12 g) pepper

Stir everything together and store in a used spice shaker bottle. Use on steaks, pork chops, burgers, or ribs—you name it. It's so good!

Yield: 16 servings, each with: 17 calories, trace fat, 1 g protein, 3 g carbohydrate, 1 g dietary fiber, 2 g usable carbs.

Cocoa Joes

You've no doubt noticed a little beef-with-cocoa theme going on here. That's because cocoa ain't just for breakfast and dessert anymore! It's a great source of antioxidants, too. These are somewhat different from the Sloppy Joes you grew up with.

2 pounds (900 g) ground chuck

1 medium onion, chopped

2 cloves garlic, crushed

1 tablespoon (6 g) cocoa powder

1 teaspoon instant coffee granules or powder

1 1/2 teaspoons cumin

1/4 teaspoon cinnamon

1 can (8 ounces, or 225 g) tomato sauce

In your big, heavy skillet, over medium heat, start browning and crumbling the ground chuck.

In the meantime, chop your onion and crush your garlic.

When the meat is browned, drain it a bit—leave maybe a third of the fat. Dump this in your slow cooker.

Add everything else and stir. Cover the pot, set to low, and let it cook for 5 to 6 hours.

Yield: 6 servings, each with: 424 calories, 32 g fat, 28 g protein, 5 g carbohydrate, 1 g dietary fiber, 4 g usable carbs. (Analysis is exclusive of coleslaw.)

Coffee Beef

This is so tender and just so good!

> 2 pounds (900 g) beef chuck
>
> 2 tablespoons (28 g) bacon grease or (28 ml) olive oil or (28 g) coconut oil
>
> 1/2 medium onion, chopped
>
> 1/2 cup (120 ml) water
>
> 1 rounded teaspoon instant coffee granules or powder
>
> 1/2 teaspoon molasses
>
> 2 tablespoons (3 g) Splenda or other sugar-free sweetener to equal
>   2 tablespoons (26 g) of sugar
>
> 2 tablespoons (28 ml) balsamic vinegar
>
> 2 tablespoons (22 g) brown mustard
>
> 2 tablespoons (28 ml) soy sauce
>
> 1 1/2 teaspoons Worcestershire sauce
>
> 1 1/2 teaspoons hot sauce—Tabasco or Frank's, or other Louisiana style
>
> 2 cloves garlic, crushed

In your big, heavy skillet, over medium-high heat, start searing your beef in the bacon grease or oil.

In the meantime, chop the half an onion and throw it in your slow cooker.

Measure everything else and stir it all together.

When your beef is seared on both sides, place it on top of the chopped onion. Pour the coffee mixture over it, cover, set to low, and cook for 5 to 6 hours.

Thicken up the pan juices just a little with your guar or xanthan shaker to the consistency of heavy cream and serve over the beef—and *Fauxtatoes* (see recipe page 343), if you have some.

Yield: 6 servings, each with: 374 calories, 28 g fat, 25 g protein, 4 g carbohydrate, trace dietary fiber, 4 g usable carbs.

chapter five

Slow Cooker Pork

This is one big chapter and with good reason. Pork is delicious, nutritious, versatile, and slow cooks really well. You'll find everything from simple family suppers to company food in this chapter!

Braised Pork with Fennel

This was one of my first great slow-cooking triumphs, and it still ranks as one of the two or three best dishes I've ever cooked in my slow cooker. This is easily good enough to serve to company. By the way, some grocery stores label "fennel" as "anise." It looks like a bulb at the bottom, with celery-like stalks above and feathery foliage. The stems are tough, but the foliage can be chopped up in salads or used as a garnish. It has a wonderful licorice-like taste.

4 pounds (1.8 kg) pork shoulder roast

2 tablespoons (28 ml) olive oil

1 medium onion, sliced

1 bulb fennel, sliced

1 cup (235 ml) cider vinegar

3 tablespoons (4.5 g) Splenda

1 cup (180 g) canned diced tomatoes, drained

1 cup (235 ml) chicken broth

1 teaspoon chicken bouillon concentrate

2 cloves garlic, crushed

1/2 teaspoon dried thyme

1/2 teaspoon red pepper flakes, or to taste

Guar or xanthan

In a big, heavy skillet, sear the pork in the oil over medium-high heat until it's brown all over. (This will take 20 minutes or so.) Transfer the pork to your slow cooker.

Pour off all but about 1 tablespoon (15 ml) of fat from the skillet and reduce the heat to medium-low. Sauté the onion and fennel until they're just getting a little golden. Transfer them to the slow cooker, too.

In a bowl, mix together the vinegar and Splenda. Pour the mixture over the pork. Add the tomatoes.

In a bowl, mix together the broth and bouillon until the bouillon dissolves. Stir in the garlic, thyme, and red pepper flakes. Pour this over the pork, too. Cover the slow cooker, set it to low, and let it cook for 8 hours.

When the time's up, remove the pork from the slow cooker and place it on a serving platter. Using a slotted spoon, scoop out the vegetables and pile them around the pork. Cover the platter with foil and put it in a warm place.

Ladle the liquid from the slow cooker into a saucepan. Place it over the highest heat and boil it hard for 5 to 7 minutes to reduce the sauce a bit. Add some guar or xanthan to thicken the sauce just a bit. (You want it to be about the texture of half-and-half, not a thick gravy.) Serve the sauce over the pork and vegetables.

Yield: 6 servings, each with: 621 calories, 46 g fat, 41 g protein, 10 g carbohydrate, 2 g dietary fiber, 8 g usable carbs.

Easy Pork Roast

This is basic, which is a strength, not a weakness. It would be a great supper with a big salad.

> 3 pounds (1.4 kg) boneless pork loin
> 2 tablespoons (28 ml) olive oil
> 1 can (8 ounces, or 225 g) tomato sauce
> 1/4 cup (60 ml) soy sauce
> 1/2 cup (120 ml) chicken broth
> 1/2 cup (12 g) Splenda
> 2 teaspoons dry mustard
> Guar or xanthan (optional)

In a big, heavy skillet, brown the pork on all sides in the oil. Transfer the pork to your slow cooker.

In a bowl, mix together the tomato sauce, soy sauce, broth, Splenda, and dry mustard. Pour the mixture over the pork. Cover the slow cooker, set it to low, and let it cook for 8 to 9 hours.

When the time's up, remove the pork to a serving platter. Thicken the pot liquid, if needed, with guar or xanthan. Serve the juice with the pork.

Yield: 8 servings, each with: 301 calories, 14 g fat, 37 g protein, 4 g carbohydrate, 1 g dietary fiber, 3 g usable carbs.

Pork Roast with Apricot Sauce

Here's a fabulous Sunday dinner for the family—with very little work.

    2¹/2 pounds (1.1 kg) boneless pork loin

    2 tablespoons (28 ml) olive oil

    ¹/3 cup (53 g) chopped onion

    3/4 cup (175 ml) chicken broth

    ¹/4 cup (80 g) low-sugar apricot preserves

    1 tablespoon (15 ml) balsamic vinegar

    1 tablespoon (15 ml) lemon juice

    1 tablespoon (1.5 g) Splenda

    Guar or xanthan

In a big, heavy skillet, sear the pork all over in the oil. Transfer the pork to your slow cooker. Scatter the onion around it.

In a bowl, mix together the broth, preserves, vinegar, lemon juice, and Splenda. Pour the mixture over the pork. Cover the slow cooker, set it to low, and let it cook for 7 hours.

When the time's up, remove the pork and put it on a serving platter. Season the juices with salt and pepper to taste. Thicken the juices with guar or xanthan. Ladle the juices into a sauce boat to serve.

Yield: 6 servings, each with: 338 calories, 17 g fat, 40 g protein, 5 g carbohydrate, trace dietary fiber, 5 g usable carbs.

Pork Roast with Creamy Mushroom Gravy and Vegetables

Here's a great down-home dinner the family will love!

2¹/2 pounds (1.1 kg) boneless pork loin

¹/2 cup (61 g) sliced carrots

4 ounces (115 g) sliced mushrooms

10 ounces (280 g) frozen cross-cut green beans, unthawed

1 tablespoon (18 g) beef bouillon concentrate

2 tablespoons (28 ml) water

1 can (14¹/2 ounces, or 410 g) tomatoes with roasted garlic

Guar or xanthan

¹/2 cup (120 ml) heavy cream

Put the pork in the bottom of your slow cooker. Surround the pork with the carrots, mushrooms, and green beans. (Don't bother thawing the green beans, just whack the package hard on the counter before opening so the beans are all separated.)

In a bowl, dissolve the bouillon in the water. Stir in the tomatoes. Pour the mixture over the pork and vegetables. Cover the slow cooker, set it to low, and let it cook for 8 to 9 hours.

When the time's up, remove the pork and vegetables to a platter. Thicken the juices in the pot with guar or xanthan and then whisk in the cream. Add salt and pepper to taste. Serve the juices with the pork and vegetables.

Yield: 8 servings, each with: 284 calories, 19 g fat, 23 g protein, 5 g carbohydrate, 1 g dietary fiber, 4 g usable carbs.

Orange Rosemary Pork

One day I saw the adorable Rachael Ray (whose Food Network show I love) grilling some pork chops for one of her 30-minute meals, and she was saying that orange and rosemary were great for basting pork. Well, hey, Rachael knows what she's talking about, so I decided to borrow those flavors for a low-carb slow cooker dish. Oh, boy, did it work out well! Thanks for the idea, Rachael!

1½ pounds (680 g) boneless pork loin

2 tablespoons (28 ml) olive oil

¼ cup (60 ml) white wine vinegar

¼ cup (60 ml) lemon juice

3 tablespoons (4.5 g) Splenda

¼ teaspoon orange extract

½ teaspoon ground, dried rosemary

1 clove garlic, crushed

1 teaspoon soy sauce

¼ teaspoon pepper

¼ teaspoon salt or Vege-Sal

In a big, heavy skillet, brown the pork in the oil over medium-high heat. Transfer the pork to your slow cooker.

In a bowl, stir together the vinegar, lemon juice, Splenda, orange extract, rosemary, garlic, soy sauce, pepper, and salt or Vege-Sal and pour over the pork. Cover the slow cooker, set it to low, and let it cook for 5 to 6 hours.

Yield: 4 servings, each with: 317 calories, 23 g fat, 23 g protein, 3 g carbohydrate, trace dietary fiber, 3 g usable carbs.

Sweet and Tangy Mustard Pork Roast

This is simple and great. I love Boston butt—which is really just a shoulder roast.

> 2¹/₂ pounds (1.1 kg) Boston butt roast
>
> 2 tablespoons (28 g) bacon grease or coconut oil
>
> ¹/₄ cup (60 g) erythritol, xylitol, or similar sweetener
>
> 1¹/₂ tablespoons (17 g) brown mustard
>
> 1 tablespoon (15 ml) lemon juice
>
> ¹/₄ teaspoon molasses
>
> ¹/₄ teaspoon ground rosemary
>
> ¹/₄ teaspoon sage
>
> ¹/₄ teaspoon thyme
>
> ¹/₄ teaspoon pepper
>
> 1 teaspoon soy sauce

In your big, heavy skillet, over medium-high heat, start your pork roast searing in the bacon grease. You want to brown it on all sides.

In the meantime, measure the erythritol, mustard, lemon juice, molasses, rosemary, sage, thyme, pepper, and soy sauce into a small dish. Stir together well.

When your roast is browned all over, smear the erythritol mixture evenly over all sides except the fatty side. Place the roast, fatty side up, in the slow cooker and spoon the rest of the mixture evenly over the fatty side.

Cover and set the slow cooker to low. Cook five hours. That's it! Put it on a platter, carve, and serve.

Yield: 6 servings, each with: 339 calories, 20 g fat, 37 g protein, 1 g carbohydrate, trace dietary fiber, 1 g usable carbs.

Pork with Cabbage

Need I point out that this recipe is for cabbage lovers?

> 4 pounds (1.8 kg) boneless pork shoulder roast, trimmed of fat
>
> 2 tablespoons (28 ml) olive oil
>
> 2 carrots, cut into 1-inch (2.5 cm) pieces
>
> 2 cloves garlic, crushed
>
> 2 stalks celery, cut 1/2-inch (6 mm) thick
>
> 1 envelope (1 ounce, or 28 g) onion soup mix
>
> 1 1/2 cups (355 ml) water
>
> 1 1/2 pounds (680 g) cabbage, coarsely chopped
>
> Guar or xanthan

In a big, heavy skillet, start browning the pork in the oil.

Place the carrots, garlic, and celery in your slow cooker. Add the soup mix and water.

When the pork is brown all over, put it on top of the vegetables in the slow cooker. Cover the slow cooker, set it to low, and let it cook for 7 hours.

When the time's up, stir in the cabbage, pushing it down into the liquid. Re-cover the slow cooker and let it cook for another 45 minutes to 1 hour.

Remove the pork and put it on a platter. Use a slotted spoon to pile the vegetables around the pork. Thicken the liquid in the slow cooker with guar or xanthan. Add salt and pepper to taste. Pour the liquid into a sauce boat and serve with the pork and vegetables.

Yield: 8 servings, each with: 478 calories, 35 g fat, 31 g protein, 10 g carbohydrate, 3 g dietary fiber, 7 g usable carbs.

Kalua Pig with Cabbage

No, no, that's not Kahlua; there's no coffee liqueur involved. Rather, it's a slow-cooker adapted version of a traditional Hawaiian dish. Super-simple, super-low carb, and utterly delicious—that Nice Boy I Married rated it a perfect 10. Feel free to use a 6 pound (2.7 kg) pork shoulder, more salt, more liquid smoke, and more cabbage and serve an army. Just increase the cooking times a bit.

3 pounds (1.4 kg) Boston butt pork roast

2 teaspoons sea salt

1 tablespoon (15 ml) liquid smoke flavoring

1 head cabbage, chopped fairly coarsely

1/4 medium onion, minced

Take a carving fork and stab your pork roast viciously all over. Do your best slasher movie imitation. You're making lots of holes to let the smoky flavor in.

Now sprinkle the salt all over the roast, getting every bit of the surface, and rub it in a little. Do the same with the smoke flavoring.

Lay your roast on the bottom of your slow cooker, cover it, set it to low, and forget about it for a good 7 to 8 hours, minimum. Then flip the roast, re-cover, and forget about it for another 7 to 8 hours.

An hour or 90 minutes before serving time, chop up your cabbage and onion.

Haul out your pork, put it in a big bowl, and shred it up with a fork. Scoop out a bit of the liquid from the pot to moisten it if it seems to need it. Then keep it somewhere warm (or you can rewarm it later in the microwave).

Throw the cabbage and onion in the remaining liquid and toss it to coat. Cover the pot, set it on high, and let it cook for at least an hour—you want it wilted but still a little crunchy.

Serve the meat and cabbage together.

Yield: 8 servings, each with: 384 calories, 27 g fat, 33 g protein, 1 g carbohydrate, trace dietary fiber, 1 g usable carbs.

Pork with Rutabaga

If you haven't tried rutabaga, you simply must. Also sometimes called a "swede" or a "yellow turnip," rutabaga is similar to a turnip, except that it has an entrancing bitter-sweet flavor. Anyway, it's fun confusing grocery store checkout clerks who can't figure out what that big yellow root is! It's actually delicious to make this with half rutabaga and half a fresh, cubed pumpkin, but it's just not possible to find fresh pumpkin some seasons of the year.

2½ pounds (1.1 kg) rutabaga, peeled and cubed

3 pounds (1.4 kg) boneless pork shoulder roast, tied or netted

½ teaspoon blackstrap molasses

½ cup (12 g) Splenda

¼ teaspoon cayenne

1 clove garlic, minced

Put the rutabaga in the bottom of your slow cooker. Put the pork on top. Drizzle the molasses over the pork and rutabega.

In a bowl, mix together the Splenda, cayenne, and garlic. Sprinkle the mixture over the pork and rutabaga. Cover the slow cooker, set it to low, and let it cook for 8 to 9 hours.

When the time's up, remove the pork from the slow cooker, cut off the string or net, and slice or pull the pork apart. Serve the pork over the rutabaga with the pot liquid.

Yield: 6 servings, each with: 472 calories, 31 g fat, 32 g protein, 16 g carbohydrate, 5 g dietary fiber, 11 g usable carbs.

"Honey" Mustard Ham

You may wonder how to roast a ham when you're not going to be around for hours to tend the oven. The answer is in your slow cooker, of course. You'll need a big slow cooker for this.

> 5 pounds (2.3 kg) fully cooked, bone-in ham
>
> 1/3 cup (75 ml) apple cider vinegar
>
> 1/2 cup (12 g) Splenda
>
> 1 tablespoon (11 g) brown mustard
>
> 1/2 teaspoon blackstrap molasses
>
> 1 teaspoon water

Place the ham in your slow cooker.

In a bowl, mix together the vinegar and 2 tablespoons (3 g) of the Splenda. Add the mixture to the slow cooker. In the same bowl, mix together the mustard, molasses, remaining Splenda, and water and spread the mixture over the ham. Cover the slow cooker, set it to low, and let it cook for 7 hours.

Yield: 6 servings, each with: 683 calories, 41 g fat, 68 g protein, 6 g carbohydrate, trace dietary fiber, 6 g usable carbs.

Ham with Rutabaga and Turnips

If you're roasting a ham in your slow cooker, you may as well roast your vegetables, too, right?

> 4 turnips, cubed
>
> 1½ pounds (680 g) rutabaga, peeled and cubed
>
> 6½ pounds (3 kg) shank half ham

Put the turnips and rutabaga in the bottom of your slow cooker. Place the ham on top, flat side down. Cover the slow cooker, set it to low, and let it cook for 5 to 6 hours. Again, you'll need a big slow cooker.

Yield: 10 servings, each with: 674 calories, 51 g fat, 43 g protein, 9 g carbohydrate, 3 g dietary fiber, 6 g usable carbs.

Creamy Ham Casserole

I made this up to use the end of a ham I'd slow cooked, and it was a hit with my husband.

1 head cauliflower

1 medium onion, chopped

1 large stalk celery, with leaves

2 cups (475 ml) Carb Countdown dairy beverage

1 cup (235 ml) chicken broth

6 teaspoons guar or xanthan

1 teaspoon dry mustard

1 teaspoon salt or Vege-Sal

1/2 teaspoon pepper

8 ounces (225 g) Gruyère cheese, shredded

Run the cauliflower through the slicing blade of your food processor. Transfer it to a bowl and replace the slicing disc with the S-blade. Chop the onion and celery fine in the food processor.

With a hand blender or regular blender, blend the Carb Countdown and broth. Add the guar or xanthan and blend it until there are no lumps. Pour the mixture it into a saucepan and heat it over medium-low heat. (If you do have a hand blender, you may as well just dump the Carb Countdown and the chicken broth in the saucepan and use the hand blender to blend in the thickener in the pot to save a little dishwashing.) Stir in the dry mustard, salt or Vege-Sal, and pepper. When the sauce is hot, stir in the cheese, a little at a time, until it's all melted. Turn off the burner.

Spray your slow cooker with nonstick cooking spray. Put in a layer of cauliflower, a lighter layer of onion and celery, and then a generous layer of ham. Repeat these layers until everything's gone and the slow cooker is full. Pour half of the sauce over the top. It won't immediately flow down into the food in the slow cooker, so poke down into it several times with the handle of a rubber scraper or spoon, piercing the layers to the bottom. The sauce will start to seep down. When there's more room on top, pour in the rest of the sauce and poke down through the layers again. Cover the slow cooker, set it to low, and let it cook for 6 to 7 hours.

Yield: 8 servings, each with: 287 calories, 19 g fat, 24 g protein, 5 g carbohydrate, 1 g dietary fiber, 4 g usable carbs.

Creamy Ham Hash

This is really wonderful. You'll thank me the day after a ham-roasting holiday, when you're trying to figure out what to do with all those leftovers. Throw this in the slow cooker and take all those holiday guests out to a movie or something, knowing that supper is taken care of. This would make a good brunch dish, too, if you made it ahead and then warmed it up.

2 large turnips

1 medium rutabaga

1 medium onion

1 medium red bell pepper

1 medium green bell pepper

2 pounds (900 g) cooked ham

2 packages (8 ounces, or 225 g each) cream cheese

1¹/₂ cups (355 ml) half and half

¹/₂ cup (120 ml) heavy cream

¹/₂ teaspoon pepper

3 tablespoons (33 g) brown mustard

This involves a lot of cutting things in little cubes. If you prefer, you can use a food processor, but you won't get the nice, even texture that you get from turning on some music or the television and just giving yourself over to dicing things.

Peel the turnips and cut them in ¹/₄-inch (6 mm) dice. Do the same with the rutabaga. You'll want to start dumping these in your slow cooker as you go, or you'll run out of space on your cutting board long before you're done dicing. Dice the onion and peppers and throw them in, too.

Now cut your ham in ¹/₄-inch (6 mm) cubes, too—I got about 5 cups (750 g) of ham cubes. Add to the slow cooker and stir everything together.

In a microwaveable bowl or big measuring cup, nuke one 8-ounce (225 g) package of the cream cheese with the half and half, heavy cream, pepper, and mustard. Give it a good 2 to 3 minutes on high and then whisk the whole thing until it's smooth. Pour this mixture evenly over the ham and veggies.

Plunk the second 8-ounce (225 g) block of cream cheese on top of the stuff in the slow cooker. Slap on the lid and set the cooker for low. Let it go for 7 to 8 hours.

At the end of the cooking time, stir the whole thing up. At first it will seem watery and curdled, but as you stir, the sauce will turn creamy and delicious. Once the sauce is creamy, serve in bowls, with soup spoons.

Yield: 8 servings, each with: 549 calories, 43 g fat, 27 g protein, 14 g carbohydrate, 2 g dietary fiber, 12 g usable carbs.

Sweet and Sour Pork

Here's another stir-fry dish turned into a slow cooker meal. This lacks the chunks of pineapple you often find in sweet-and-sour dishes. They're just too high carb. But the crushed pineapple in the sauce gives the right flavor!

> 1¹/2 pounds (680 g) boneless pork loin, cut into 1-inch (2.5 cm) cubes
> 1 green bell pepper, diced
> ¹/4 cup (6 g) Splenda
> 1 tablespoon (8 g) grated ginger root
> 1 clove garlic, crushed
> ¹/4 cup (60 ml) rice vinegar
> 3 tablespoons (45 ml) soy sauce
> ¹/4 teaspoon blackstrap molasses
> ¹/3 cup (80 g) canned crushed pineapple in juice
> ¹/2 head cauliflower
> Guar or xanthan

Put the pork and pepper in your slow cooker.

In a bowl, mix together the Splenda, ginger, garlic, vinegar, soy sauce, molasses, and pineapple. Pour the mixture over the pork and pepper. Cover the slow cooker, set it on low, and let it cook for 6 hours.

When the time's up, run the cauliflower through the shredding blade of a food processor and put it in a microwaveable casserole dish with a lid. Add a couple of tablespoons of water (28 ml), cover, and microwave on high for 7 minutes. This is your *Cauli-Rice*!

Meanwhile, thicken up the pot juices with guar or xanthan until they're about the texture of commercial Chinese food. Serve the pork mixture over the *Cauli-Rice*.

Yield: 4 servings, each with: 283 calories, 11 g fat, 36 g protein, 9 g carbohydrate, 1 g dietary fiber, 8 g usable carbs.

Curried Pork Stew

This is not terribly authentic, but it's awfully good. Try one of the chutneys (see recipe pages 309 and 310) with this.

  1 pound (455 g) boneless pork loin, cubed

  1/2 teaspoon salt

  2 tablespoons (12 g) curry powder

  1 tablespoon (15 ml) olive oil

  1 onion, sliced

  2 small turnips, cubed

  1 cup (180 g) canned diced tomatoes

  1/2 cup (120 ml) cider vinegar

  2 tablespoons (3 g) Splenda

  2 cups (200 g) diced cauliflower

Season the pork with the salt and sprinkle with 1 tablespoon (6 g) of the curry powder.

In a big, heavy skillet, heat the oil and brown the pork over medium-high heat.

Place the onion and turnips in your slow cooker. Top with the pork and tomatoes.

In a bowl, stir together the vinegar, Splenda, and the remaining 1 tablespoon (6 g) curry powder. Pour the mixture over the pork. Cover the slow cooker, set it to low, and let it cook for 7 hours.

When the time's up, stir in the cauliflower. Re-cover the slow cooker and cook for 1 more hour or until the cauliflower is tender.

Yield: 6 servings, each with: 177 calories, 8 g fat, 17 g protein, 11 g carbohydrate, 3 g dietary fiber, 8 g usable carbs.

Pork and "Apple" Stew

The apple flavor here comes from the apple cider vinegar. Our tester, Maria, cut her turnips into apple-slice shapes, and her family thought they were apples! They loved the whole thing.

2 pounds (900 g) pork loin, cut into 1-inch (2.5 cm) cubes

2 medium turnips, cubed

2 medium carrots, cut 1/2-inch (13 mm) thick

1 medium onion, sliced

1/2 cup (50 g) sliced celery

1 cup (235 ml) apple cider vinegar

3 tablespoons (4.5 g) Splenda

1 cup (235 ml) chicken broth

1 teaspoon chicken bouillon concentrate

1 teaspoon caraway seeds

1/4 teaspoon pepper

Combine the pork, turnips, carrots, onion, and celery in your slow cooker.

In a bowl, stir together the vinegar, Splenda, broth, and bouillon. Pour the mixture over the pork and vegetables. Add the caraway seeds and pepper and stir everything. Cover the slow cooker, set it to low, and let it cook for 8 hours.

Yield: 6 servings, each with: 226 calories, 6 g fat, 34 g protein, 10 g carbohydrate, 2 g dietary fiber, 8 g usable carbs.

Easy Southwestern Pork Stew

Our tester gave this a 10—and so did her family!

> 1 medium onion, chopped
>
> 3 cloves garlic, crushed
>
> 2 pounds (900 g) boneless pork loin, cut into 1-inch (2.5 cm) cubes
>
> 2 teaspoons ground cumin
>
> 1 tablespoon (4 g) dried oregano
>
> 1/2 teaspoon salt
>
> 1 can (15 ounces, or 425 g) black soybeans
>
> 1 can (14 1/2 ounces, or 410 g) tomatoes with green chiles
>
> 1 cup (235 ml) chicken broth
>
> 1 teaspoon chicken bouillon concentrate

Put the onion and garlic in your slow cooker and place the pork on top.

In a bowl, stir together the cumin, oregano, salt, soybeans, tomatoes, broth, and bouillon. Pour the mixture over the pork and vegetables. Cover the slow cooker, set it to low, and let it cook for 8 to 9 hours.

Yield: 6 servings, each with: 257 calories, 10 g fat, 34 g protein, 6 g carbohydrate, 1 g dietary fiber, 5 g usable carbs.

Orange Pork Loin

Boneless pork loin frequently goes on sale. It's very lean, however, so it's often both bland and dry. Slow cooking takes care of that little problem! Sadly, fresh pumpkin is only available for a couple of months in the autumn, so that's when you'll need to make this dish. Buy a small pumpkin, or you'll have piles of it leftover.

1 pound (455 g) pumpkin, peeled and cut into ¹/₂-inch (13 mm) cubes

1 pound (455 g) rutabaga, cut into ¹/₂-inch (13 mm) cubes

2 tablespoons (28 ml) olive oil

2 pounds (900 g) pork loin

2 tablespoons (40 g) low-sugar marmalade or orange preserves

¹/₄ teaspoon orange extract

2 teaspoons Splenda

2 cloves garlic, crushed

¹/₂ teaspoon salt

¹/₂ cup (120 ml) chicken broth

Guar or xanthan

Put the pumpkin and rutabaga in the bottom of your slow cooker.

In a big, heavy skillet, heat the oil over medium-high heat and brown the pork all over. Put the pork in the slow cooker on top of the pumpkin and rutabaga.

In a bowl, stir together the marmalade, orange extract, Splenda, garlic, salt, and broth. Pour the mixture over the pork. Cover the slow cooker, set it to low, and let it cook for 8 hours.

When the time's up, carefully remove the pork to a platter and use a slotted spoon to pile the vegetables around it. Use guar or xanthan to thicken the liquid in the pot to the consistency of heavy cream. Serve the liquid with the pork and vegetables.

Yield: 6 servings, each with: 281 calories, 10 g fat, 34 g protein, 13 g carbohydrate, 2 g dietary fiber, 11 g usable carbs.

Spinach-Stuffed Pork Loin

Pork loin is a little lean for my tastes. On the other hand, it's a nice, solid chunk of meat in a handy shape, just right for stuffing. It makes a great company dish. Feel free to use this basic method with other low-carb stuffings.

2 pounds (900 g) boneless pork loin in one chunk

Salt and pepper

2 tablespoons (28 ml) olive oil

10 ounces (280 ml) frozen chopped spinach, thawed

2 tablespoons (14 g) sun-dried tomatoes, oil-packed, diced

4 pieces pepperoncini peppers, topped and chopped

4 cloves garlic, crushed

1/2 onion, chopped

1/3 cup (50 g) crumbled feta cheese

Salt and pepper

2 tablespoons (28 ml) lemon juice

2 tablespoons (28 ml) olive oil

1/2 teaspoon chicken bouillon concentrate

1 pinch pepper

1/3 cup (45 g) pine nuts

First, slice your pork loin down one long side, cutting it almost all the way through, so you can open it up like a book. Open it up, place it with the inside down on your cutting board, and salt and pepper the outside surface.

In your big, heavy skillet, heat the olive oil over medium-high heat. Lay the pork, outside down, in the hot oil. You're browning the outside a bit.

While that's happening, drain your spinach very well—I dump mine into a colander in the sink and then use clean hands to squeeze it dry. Put it in a big mixing bowl. Now go check your pork! If it's nicely golden, turn off the heat.

Now go back to the mixing bowl. Add the sun-dried tomatoes, chopped pepperoncini, crushed garlic, chopped onion, and crumbled feta. Mix this all up well.

Lay three lengths of string, big enough to tie around your pork roast, on your cutting board and lay your pork, the cut, unbrowned side up, on top of them. Spoon about half the spinach mixture evenly over one side and then close the other side over it. Use the string to tie your roast shut and then carefully transfer it to the slow cooker.

Mix together the lemon juice, olive oil, chicken bouillon concentrate, and pepper, stirring until the bouillon is dissolved. Pour this evenly over the roast. Cover the pot and set to low. Forget about it for 4 to 5 hours.

You'll notice you still have a bunch of spinach mixture left. Not to worry. Get a big sheet of aluminum foil and lay it out on that cutting board. Spoon the rest of the spinach mixture onto half of it, fold the other half over it, and fold up all the edges, making a nice, tight packet. Stash this in the fridge for a few hours.

About an hour before you want to serve your roast—about 4 to 5 hours after you started cooking your roast—place your packet of leftover spinach stuffing on top of the pork, replace the lid, and let the whole thing cook another hour.

Ten minutes before you're getting ready to serve, put your pine nuts in a dry skillet over medium heat and stir them until they're touched with gold. (Or just buy them already toasted, if your store has them that way.)

Pull the packet out of the slow cooker and set it aside for a moment. Use a big spatula to carefully lift out the roast and put it on a platter. Snip the strings and pull them out, discarding them. Now open your packet and pile the extra spinach around the roast.

Now it's back to that slow cooker. However you can, get the yummy lemony-olive-oil-y juices into a pitcher or sauce dish! I used two hot mitts, picked up the whole crockery liner, and poured! Put the pine nuts in a little serving dish with a spoon, too.

Serve slices of the stuffed roast with a little of the extra stuffing with each slice. Pour pot juices over each serving and sprinkle with a spoonful of pine nuts.

Yield: 6 servings, each with: 298 calories, 20 g fat, 24 g protein, 6 g carbohydrate, 2 g dietary fiber, 4 g usable carbs.

Pork Slow Cooker Chili

Try this when you want to have people over after the kids' soccer game!

1 tablespoon (15 ml) olive oil

2¹/2 pounds (1.1 kg) boneless pork loin, cut into 1-inch (2.5 cm) cubes

1 can (14¹/2 ounces, or 410 g) tomatoes with green chiles

¹/4 cup (40 g) chopped onion

¹/4 cup (38 g) diced green bell pepper

1 clove garlic, crushed

1 tablespoon (8 g) chili powder

In a big, heavy skillet, heat the oil and brown the pork all over. Transfer the pork to your slow cooker. Stir in the tomatoes, onion, pepper, garlic, and chili powder. Cover the slow cooker, set it to low, and let it cook for 6 to 8 hours.

Serve this with sour cream and shredded Monterey Jack cheese, if you like, but it's darned good as is.

Yield: 8 servings, each with: 189 calories, 8 g fat, 25 g protein, 3 g carbohydrate, 1 g dietary fiber, 2 g usable carbs.

Orange and Tomatillo Pork Chili

2 pounds (900 g) pork loin

1 tablespoon (15 g) bacon grease

1 medium onion

1 jalapeño pepper

1 pound (455 g) tomatillos, husks removed

1 can (14 ounces, or 390 g) diced tomatoes

1 can (15 ounces, 425 g) Eden Organic black soy beans

4 cloves garlic

2 teaspoons grated orange rind

2 tablespoons (28 ml) orange juice

1/4 cup (60 ml) lemon juice

1/4 teaspoon orange extract

1 tablespoon (1.5 g) Splenda or the equivalent in another sugar-free sweetener

1/2 cup (8 g) chopped fresh cilantro

12 fluid ounces (355 ml) light beer

Cut your pork in bite-sized cubes. In your big, heavy skillet, over medium-high heat, start browning your pork cubes in the bacon grease. Don't crowd them; do them in a few batches, transferring them to the slow cooker as they're done. Add more bacon grease if you need to.

While the pork is browning, chop your onion and seed and mince your jalapeño. Add these to the slow cooker. (Then wash your hands thoroughly with soap and water, or you'll be sorry the next time you touch your eyes or nose. You must always wash your hands well after handling hot peppers.) Husk your tomatillos, cut them in quarters, and throw those in, too.

Add the diced tomatoes, undrained. Drain your soybeans and add them to the pot.

Now grate your orange rind and squeeze 2 tablespoons (28 ml) of orange juice. Mix the rind and orange juice with the lemon juice, orange extract, Splenda or other sweetener, cilantro, and beer. Pour this mixture over everything in the slow cooker.

Cover, set cooker to low, and let it go for a good 7 to 8 hours. You can serve with sour cream, if you like, but it's good as is.

Yield: 6 servings, each with: 224 calories, 8 g fat, 21 g protein, 13 g carbohydrate, 2 g dietary fiber, 11 g usable carbs.

Note: Feel free to kick up the heat in this by adding some red pepper flakes or cayenne—or for that matter, another jalepeño pepper.

Slow Cooker Mu Shu Pork

This isn't authentic, by any means, but it's very tasty. My husband, not a big Chinese food guy, really liked this.

> 2 plums, pitted and chopped
>
> 1 clove garlic, crushed
>
> 2 tablespoons (16 g) grated ginger root
>
> 1/4 cup (60 ml) soy sauce
>
> 2 tablespoons (28 ml) dry sherry
>
> 2 teaspoons dark sesame oil
>
> 1/8 teaspoon five-spice powder
>
> 1 tablespoon (15 ml) rice vinegar
>
> 3 tablespoons (4.5 g) Splenda
>
> 2 pounds (900 g) boneless pork loin, cut into a few big chunks across the grain
>
> Guar or xanthan
>
> 5 eggs, beaten
>
> 2 cups (208 g) bean sprouts
>
> 2 cups (150 g) shredded napa cabbage
>
> 16 low-carb tortillas, 6-inch
>
> 3/4 cup (75 g) sliced scallions
>
> *Hoisin Sauce* (optional, see recipe page 337)

Put the plums, garlic, ginger, soy sauce, sherry, sesame oil, five-spice powder, vinegar, and Splenda in a food processor with the S-blade in place and run until the plum is puréed.

Place the pork in your slow cooker. Pour the plum sauce over the pork. Cover the slow cooker, set it to low, and let it cook for 7 to 8 hours.

When the time's up, scoop out the pork with a slotted spoon and put it on a big plate. Use a couple of forks to tear the pork into little shreds. Thicken the sauce in the slow cooker to about ketchup consistency with guar or xanthan. Stir the shredded pork back into the slow cooker. Re-cover the slow cooker, set it to high, and let it cook for 30 minutes.

Meanwhile, spray a big, heavy skillet well with nonstick cooking spray. (A nonstick skillet is even better for this.) Put it over medium-high heat and let it get hot. Pour in enough of the eggs to form a thin layer on the bottom and let it cook, not stirring, until it's a solid sheet. Lift the eggs out and set them on a plate. Cook the rest of the eggs into a thin sheet as well. Use a sharp knife to cut these sheets of cooked egg into strips about 1/4 inch (6 millimeters) wide. Reserve.

When the 30 minutes are up, stir the bean sprouts, cabbage, and shredded eggs into the pork mixture. Re-cover the slow cooker and let it cook for just another 10 to 15 minutes. (You want the bean sprouts to be hot through but still have some crispness.) While that's happening, slice your scallions. (If you're not going to be eating all of this right away, only slice enough scallions for immediate use.)

To serve, spread 1/3 cup (85 g) of the pork-and-egg-and-vegetable mixture on a tortilla, sprinkle with sliced scallions, wrap, and eat! If you want to be more authentic, you could spread a little *Hoisin Sauce* on each tortilla before filling, but it's hardly essential.

Yield: 16 servings, each with: 175 calories, 8 g fat, 19 g protein, 14 g carbohydrate, 9 g dietary fiber, 5 g usable carbs.

⏻ Slow Cooker Pulled Pork

Pulled pork is a Carolina tradition, and it usually involves many, many hours of long, slow smoking. This is not authentic, but it is tasty, and thanks to liquid smoke flavoring, it has an appealingly smoky flavor. This recipe requires a meat injector, a big, scary-looking syringe that looks like your doctor got way out of hand. You can buy inexpensive ones at housewares stores.

> 1/3 cup (80 ml) liquid smoke flavoring
>
> 3 pounds (1.4 kg) pork shoulder
>
> Sauces, such as *Eastern Carolina Vinegar Sauce* (see recipe page 336),
>
>   *Dana's "Kansas City" Barbecue Sauce* (see recipe page 335),
>
>   and *Piedmont Mustard Sauce* (see recipe page 336)

Slurp up a syringe-full of the liquid smoke flavoring and inject it into a dozen sites all over the pork shoulder. Season the pork with salt and pepper. Place the pork in your slow cooker and pour another tablespoon or two (15 to 28 ml) of liquid smoke over it. Cover the slow cooker, set it to low, and let it cook for 8 hours.

When the time's up, remove the pork from the slow cooker and pull out the bone, which will be very easy to do at this point. Discard the bone, along with any surface fat. Use two forks to pull the meat into shreds. Toss it with one of the sauces.

You can serve *Slow Cooker Pulled Pork* in one of a few ways: You can wrap it in low-carb tortillas, serve it on low-carb buns, or my favorite, serve it on a bed of coleslaw.

Yield: 6 servings, each with: 405 calories, 31 g fat, 29 g protein, trace carbohydrate, trace dietary fiber, 0 g usable carbs.

Hot Asian Ribs

This is full-bodied Chinese flavor. If your family loves Chinese spareribs, you have to make this!

 3½ pounds (1.6 kg) country-style pork ribs

 4 scallions, sliced

 ¼ cup (60 ml) soy sauce

 ⅓ cup (8 g) Splenda

 1 teaspoon blackstrap molasses

 2 tablespoons (28 ml) white wine vinegar

 2 teaspoons toasted sesame oil

 2 teaspoons lemon juice

 ½ teaspoon hot sauce

 1 clove garlic

 ½ teaspoon ground ginger

 ½ teaspoon chili powder

 ¼ teaspoon red pepper flakes

 6 teaspoons (30 g) *Hoisin Sauce* (see recipe page 337)

Put the ribs in your slow cooker.

In a bowl, mix together the scallions, soy sauce, Splenda, molasses, vinegar, sesame oil, lemon juice, hot sauce, garlic, ginger, chili powder, red pepper flakes, and *Hoisin Sauce*. Pour the sauce over the ribs. Cover the slow cooker, set it to low, and let it cook for 8 to 9 hours.

Yield: 6 servings, each with: 469 calories, 35 g fat, 32 g protein, 4 g carbohydrate, 1 g dietary fiber, 3 g usable carbs.

Chili-Apricot Glazed Ribs

As you'll probably notice, ribs are one of my favorite things to do in the slow cooker. That's partly because ribs are one of my favorite things, partly because they take really well to slow cooking, partly because they're often cheap, and partly because you can do so many great things with them. These are both spicy and fruity.

4 pounds (1.8 kg) pork spareribs

1 tablespoon (9 g) garlic powder

1 teaspoon dried thyme

1 tablespoon (7 g) paprika

1 tablespoon (15 g) erythritolor other sugar-free sweetener to equal

   1 tablespoon (13 g) sugar

2 teaspoons salt or Vege-Sal

1/2 teaspoon cayenne

1 teaspoon pepper

1 tablespoon (9 g) dry mustard

1/3 cup (107 g) low-sugar apricot preserves

1/4 cup (60 ml) cider vinegar

2 tablespoons (28 ml) water

15 drops apricot nectar stevia drops

1 teaspoon red pepper flakes

1 tablespoon (11 g) brown mustard

1/4 teaspoon salt or Vege-Sal

Cut your ribs into sections that fit in your slow cooker.

Mix together everything from the garlic powder through the dry mustard and sprinkle the ribs liberally all over with this mixture. If you have any left over, save it to season the ribs at the table later on. Throw your rub coated ribs in the slow cooker and set it on low. Let them cook for a good 6 to 7 hours.

When dinnertime rolls around, combine the rest of the ingredients in a small, nonreactive sauce pan and whisk them over low heat until you have a syrupy sauce.

Fish the ribs out of the slow cooker and lay them meaty side up on your broiler rack—you may have to do them in a couple of batches. Coat them with the sauce, run them under a high broiler just for five minutes or so, and then serve.

Yield: 6 servings, each with: 573 calories, 45 g fat, 33 g protein, 8 g carbohydrate, 1 g dietary fiber, 7 g usable carbs.

Slow Cooker Pork Ribs Adobado

This is my favorite seasoning mixture for cooking ribs in the oven, so I thought it would be good in the slow cooker, too. It is!

3 pounds (1.4 kg) pork spareribs

2 to 3 tablespoons (28 to 45 ml) olive oil

2 teaspoons garlic powder

1 tablespoon (7 g) paprika

1 teaspoon ground cumin

1 teaspoon dried oregano

1 teaspoon salt or Vege-Sal

1/2 teaspoon pepper

Cut your slab of ribs into sections that will fit in your slow cooker, stacked. Rub them with the oil, lay them on your broiler rack, and slide them under the broiler, about 4 inches (10 cm) from the heat. You're just browning them a little on both sides.

In the meantime, mix together everything else in a small dish.

When the ribs are brown, sprinkle them liberally all over with the rub. Stack them up in the slow cooker, slap on the lid, set it to low, and forget about them for 6 to 7 hours. That's it! Cut them into individual ribs and serve with plenty of napkins.

Yield: 4 to 5 servings; Assuming 5, each will have: 565 calories, 48 g fat, 29 g protein, 2 g carbohydrate, 1 g dietary fiber, 1 g usable carbs.

Satay-Flavored Pork

I totally cribbed this combination of seasonings from a recipe for pork satay. It's exotic and great; if you like curry, you'll like this.

3 pounds (1.4 kg) pork country-style ribs

2 tablespoons (28 g) coconut oil

1 tablespoon (1.5 g) Splenda

1/4 teaspoon molasses

2 teaspoons fish sauce

1 tablespoon (15 ml) lemon juice

1/2 small onion, chopped

1 tablespoon (16 g) chili garlic paste

1 teaspoon ground turmeric

1 can (13 1/2 ounces, or 380 ml) coconut milk, unsweetened

1 teaspoon soy sauce

1 teaspoon chicken bouillon concentrate

In your big, heavy skillet, start the ribs browning a bit in the coconut oil.

While that's happening, mix together everything else, stirring it up well.

Transfer the browned ribs to the slow cooker and pour the sauce over them. Turn them over once or twice, using tongs, to coat well. Cover the pot, set to low, and let it go 6 to 7 hours.

You'll find your ribs have turned a lovely golden color. Serve with the sauce spooned over them. *Cauli-Rice* (see recipe page 343) would be nice with this to soak up the extra sauce.

Yield: 6 to 8 servings; Assuming 6, each will have: 478 calories, 33 g fat, 41 g protein, 2 g carbohydrate, trace dietary fiber, 2 g usable carbs.

Key West Ribs

Citrusy barbecue sauce gives this a Florida kind of taste!

 3 pounds (1.4 kg) country-style pork ribs

 1/4 cup (40 g) finely chopped onion

 1/4 cup (65 g) low-carb barbecue sauce (recipe from page 343 or purchased)

 1 teaspoon grated orange peel

 1 teaspoon grated lemon rind

 1/2 teaspoon salt

 2 tablespoons (28 ml) white wine vinegar

 2 tablespoons (28 ml) lemon juice

 2 tablespoons (28 ml) lime juice

 1 1/2 tablespoons (2 g) Splenda

 1/8 teaspoon orange extract

 2 tablespoons (28 ml) olive oil

In a big, heavy skillet, brown the ribs over medium-high heat. Transfer them to your slow cooker.

In a bowl, mix together the onion, barbecue sauce, orange peel, lemon rind, salt, vinegar, lemon juice, lime juice, Splenda, orange extract, and oil. Pour the mixture over the ribs. Cover the slow cooker, set it to low, and let it cook for 7 to 9 hours.

Serve the ribs together with the sauce.

Yield: 6 servings, each with: 421 calories, 33 g fat, 26 g protein, 3 g carbohydrate, trace dietary fiber, 3 g usable carbs.

Maple-Spice Country-Style Ribs

My pal Ray Stevens, who has tested many recipes for me, raves about this. It's shaping up to be the recipe by which all other recipes are judged!

    3 pounds (1.4 kg) country-style pork ribs

    1/2 cup (160 g) sugar-free pancake syrup

    3 tablespoons (4.5 g) Splenda

    2 tablespoons (28 ml) soy sauce

    1/4 cup (40 g) chopped onion

    1/2 teaspoon ground cinnamon

    1/2 teaspoon ground ginger

    1/2 teaspoon ground allspice

    3 cloves garlic, crushed

    1/4 teaspoon pepper

    1/8 teaspoon cayenne

Put the ribs in your slow cooker.

In a bowl, mix together the syrup, Splenda, soy sauce, onion, cinnamon, ginger, allspice, garlic, pepper, and cayenne. Pour the mixture over the ribs. Cover the slow cooker, set it to low, and let it cook for 9 hours.

Yield: 6 servings, each with: 382 calories, 29 g fat, 27 g protein, 2 g carbohydrate, trace dietary fiber, 2 g usable carbs. (Analysis does not include the polyols in the sugar-free pancake syrup.)

Maple Chili Ribs

This barbecue sauce is so good, you'll make it for cooking ribs on the grill, too. Feel free to double the sauce and do a full slab.

> 3 pounds (1.4 kg) pork spareribs (about half a slab)
>
> Salt and pepper
>
> 2 tablespoons (30 g) *Dana's No-Sugar Ketchup* (see recipe page 332.)
>
> 2 chipotle chiles canned in adobo, plus 2 teaspoons of the sauce
>
> 1 teaspoon onion powder
>
> 1/4 cup (80 g) sugar-free pancake syrup
>
> 2 teaspoons Worcestershire sauce
>
> 2 tablespoons (28 ml) soy sauce
>
> 1 1/2 teaspoons dry mustard
>
> 1/2 teaspoon chili powder

Cut the ribs into lengths that will fit, stacked, in your slow cooker. Salt and pepper them and put them on your broiler rack. Give them about 12 minutes per side 4 to 5 inches (10 to 13 cm) from the broiler, set on high. In the meantime, do to the next step.

Mix together everything else in a small dish. You know to chop up the chipotle, right? And then wash your hands really well?

When the ribs are browned, place the first chunk in the bottom of the slow cooker and spread some of the sauce all over it, edge to edge. Repeat with the rest of the ribs. Reserve half of the sauce.

Cover the slow cooker, set it to low, and let it go 6 hours or so. Serve with the reserved sauce.

Yield: 4 servings, each with: 629 calories, 50 g fat, 37 g protein, 4 g carbohydrate, 1 g dietary fiber, 3g usable carbs. (Analysis does not include the polyols in the sugar-free pancake syrup.)

Orange-Glazed Country Ribs

Fruit flavors of all kinds bring out the best in pork.

2 pounds (900 g) boneless pork country-style ribs

1/2 small onion, sliced

1 clove garlic, crushed

1/2 tablespoon (7 g) butter

1/2 cup (75 g) finely chopped green bell pepper

1/2 clove garlic, crushed

3 tablespoons (60 g) low-sugar orange marmalade

1/4 cup (60 ml) lemon juice

1 tablespoon (1.5 g) Splenda

1/4 teaspoon orange extract

1 tablespoon (8 g) grated ginger root

Guar or xanthan

Spray your slow cooker with nonstick cooking spray. Add the ribs, onion, and garlic. Cover the slow cooker, set it to low, and let it cook for 7 to 8 hours.

When the time's up, melt the butter in a medium-size nonreactive saucepan. Add the pepper and garlic and sauté until it's just soft. Add the marmalade, lemon juice, Splenda, orange extract, and ginger, bring to a simmer, and let it cook for 5 minutes. Thicken the sauce a little with guar or xanthan.

Remove the ribs from the slow cooker and put them on a broiler rack. Brush them with the sauce and run them under the broiler, set on high, for 5 minutes to glaze. Serve with the rest of the sauce.

Yield: 6 servings, each with: 304 calories, 20 g fat, 27 g protein, 3 g carbohydrate, trace dietary fiber, 3 g usable carbs.

Cranberry-Orange Ribs

You'll need cranberries for this, obviously, and they're only available for a few months in the fall. They freeze well, though, so grab several extra bags and throw them in the freezer. Or just make this in the fall.

2½ pounds (1.1 kg) pork boneless country-style ribs

2 tablespoons (28 g) coconut oil

¼ cup (80 g) low-sugar orange marmalade

¼ cup (60 ml) rice vinegar

¼ teaspoon orange extract

½ cup (12 g) Splenda or other sugar-free sweetener to equal ½ cup (100 g) sugar

1 tablespoon (11 g) brown mustard

2 cups (200 g) cranberries

½ onion, chopped

In your big, heavy skillet over medium-high heat, start browning the pork in the coconut oil.

In the meantime, mix together the orange marmalade, vinegar, orange extract, Splenda or other sweetener, and mustard.

Dump the cranberries in the slow cooker, add the onion, and pour the orange mixture over them. Give it all a stir.

When the ribs are browned all over, transfer them to the pot with tongs and lay them on top of the cranberries and onion. Cover the pot, set to low, and let it cook for 6 hours.

Serve the ribs with the sauce and cranberries spooned over them.

Yield: 6 servings, each with: 395 calories, 29 g fat, 22 g protein, 11 g carbohydrate, 2 g dietary fiber, 9 g usable carbs.

Ribs 'n' Kraut

If you like, you can make this with smoked sausage instead of the country-style ribs. If you do, read the labels to find the lowest carb smoked sausage.

2 pounds (900 g) country-style pork ribs

1 medium Granny Smith apple, diced

1/2 medium onion, sliced

16 ounces (455 g) sauerkraut, rinsed and drained

3 tablespoons (4.5 g) Splenda

1/2 teaspoon blackstrap molasses

1 teaspoon caraway seeds

1/4 cup (60 ml) dry white wine

Put the ribs, apple, and onion in your slow cooker. Cover with the sauerkraut.

In a bowl, stir together the Splenda, molasses, caraway seeds, and wine. Pour the mixture over the sauerkraut and ribs. Cover the slow cooker, set it to low, and let it cook for 8 hours.

Yield: 6 servings, each with: 286 calories, 19 g fat, 18 g protein, 7 g carbohydrate, 3 g dietary fiber, 4 g usable carbs.

Soy and Sesame Ribs

Here's another Asian take on ribs. The toasted sesame seed topping really sets this recipe apart.

3 pounds (1.4 kg) pork spareribs

1/3 cup (8 g) Splenda

1/4 cup (60 g) *Dana's No-Sugar Ketchup* (see recipe page 332) or prepared low-carb ketchup

1 tablespoon (21 g) sugar-free imitation honey

1 tablespoon (28 ml) cider vinegar

1 clove garlic, crushed

1/2 teaspoon ground ginger

1/2 teaspoon red pepper flakes

1/2 teaspoon dark sesame oil

1 tablespoon (8 g) sesame seeds

4 scallions, thinly sliced

Cut the ribs into portions if needed to fit them in your slow cooker. Broil the ribs about 6-inches (15 cm) from high heat until browned, about 10 minutes per side. Transfer them to your slow cooker.

In a bowl, mix together the Splenda, ketchup, honey, vinegar, garlic, ginger, red pepper flakes, and sesame oil. Pour the mixture over the ribs, turning to coat if needed. Cover the slow cooker, set it to low, and let it cook for 5 to 6 hours.

Toast the sesame seeds by stirring them in a dry skillet over medium-high heat until they start to make popping sounds and jump around a bit. Serve the ribs with sesame seeds and scallions scattered over them.

Yield: 4 servings, each with: 646 calories, 52 g fat, 37 g protein, 7 g carbohydrate, 1 g dietary fiber, 6 g usable carbs. (Analysis does not include the polyols in the imitation honey.)

Teriyaki-Tangerine Ribs

This is an easy twist on plain old teriyaki.

> 4 pounds (900 g) country-style pork ribs
>
> *Low-Carb Teriyaki Sauce* (see recipe page 337)
>
> *Florida Sunshine Tangerine Barbecue Sauce* (see recipe page 334)

Put the ribs in your slow cooker.

In a bowl, mix together the *Low-Carb Teriyaki Sauce* and the *Florida Sunshine Tangerine Barbecue Sauce*. Pour the mixture over the ribs. Cover the slow cooker, set it to low, and let it cook for 7 to 8 hours.

When the time's up, remove the ribs. Transfer the sauce to a nonreactive saucepan and put it over high heat. Boil it hard until it thickens up a bit and serve the sauce over the ribs.

Yield: 8 servings, each with: 415 calories, 29 g fat, 28 g protein, 8 g carbohydrate, 1 g dietary fiber, 7 g usable carbs.

Slow Cooker Teriyaki Ribs

This dish is sweet, spicy, and tangy and falling-off-the-bone tender.

6 pounds (2.7 kg) pork spareribs, cut into 3 or 4 pieces so they fit in the slow cooker

3/4 cup (180 g) *Dana's No-Sugar Ketchup* (see recipe page 332) or purchased low-carb ketchup

1 batch *Low-Carb Teriyaki Sauce* (see recipe page 337)

1/4 cup (6 g) Splenda

1/4 teaspoon blackstrap molasses

1 teaspoon minced garlic or 2 cloves garlic, crushed

Guar or xanthan

Place the ribs in your slow cooker.

In a bowl, mix the ketchup, *Low-Carb Teriyaki Sauce*, Splenda, molasses, and garlic together. Pour the mixture over the ribs. Cover the slow cooker, set it to low, and let it cook for 10 hours.

When the time's up, use tongs to pull out the now unbelievably tender and flavorful ribs. Ladle out as much of the pot liquid as you think you'll use and thicken it using guar or xanthan. Serve the sauce over the ribs.

Yield: 8 servings, each with: 650 calories, 50 g fat, 38 g protein, 9 g carbohydrate, 1 g dietary fiber (depending on how much of the liquid you eat), about 8 g usable carbs.

Fruity, Spicy Ribs

This recipe is a little hot, a little sweet, a little Southwestern, and a little Asian—but all tasty.

6 pounds (2.7 kg) pork spareribs, cut in pieces so they fit in your slow cooker

6 tablespoons (120 g) low-sugar apricot preserves

1/3 cup (80 ml) lemon juice

2 tablespoons (3 g) Splenda

2 tablespoons (16 g) chili powder

2 teaspoons five-spice powder

1/4 cup (60 ml) soy sauce

1/2 cup (120 ml) chicken broth

Put the ribs on a broiler rack and broil them about 6 inches (15 cm) from high heat for about 7 to 8 minutes per side or until browned. Transfer the ribs to your slow cooker.

In a bowl, mix together the preserves, lemon juice, Splenda, chili powder, five-spice powder, soy sauce, and broth. Pour the mixture over the ribs. Cover the slow cooker, set it to low, and let it cook for 6 to 7 hours.

When the time's up, remove the ribs to a platter. Pour off the liquid in the pot into a deep, clear container and let the fat rise to the top. Skim off the fat. Now pour the liquid into a saucepan. Boil it hard until it's reduced by at least half and starting to thicken. Serve the sauce with the ribs.

Yield: 8 servings, each with: 636 calories, 50 g fat, 37 g protein, 7 g carbohydrate, 1 g dietary fiber, 6 g usable carbs.

Rosemary-Ginger Ribs with Apricot Glaze

This recipe originally appeared in *15-Minute Low-Carb Recipes*. Feel free to use a full-size slab of ribs—about 6 pounds (2.7 kilograms) worth—and double the seasonings if you're feeding a family.

1 slab baby back ribs, about 2¹/₂ pounds (about 1 kg)

Rosemary-ginger rub (I use a brand called Stubb's.)

2 tablespoons (40 g) low-sugar apricot preserves

1¹/₂ teaspoons spicy brown mustard

1 teaspoon Splenda

1¹/₂ teaspoons soy sauce

Sprinkle both sides of the ribs generously with the rosemary-ginger rub. Curl the slab of ribs around and fit it down into your slow cooker. Cover the slow cooker, set it to low, and let it cook for 9 to 10 hours. (No, I didn't forget anything. You don't put any liquid in the slow cooker. Don't sweat it.)

When the time's up, mix together the preserves, mustard, Splenda, and soy sauce. Carefully remove the ribs from the slow cooker. (They may fall apart on you a bit because they'll be so tender.) Arrange the ribs meaty-side-up on a broiler rack. Spread the apricot glaze evenly over the ribs and run them under a broiler set on high, 3 to 4 inches (8 to 10 centimeters) from the heat, for 7 to 8 minutes.

Yield: 3 servings, each with: 689 calories, 56 g fat, 40 g protein, 4 g carbohydrate, trace dietary fiber, 4 g usable carbs.

Slow Cooker "Barbecued" Ribs

Okay, it's not really barbecue because it's not done over a fire. But this recipe tastes great and lets you dig into your ribs within minutes of walking in the door.

> 2¹/₂ pounds (1.1 kg) pork spare ribs
>
> 2 tablespons (12 g) *Classic Rub* (see recipe page 338) or purchased dry rub
>
> ¹/₃ cup (85 g) *Dana's "Kansas City" Barbecue Sauce* (see recipe page 335) or purchased low-carb barbecue sauce

Sprinkle the slab of ribs liberally on both sides with the dry rub, coil the ribs up, and slide them into your slow cooker. Cover the slow cooker, set it to low, and let it cook for 9 to 10 hours.

When the time's up, pull the ribs out of the slow cooker. (Do this carefully because they'll be falling-apart tender.) Lay the ribs on a broiler rack, meaty-side-up, and spread the barbecue sauce over them. Broil 3 to 4 inches (8 to 10 centimeters) from the broiler set on high for 7 to 8 minutes.

Note: If you'd like to give these a smoked flavor, you can buy liquid smoke flavoring at your grocery store. Simply brush the ribs with the liquid smoke before you sprinkle on the dry rub.

Yield: 3 servings, each with: 688 calories, 56 g fat, 40 g protein, 4 g carbohydrate, 1 g dietary fiber, 3 g usable carbs. (Your carb count will be a bit different depending on whether you use homemade sugar-free barbecue sauce or commercial low-carb sauce.)

About Pork Neckbones

Unless you grew up on soul food, you may never have tried pork neckbones. They're another one of those cuts that are perfect for the slow cooker. They're bony and tough and cheap. My grocery store has them for 59 cents a pound week in and week out. Yet cooked with slow moist heat, they're incredibly flavorful, and because the meat falls right off the bone, who cares that they're bony?

I did have one teeny problem with pork neckbones: I simply could not find any nutritional statistics for them, and I even wrote to a big pork producer! However, you can count on them being carb-free, so these carb counts are accurate. It's the protein and calorie counts that I couldn't get, so that's why they're missing in these neckbone recipes.

Stewed Pork Neckbones with Turnips and Cabbage

This one-pot meal is not a beautiful dish to look at, but boy, does it taste good! Plenty of Tabasco is essential.

> 3 turnips, diced
>
> 3 pounds (1.4 kg) meaty pork neckbones
>
> 1 teaspoon red pepper flakes
>
> 1¹/₂ teaspoons salt or Vege-Sal
>
> 3 cups (700 ml) water
>
> 1/₂ head cabbage, cut in wedges
>
> Tabasco sauce

Put the turnips in the bottom of your slow cooker. Put the neckbones on top of them. Sprinkle the red pepper flakes and salt or Vege-Sal over it and then pour the water over that. Now arrange the cabbage wedges on top of that. Cover the slow cooker, set it to low, and let it cook for 7 to 8 hours.

Scoop everything out onto a platter together with a slotted spoon and dose it well with Tabasco sauce before serving.

Yield: 4 servings, each with: 6 g carbohydrate, 2 g dietary fiber, 4 g usable carbs.

Neckbones and "Rice"

I adapted this recipe from one on a soul food website. I have no experience with genuine soul food, so I can't tell you how close this comes, but it's great in its own right.

2½ pounds (1.1 kg) meaty pork neckbones

½ cup (120 ml) oil

1 medium onion, sliced

1 tablespoon (9 g) garlic powder

1 teaspoon salt or Vege-Sal

1 teaspoon pepper

2 cups (475 ml) chicken broth

½ head cauliflower

Guar or xanthan

In a big, heavy skillet, brown the pork neckbones in the oil over medium-high heat, in batches. Transfer the neckbones to your slow cooker.

Add the onion and sprinkle the garlic powder, salt or Vege-Sal, and pepper over the whole thing. Pour in the broth and give the whole thing a stir. Cover the slow cooker, set it to low, and let it cook for 6 to 7 hours.

When the time's up, run the cauliflower through the shredding blade of a food processor. Put the resulting *Cauli-Rice* in a microwaveable casserole dish with a lid. Add a couple of tablespoons of water (28 ml), cover, and microwave on high for 7 minutes.

Meanwhile, remove the neckbones to a platter. Thicken the liquid a little with guar or xanthan. Serve the neckbones, onions, and gravy over the Cauli-Rice.

Yield: 3 servings, each with: 7 g carbohydrate, 1 g dietary fiber, 6 g usable carbs.

Italian Neck Bones

Pork neck bones are so wonderfully succulent and flavorful. Traditionally poor people's food, they're better than most of the expensive cuts. These are particularly sumptuous.

    4 pounds (1.8 kg) pork neck bones

    1 large onion, diced

    5 cloves garlic, crushed

    1/2 cup (120 ml) olive oil, or as needed

    1 can (14 1/2 ounces, or 410 g) diced tomatoes

    2 tablespoons (28 ml) balsamic vinegar

    1/4 cup (60 ml) dry red wine

    1/4 teaspoon pepper

    1/4 teaspoon red pepper flakes

    1 teaspoon chicken bouillon concentrate

    1 tablespoon (6 g) Italian seasoning

Lay your neck bones on your broiler rack and slide them under a high broiler, 4 to 5 inches (10 to 13 cm) from the heat, to brown a bit—maybe 5 minutes per side.

In the meantime, chop your onion—what the heck? In your big, heavy skillet, start the onions and garlic sautéing in all that nice olive oil.

Use tongs to transfer your neckbones to the slow cooker. When the onion is translucent, add it to the pot. Put the skillet back over the heat. Dump in the tomatoes, vinegar, wine, pepper, bouillon concentrate, and Italian seasoning. Stir it all around, scraping up any nice browned bits, and keep stirring until the bouillon is dissolved. Pour it all over the neckbones.

Cover the pot, set it for low, and let it go for a good 7 to 8 hours until it is falling off the bone succulent! Serve with the pot liquor spooned over the neck bones, with plenty of napkins.

Yield: 5 servings, each with: 238 calories, 22 g fat, 1 g protein, 9 g carbohydrate, 1 g dietary fiber, 8 g usable carbs.

Cocido de Puerco

This pork stew appeared in *500 Low-Carb Recipes*, but I hadn't thought of slow cooking it yet. It worked out great!

3 pounds (1.4 kg) pork neckbones

2 tablespoons (28 ml) olive oil

1 small onion, chopped

1 clove garlic, crushed

1 green bell pepper, diced

2 medium zucchini, chunked

1 can (14$\frac{1}{2}$ ounces, or 410 g) diced tomatoes

2 teaspoons cumin

2 teaspoons dried oregano

$\frac{1}{2}$ teaspoon red pepper flakes

1 large onion, sliced

In a big, heavy skillet, brown the pork neckbones in the oil.

While that's happening, put the onion and garlic in the bottom of your slow cooker. When the neckbones are browned, put them in the slow cooker on top of the onions. Put the pepper and zucchini on top.

In a bowl, stir together the tomatoes, cumin, oregano, and red pepper flakes. Pour the mixture into the slow cooker. Cover the slow cooker, set it to low, and let it cook for 6 to 7 hours.

Yield: 5 servings, each with: 12 g carbohydrate, 2 g dietary fiber, 10 g usable carbs.

Stuffed Peppers

6 large green peppers

1 1/2 pounds (680 g) bulk Italian sausage

1/2 head cauliflower

2 cups (490 g) no-sugar-added spaghetti sauce

2/3 cup (100 g) crumbled feta cheese

1/2 cup (80 g) chopped onion

1/4 cup (90 g) chopped tomato

1/4 cup (15 g) chopped fresh parsley

2 tablespoons (12 g) chopped black olives

1 clove garlic, crushed

1/2 teaspoon salt or Vege-Sal

1 teaspoon Italian seasoning

1/2 teaspoon red pepper flakes

Cut the tops off the peppers. Remove the usable pepper wall from the stems and chop it, discarding the stems and seeds. Reserve the pepper shells.

In a big, heavy skillet, brown and crumble the sausage till done. Drain the fat.

Run the cauliflower through the shredding blade of a food processor. Place the resulting *Cauli-Rice* in a big mixing bowl.

Put 1 cup (245 g) of the spaghetti sauce in the slow cooker. Add the rest to the *Cauli-Rice*. Add the cheese, onion, tomato, parsley, olives, garlic, salt or Vege-Sal, Italian seasoning, red pepper flakes, cooked sausage, and the chopped bit of green pepper to the *Cauli-Rice*. Combine well. Divide the mixture between the pepper shells.

Put the stuffed peppers in the slow cooker. Cover the slow cooker, set it to low, and let it cook for 4 to 5 hours or until the peppers are tender.

Yield: 6 servings, each with: 592 calories, 51 g fat, 18 g protein, 18 g carbohydrate, 5 g dietary fiber, 13 g usable carbs.

Tangy Pork Chops

4 pounds (1.8 kg) pork chops, 1/2-inch (13 mm) thick

1/2 teaspoon salt or Vege-Sal

1/4 teaspoon pepper

1/2 cup (80 g) chopped onion

2 stalks celery, diced

1 green bell pepper, diced

1 can (14 1/2 ounces, or 410 g) diced tomatoes

1/2 cup (120 g) *Dana's No-Sugar Ketchup* (see recipe page 332) or purchased low-carb ketchup

2 tablespoons (28 ml) cider vinegar

2 tablespoons (28 ml) Worcestershire sauce

2 tablespoons (3 g) Splenda

1/4 teaspoon blackstrap molasses

1 tablespoon (15 ml) lemon juice

1 teaspoon beef bouillon concentrate

Guar or xanthan

Place the pork in the bottom of your slow cooker. Sprinkle the pork with the salt and pepper. Now add the onion, celery, green pepper, and tomatoes.

In a bowl, stir together the ketchup, vinegar, Worcestershire sauce, Splenda, molasses, lemon juice, and bouillon. Stir until the bouillon dissolves. Pour the mixture into the slow cooker. Cover the slow cooker, set it to low, and let it cook for 5 to 6 hours.

When the time's up, remove the pork and place it on a platter. Use a slotted spoon to pile the vegetables around the pork. Thicken the liquid left in the slow cooker with guar or xanthan and serve the sauce with the pork and vegetables.

Yield: 8 servings, each with: 396 calories, 23 g fat, 36 g protein, 11 g carbohydrate, 1 g dietary fiber, 10 g usable carbs.

Polynesian Pork Ribs

It's a luau in your slow cooker!

2 pounds (900 g) country-style pork ribs

1 clove garlic, crushed

1/2 medium onion, sliced

1/4 cup (60 g) canned crushed pineapple in juice

1/2 cup (120 g) *Dana's No-Sugar Ketchup* (see recipe page 332) or purchased low-carb ketchup

1 tablespoon (1.5 g) Splenda

1/2 teaspoon blackstrap molasses

1 tablespoon (15 ml) soy sauce

1 teaspoon grated ginger root

1/2 teaspoon dark sesame oil

1 tablespoon (15 ml) cider vinegar

Put the ribs in your slow cooker, along with the garlic and onion.

In a bowl, stir together the pineapple and 1/4 cup (60 g) of the ketchup. Pour the mixture over the ribs. Cover the slow cooker, set it to low, and let it cook for 8 to 10 hours.

When the time's up, pull the ribs out of the slow cooker, put them on a broiler rack, and stash them somewhere warm.

Ladle the cooking liquid into a saucepan. Stir in the remaining 1/4 (60 g) cup ketchup, the Splenda, molasses, soy sauce, ginger, sesame oil, and vinegar, bring to a simmer, and let cook until you have a passably thick sauce.

Spoon the sauce over the ribs and run them under the broiler for 5 minutes or so, just to glaze them a bit.

Yield: 6 servings, each with: 288 calories, 20 g fat, 19 g protein, 9 g carbohydrate, 1 g dietary fiber, 8 g usable carbs.

Havana Ribs

The inspiration for these ribs was a recipe for a Cuban pork roast, marinated in citrus juice and rum. I took a lot of liberties, but the results are good, so why not?

3 pounds (1.4 kg) pork spareribs

Salt and pepper

1/2 orange

2 tablespoons (28 ml) lime juice

2 tablespoons (28 ml) lemon juice

2 tablespoons (28 ml) dark rum

5 cloves (15 g) garlic, crushed

1 teaspoon cumin

1 teaspoon oregano

1/2 teaspoon pepper

4 teaspoons (1 g), or 2 packets, Splenda, or other low-carb sweetener (not aspartame) to equal 4 teaspoons sugar in sweetness

2 tablespoons (28 ml) chicken broth

2 tablespoons (38 g) low-sugar orange marmalade

Cut your ribs into sections that fit in your slow cooker, if you need to. Salt and pepper 'em all over. Plunk them in the cooker.

Grate the zest from your orange half, and squeeze the juice into a bowl. Add everything else, and stir it up well. Pour it over the ribs, and turn them all about, making sure they get coated with the citrus-rum mixture. Cover, and cook on low for 5 hours.

When time's up, use a tongs to pull your ribs out and throw them on a platter. Keep them warm while you . . .

Pour the liquid from the slow cooker into a small, non-reactive saucepan, and boil it down untill it's syrupy. If you like, you can also slide your ribs under the broiler to brown them a little while you're boiling down the sauce, but it's not essential.

Coat the ribs with the sauce, and serve.

Yield: 4 Servings, each with 654 calories, 50 g fat, 37 g protein, 8 g carbohydrate, 1 g dietary fiber, 7 grams usable carb

Ribs with Apple Kraut

Even folks who aren't wild about sauerkraut may like this. With the apple and the other vegetables, there's a lot more than just sauerkraut going on here.

3½ pounds (1.6 kg) country-style pork ribs

2 tablespoons (28 ml) oil

3/4 cup (75 g) diced cauliflower

3/4 cup (113 g) diced turnip

1 Granny Smith apple, cored and thinly sliced

2 carrots, sliced

1 medium onion, sliced

1 pound (455 g) sauerkraut, rinsed and drained

1/2 cup (120 ml) apple cider vinegar

3 tablespoons (4.5 g) Splenda

2 teaspoons caraway seeds

1/8 teaspoon ground cloves

Guar or xanthan

In a big, heavy skillet, brown the ribs in the oil over medium-high heat.

Put the cauliflower, turnip, apple, carrots, and onion in your slow cooker. Put the ribs and sauerkraut on top.

In a bowl, mix together the vinegar, Splenda, caraway seeds, and cloves. Pour the mixture over the ribs and sauerkraut. Cover the slow cooker, set it to low, and let it cook for 8 to 9 hours.

When the time's up, remove the ribs to a platter with tongs and scoop out the vegetables with a slotted spoon. Thicken the pot liquid with guar or xanthan, add salt and pepper to taste, and serve the sauce with the ribs and vegetables.

Yield: 6 servings, each with: 529 calories, 39 g fat, 32 g protein, 13 g carbohydrate, 4 g dietary fiber, 9 g usable carbs.

Hocks and Shanks with Cabbage and Apples

Ham hocks and ham shank slices (sometimes called smoked hocks) give you great ham flavor without having to wrestle with that whole ham. They're cheaper, too. And again, this kind of tough, bony meat really shines when you slow-cook it.

1¹/₂ pounds (680 g) ham hocks

1¹/₂ pounds (680 g) ham, shank half

(or 3 pounds [1.4 kg] of hocks or 3 pounds [1.4 kg] of shanks,
    whatever you can get)

1 medium head red cabbage

¹/₂ Granny smith apple

¹/₂ medium onion

1¹/₂ cups (355 ml) chicken broth

¹/₂ cup (120 ml) apple cider vinegar

4 teaspoons (2 g) Splenda or the equivalent in other sugar-free sweetener

1 tablespoon (15 g) bacon grease, melted

Throw your hocks, shanks, or both into your slow cooker. Coarsely chop your cabbage and dice your apple and onion. Throw them in, too.

Mix together everything else and then pour it over the meat and vegetables. Cover your slow cooker, set it on low, and let the whole thing cook for a good 6 to 7 hours; then serve.

Note: Use smoked hocks or shanks, whichever you can get—I used both. The shanks have more meat.

Yield: 6 servings, each with: 624 calories, 44 g fat, 44 g protein, 12 g carbohydrate, 3 g dietary fiber, 9 g usable carbs.

chapter six

Slow Cooker Lamb

You'll notice a certain reliance on lamb shanks here. Lamb shanks are the bottom-most part of a leg of lamb, and they're ideal for slow cooking for a couple reasons. They fit neatly in the pot, and they're the sort of tough, flavorful meat that really shines with slow, moist cooking.

If you're having trouble finding lamb shanks at your grocery store, ask the nice meat guys. Or you could make any of the shank recipes with a chunk of lamb leg or shoulder of the right weight. Have the meat guys cut it into a few pieces, though, so it'll fit in your pot and won't take far more cooking time than the recipe specifies. Most grocery stores will cut up a roast for you for no added charge.

Lamb Shanks in Red Wine

This is a hearty one-pot meal.

>   5 pounds (2.3 kg) lamb shank (4 shanks)
>
>   1/4 cup (60 ml) olive oil
>
>   2 stalks celery, sliced 1/2-inch (13 mm) thick
>
>   2 carrots, sliced 1/2-inch (13 mm) thick
>
>   8 cloves garlic, crushed
>
>   1/2 onion, chunked
>
>   8 ounces (225 g) sliced mushrooms
>
>   1 cup (235 ml) chicken broth
>
>   1 cup (235 ml) dry red wine
>
>   1 teaspoon beef bouillon concentrate
>
>   2 teaspoons pepper
>
>   1/2 teaspoon ground rosemary
>
>   2 bay leaves
>
>   Guar or xanthan

In a big, heavy skillet, sear the lamb all over in the oil.

Place the celery, carrots, garlic, onion, and mushrooms in your slow cooker.

When the lamb is browned all over, transfer it to the slow cooker, on top of the veggies.

In a bowl, stir together the broth, wine, bouillon, pepper, and rosemary. Pour the mixture over the lamb. Add the bay leaves. (Make sure they land in the liquid!) Cover the slow cooker, turn it to low, and let it cook for 6 hours.

When the time's up, remove the lamb to serving plates. Remove the bay leaves. Using guar or xanthan, thicken the liquid in the slow cooker to the consistency of heavy cream. Ladle the sauce and vegetables over the lamb.

Yield: 6 servings, each with: 757 calories, 50 g fat, 59 g protein, 8 g carbohydrate, 2 g dietary fiber, 6 g usable carbs.

Lemon Lamb Shanks

Lemon brings out the best in lamb!

> 4 pounds (1.8 kg) lamb shank
>
> 2 tablespoons (28 ml) olive oil
>
> 1 teaspoon lemon pepper
>
> 1/2 teaspoon dry mustard
>
> 1/2 cup (120 ml) chicken broth
>
> 1 teaspoon beef bouillon concentrate
>
> 1/2 teaspoon grated lemon peel
>
> 2 tablespoons (28 ml) lemon juice
>
> 1 teaspoon dried rosemary
>
> 2 cloves garlic, crushed
>
> Guar or xanthan

Sear the lamb all over in the oil. Place the lamb in your slow cooker.

In a bowl, mix together the lemon pepper and dry mustard. Sprinkle the mixture evenly over the lamb.

In the same bowl, mix together the broth, bouillon, lemon peel, lemon juice, rosemary, and garlic. Pour the mixture over the lamb. Cover the slow cooker, set it to low, and let it cook for 8 hours.

When the time's up, remove the lamb and thicken up the liquid in the slow cooker a bit with guar or xanthan.

Serve this dish with a salad with plenty of cucumbers and tomatoes!

Yield: 6 servings, each with: 535 calories, 37 g fat, 46 g protein, 1 g carbohydrate, trace dietary fiber, 1 g usable carbs.

Kashmiri Lamb Shanks

This was originally a recipe for a skillet curry of lamb, but it works wonderfully in the slow cooker. If you like Indian food, you have to try this. And if you've never eaten Indian food, you need to start!

2¹/₂ pounds (1.1 kg) lamb shank

2 tablespoons (28 ml) olive oil

1 cup (235 ml) chicken broth

¹/₂ teaspoon beef bouillon concentrate

1 teaspoon *Garam Masala* (see recipe page 340) or purchased garam masala

2 teaspoons ground coriander

1 tablespoon (8 g) grated ginger root

¹/₄ teaspoon cayenne

Guar or xanthan

In a big, heavy skillet, sear the lamb all over in the oil over medium-high heat. Transfer the lamb to your slow cooker.

In a bowl, mix together the broth, bouillon, garam masala, coriander, ginger, and cayenne. Pour the mixture over the lamb. Cover the slow cooker, set it to low, and let it cook for 8 hours.

Remove the lamb to a platter, thicken the sauce a bit with guar or xanthan, and serve the sauce over the lamb.

Yield: 4 servings, each with: 530 calories, 38 g fat, 44 g protein, 1 g carbohydrate, trace dietary fiber, 1 g usable carbs.

Choucroute Garni

This is a streamlined version of a traditional dish from the Alsace region of France. The name means Garnished Sauerkraut. It's so simple and so good, especially on a cold night.

> 1 can (14 ounces, or 400 g) sauerkraut, rinsed and drained
>
> 1 tablespoon (15 g) bacon grease
>
> 1/4 cup (60 ml) apple cider vinegar
>
> 1 tablespoon (1.5 g) Splenda
>
> 1/2 medium onion, thinly sliced
>
> 2 tablespoons (28 ml) gin
>
> 1/4 cup (60 ml) dry white wine
>
> 1 pound (455 g) meat (Choose any combination of kielbasa, smoked sausage, frankfurters, link sausages, 1/4-inch-thick (6 mm) ham slices, or smoked pork chops.*)

Place the sauerkraut in your slow cooker. Add the bacon grease, vinegar, Splenda, onion, gin, and wine and give it a quick stir. Place the meat on top. Cover the slow cooker, set it to low, and let it cook for 5 to 6 hours.

*I use 1/2 pound (225 g) each of the lowest carbohydrate kielbasa and smoked sausage I can find.

Note: This doesn't even start to fill my slow cooker, so feel free to double or even triple this recipe. If you increase it, I suggest arranging it with a layer of kraut, a layer of meat, a layer of kraut, and so on. And of course, you'll have to increase the cooking time by an hour, maybe two, depending on how many extra layers you use.

Yield: 3 servings, each with: 112 calories, 5 g fat, 1 g protein, 9 g carbohydrate, 4 g dietary fiber, 5 g usable carbs. (This will depend on which meats you use.)

Onion-Mustard Pork Chops

2 pounds (900 g) pork chops

1 tablespoon (15 ml) olive oil

1 medium onion, thinly sliced

4 cloves garlic, crushed

1 teaspoon dry mustard

1/2 teaspoon salt or Vege-Sal

1 teaspoon pepper

1 dash hot sauce

1 tablespoon (15 ml) cider vinegar

1/2 cup (120 ml) dry white wine

2 tablespoons (22 g) brown mustard

1/2 cup (120 ml) heavy cream

Guar or xanthan

In a big, heavy skillet, brown the pork on both sides in the oil over medium-high heat. Transfer the pork to your slow cooker.

Turn the heat down to medium-low and add the onion to the skillet. Sauté it until it's translucent. Then stir in the garlic, dry mustard, salt or Vege-Sal, pepper, and hot sauce and let the whole thing sauté for another minute or so. Transfer the mixture to the slow cooker on top of the pork.

In a bowl, stir together the vinegar and wine. Pour the mixture into the slow cooker. Cover the slow cooker, set it to low, and let it cook for 6 hours.

When the time's up, remove the pork to a platter. Stir the mustard and cream into the juice in the pot. Thicken the juice a tad with guar or xanthan and serve the sauce over the pork.

Yield: 6 servings, each with: 352 calories, 25 g fat, 25 g protein, 4 g carbohydrate, 1 g dietary fiber, 3 g usable carbs.

Caribbean Slow Cooker Lamb

Lamb and goat are very popular in the Caribbean, and this is my slow cooker interpretation of a Caribbean lamb dish. Look for tamarind concentrate in a grocery store with a good international section. I found it in a medium-size town in southern Indiana, so you may well find it near you! If you can't find it, you could use a tablespoon (15 ml) of lemon juice and a teaspoon of Splenda instead. Your lamb will be less authentically Caribbean-tasting, but still yummy.

2- to 3-pound section (0.9 to 1.4 kg) of a leg of lamb

1/2 medium onion, chopped

1/2 teaspoon minced garlic or 1 clove garlic, crushed

1 teaspoon tamarind concentrate

1 tablespoon (11 g) spicy brown mustard

1 cup (180 g) canned diced tomatoes

1 teaspoon hot sauce—preferably Caribbean Scotch Bonnet sauce—or more or less to taste

Guar or xanthan (optional)

Place the lamb in your slow cooker.

In a bowl, stir together the onion, garlic, tamarind, mustard, tomatoes, and hot sauce. Pour the mixture over the lamb. Cover the slow cooker, set it to low, and let it cook for a good 8 hours.

When it's done, remove the lamb to a serving platter, thicken the pot juices with the guar or xanthan if it seems necessary, and add salt and pepper to taste.

Yield: 6 servings, each with: 357 calories, 26 g fat, 27 g protein, 3 g carbohydrate, 1 g dietary fiber, 2 g usable carbs.

Greek Stuffed Peppers

This is really a one-dish meal since it has so many vegetables in it. Feel free to use this method of cooking with any stuffed pepper recipe.

4 large green bell peppers

1 small onion, chopped

1¹/4 (570 g) pounds ground lamb

1 cup (150 g) crumbled feta cheese

1 can (14¹/2 ounces, or 410 g) diced tomatoes, drained

2 cloves garlic, crushed

2 teaspoons dried oregano

¹/4 cup (15 g) chopped fresh parsley

1 teaspoon salt, or to taste

¹/2 teaspoon pepper

Whack the tops off the peppers. Scoop out and discard the cores. Trim the useable flesh from around the stems and throw it in your food processor with the S-blade in place.

Peel your onion and cut it in chunks; throw it in the food processor, too. Pulse to chop everything medium-fine.

Throw the chopped pepper and onion in a big mixing bowl. Add the lamb, feta, drained tomatoes, garlic, oregano, parsley, salt, and pepper and use clean hands to mash everything together really well.

Stuff this mixture into your peppers, mounding it a bit on top. Settle them down into your slow cooker, cover, and set to low. Cook for 5 to 6 hours and then serve. You can crumble a little extra feta over the tops, if you like, but it's not essential.

Yield: 4 servings, each with: 575 calories, 42 g fat, 31 g protein, 19 g carbohydrate, 3 g dietary fiber, 16 g usable carbs.

chapter seven

Slow Cooker Fish and Seafood

I don't generally think of fish when I think of long, slow cooking, and indeed who wants to leave fish in a slow cooker all day? But the gentle, even heating of your slow cooker, used judiciously, can yield fish and seafood that's remarkably moist and tender. When you don't need to have dinner waiting, try these recipes!

Or as in a few of these recipes, you can cook everything else all day and then just stir in the seafood for the last little bit of cooking time. It doesn't take long to cook fish or seafood through!

Lime-Basted Scallops

My seafood-loving husband thought these were some of the best scallops he'd ever had.

> 1/4 cup (60 ml) lime juice
>
> 3 tablespoons (45 g) butter
>
> 2 cloves garlic
>
> 24 ounces (680 g) sea scallops
>
> Guar or xanthan
>
> 1/4 cup (4 g) chopped fresh cilantro

Put the lime juice, butter, and garlic in your slow cooker. Cover the slow cooker, set it to high, and let it cook for 30 minutes.

Uncover the slow cooker and stir the butter, lime juice, and garlic together. Now add the scallops, stirring them around to coat them with the sauce. Spread them in a single layer on the bottom of the slow cooker. (If the sauce seems to pool in one or two areas, try to cluster the scallops there. In my pot, the sauce liked to stay around the edges.) Re-cover the pot, set it to high, and let it cook for 45 minutes.

When the time's up, remove the scallops to serving plates. Thicken the pot liquid just a tiny bit with guar or xanthan and spoon the sauce over the scallops. Top each serving with a tablespoon of cilantro.

Yield: 4 servings, each with: 233 calories, 10 g fat, 29 g protein, 6 g carbohydrate, trace dietary fiber, 6 g usable carbs.

Scallops Florentine

This is a simple creamed spinach recipe with scallops. This would make a nice romantic dinner since it serves two.

- 10 ounces (280 g) frozen chopped spinach, thawed
- 1 clove garlic, crushed
- 1/4 cup (60 ml) heavy cream
- 1/4 cup (25 g) grated Parmesan cheese
- 1 tablespoon (7 g) Old Bay seafood seasoning
- 12 ounces (340 g) sea scallops

Dump your thawed spinach into a strainer and press it really well to get out all the water—you could even pick it up with clean hands and squeeze it hard. Just drain it really well. Then dump it in your slow cooker.

Add the garlic, cream, Parmesan, and Old Bay seasoning. Stir this mixture together well. Cover the pot, set to low, and let it cook for 30 to 45 minutes until the spinach mixture is getting hot.

Lay the scallops in a single layer on top of the spinach, re-cover the pot, and let the whole thing cook for an hour. Serve the scallops on a bed of the spinach.

Yield: 2 servings, each with: 334 calories, 16 g fat, 37 g protein, 11 g carbohydrate, 4 g dietary fiber, 7 g usable carbs.

Lemon-Mustard Salmon Steaks

This is so simple and classic. The salmon comes out tender and moist.

2 tablespoons (28 g) butter

1 tablespoon (15 ml) lemon juice

1 teaspoon Dijon mustard

1 pinch salt or Vege-Sal

2 salmon steaks (totaling about 1 pound, or 455 g)

2 tablespoons (8 g) chopped fresh parsley

Combine the butter, lemon juice, mustard, and salt or Vege-Sal in your slow cooker. Cover the slow cooker, set it to low, and let it cook for 30 to 40 minutes. Stir together.

Now put the salmon steaks in the slow cooker and turn them once or twice to coat. Re-cover the slow cooker and let it cook for 1 hour. Spoon some of the pot liquid over the salmon and sprinkle with the parsley before serving.

Yield: 2 servings, each with: 369 calories, 19 g fat, 46 g protein, 1 g carbohydrate, trace dietary fiber, 1 g usable carbs.

Orange Basil Salmon

Keith the Organic Gardening God next door always plants a ton of basil, and we get the overflow. Here's one way to use some of it!

> 1 orange
>
> 1/3 cup (80 ml) extra virgin olive oil
>
> 1/2 cup (20 g) minced fresh basil
>
> 24 ounces (680 g) salmon fillets
>
> Salt and pepper

Grate the zest of your orange and reserve.

Pour the olive oil into your slow cooker. Now whack the orange in half and squeeze in the juice. (If you use a navel orange, you won't have to worry about pits.) Throw in the zest, too. Cover the pot, set to low, and let it heat for a half an hour.

When the half an hour is up, cut your salmon fillets into servings and salt and pepper them on both sides. Mince your basil. Open up your slow cooker and give the oil and orange a stir to make sure it's well-blended. Add the basil to the pot and then put in the salmon. Flip it over a few times to make sure the salmon's well-coated on both sides. Now lay it, skin-side up, flat on the bottom of the slow cooker in the olive oil/orange mixture.

Re-cover the pot and let the salmon cook for 60 to 90 minutes. Serve with the pot juices spooned over it.

Yield: 4 servings, each with: 373 calories, 24 g fat, 34 g protein, 4 g carbohydrate, 1 g dietary fiber, 3 g usable carbs.

Maple-Balsamic Salmon

This started as a recipe for grilled salmon in *The Low-Carb Barbecue Book*, but it works brilliantly in the slow cooker, as well.

> 2 salmon steaks (totaling about 1 pound, or 455 g)
>
> 1 tablespoon (15 ml) olive oil
>
> 2 tablespoons (40 g) sugar-free pancake syrup
>
> 1 clove garlic, crushed
>
> 1 tablespoon (15 ml) balsamic vinegar

In your slow cooker, combine everything but the salmon. Cover the slow cooker, set it to low, and let it cook for 30 minutes.

Now add the salmon, turning the steaks to coat them with the sauce. Re-cover the pot and let it cook for 1 hour. Spoon some of the pot liquid over the steaks before serving.

Yield: 2 servings, each with: 326 calories, 15 g fat, 45 g protein, 1 g carbohydrate, trace dietary fiber, 1 g usable carbs. (Analysis does not include the polyols in the sugar-free pancake syrup.)

Balsamic-Vanilla Salmon

Cooking is a remarkably trend-driven business, and a recent fashion has been using vanilla in main-dish recipes. It works so well for chocolate, I thought I'd give it a try. It turned out great!

2 tablespoons (28 ml) extra virgin olive oil

1/4 teaspoon Splenda

1/2 teaspoon Worcestershire sauce

2 drops molasses

2 teaspoons balsamic vinegar

1/2 teaspoon spicy brown or dijon mustard

1/2 teaspoon vanilla extract

1 clove garlic, crushed

2 tablespoons (20 g) minced onion

2 tablespoons (6 g) minced fresh basil

2 tablespoons (8 g) minced fresh parsley

24 ounces (680 g) salmon fillets

Measure and whisk together everything from the olive oil through the garlic.

Place the onion, basil, and parsley in the bottom of your slow cooker and pour in the vinaigrette. Stir it all together a little.

Add your salmon fillets and flip them once or twice to coat. Arrange them skin-side up. Then cover the pot, set it to low, and let it cook for an hour.

Serve with the liquid and herbs from the pot spooned over the fish.

Yield: 4 servings, each with: 264 calories, 13 g fat, 34 g protein, 1 g carbohydrate, trace dietary fiber, 1 g usable carbs.

Salmon in Sweet Chili Sauce

That *Not-Quite-Asian Sweet Chili Sauce* is quick and easy; so don't hesitate!

> 1/2 batch *Not-Quite-Asian Sweet Chili Sauce* (see recipe below.)
> 24 ounces (680 g) salmon fillets

Simply put the sauce in the slow cooker, lay the fillets in it, and flip them a couple of times to coat. Arrange them skin-side up, cover the pot, set to low, and let it cook for 60 to 90 minutes. That's it!

Yield: 4 servings, each with: 222 calories, 6 g fat, 35 g protein, 3 g carbohydrate, trace dietary fiber, 2 g usable carbs. (Analysis does not include the polyols in the *Not-Quite-Asian Sweet Chili Sauce.*)

Not-Quite-Asian Sweet Chili Sauce

This is great with fish, chicken, and pork—all sorts of stuff.

> 5 dried Thai bird peppers (the little skinny pointy hot peppers)
> 1/2 cup (160 g) sugar-free pancake syrup
> 1/2 cup (120 g) erythritol
> 3 tablespoons (45 ml) cider vinegar
> 1/4 cup (60 ml) dry sherry
> 1/4 cup (60 ml) soy sauce
> 1 tablespoon (28 g) fresh ginger root—a chunk a little bigger than a whole
>   shell-on walnut
> 3 garlic cloves
> 1/4 teaspoon pepper

Just throw everything in your blender or food processor and run until the peppers, ginger, and garlic are pulverized. Keep in a screw-top jar in the fridge.

Yield: 1 1/2 cups, or 24 servings of 1 tablespoon, each with: 8 calories, trace fat, trace protein, 1g carbohydrate, trace dietary fiber, 1 g usable carbs. (Analysis does not include the polyols in the sugar-free pancake syrup.)

Sweet and Sour Shrimp

Adding the shrimp and snow peas at the last moment keeps them from becoming desperately overcooked.

1 cup (170 g) peaches, peeled and cubed (Frozen unsweetened peaches work well. Just cut them into smaller chunks—1/2 inch [13 mm].)

1/2 cup (80 g) chopped onion

1 green bell pepper, diced

1/2 cup (50 g) chopped celery

1/2 cup (120 ml) chicken broth

2 tablespoons (28 ml) dark sesame oil

1/4 cup (60 ml) soy sauce

2 tablespoons (28 ml) rice vinegar

1/4 cup (60 ml) lemon juice

1 teaspoon red pepper flakes

1 tablespoon (1.5 g) Splenda

6 ounces (170 g) fresh snow pea pods, trimmed

1 1/2 pounds (700 g) shrimp, shells removed

1/3 cup (37 g) slivered almonds, toasted

Guar or xanthan

Put the peaches, onion, pepper, celery, broth, sesame oil, soy sauce, vinegar, lemon juice, red pepper flakes, and Splenda in your slow cooker and stir them together. Cover the slow cooker, set it to low, and let it cook for 4 hours. (Or you could cook it on high for 2 hours.)

When the time's up, turn the pot up to high while you trim the snow peas and cut them in 1-inch (2.5 cm) lengths. Stir them in and let it cook for 15 to 20 minutes. Now stir in the shrimp. If they're uncooked, give them 10 minutes or until they're pink through. If they're cooked already, just give them 5 minutes or so to get hot through.

You can serve this over rice for the carb-eaters in the family, of course. If you like, you can have yours on *Cauli-Rice* (see recipe page 343), but this dish is high-carb enough already that I'd probably eat it plain.

Yield: 6 servings, each with: 257 calories, 11 g fat, 27 g protein, 13 g carbohydrate, 3 g dietary fiber, 10 g usable carbs.

Super-Simple Catfish

Catfish is That Nice Boy I Married's favorite, but breading and frying it is a big production. This is a whole lot easier and tastes great. And there's no carbs at all!

> 2 tablespoons (28 g) bacon grease
>
> 2 pounds (900 g) catfish fillets
>
> Creole seasoning (I used Tony Cachere's.)

This is so easy, but my husband loved it! Turn on your slow cooker to low and throw in the bacon grease. Let it heat for 30 minutes.

If you need to, cut your catfish into pieces that will fit flat in the bottom of the slow cooker. Sprinkle it liberally on both sides with the Creole seasoning. Then lay it in the bacon grease, flipping it once to coat. Cover the pot and let it cook for 45 minutes to an hour and then serve.

Yield: 4 servings, each with: 275 calories, 13 g fat, 37 g protein, 0 g carbohydrate, 0 g dietary fiber, 0 g usable carbs.

Bacon-Almond Flounder Rolls

6 tablespoons (85 g) butter, divided

2 tablespoons (28 g) bacon grease

6 flounder fillets

6 scallions

2 small celery ribs

1 cup (112 g) almond meal

6 slices bacon

1 teaspoon dried thyme

Salt and pepper

Paprika

Start 2 tablespoons (28 g) of the butter and the bacon grease heating in your slow cooker on high.

Lay your bacon on a microwave bacon rack or in a Pyrex pie plate and give them 6 to 8 minutes on high—you want it crisp but not burnt.

Trim the scallions and celery, throw them in your food processor, and chop them fairly fine.

Okay, melt another 2 tablespoons (28 g) of the butter in a small skillet over medium-low heat. Add the almond meal and stir until it smells toasty. Transfer to a plate.

Melt the last 2 tablespoons (28 ml) of butter and sauté the scallions and celery until softened. Add the almond meal back to the skillet and stir to combine. Now use your kitchen shears to snip in the bacon in little bits. Add the thyme, stir it up, and salt and pepper to taste.

Lay a fillet flat on a plate, put a couple tablespoons (28 g) of stuffing across it about 2 inches (5 cm) from one end, and wrap those 2 inches (5 cm) around it. Wrap the other end around. Carefully transfer to the slow cooker, placing it seam-side down. Repeat with the rest of the fish and stuffing.

Sprinkle the rolls lightly with paprika. Then cover the pot and let them cook an hour. Spoon some of the grease/liquid in the pot over each roll when you serve them and snip a few scallion tops over them to make them look pretty.

Yield: 6 servings, each with: 427 calories, 25 g fat, 42 g protein, 8 g carbohydrate, 1 g dietary fiber, 7 g usable carbs.

Almond-Stuffed Flounder Rolls with Orange Butter Sauce

    4 tablespoons (55 g) butter, divided

    2 tablespoons (28 ml) lemon juice

    1/8 teaspoon orange extract

    1 teaspoon Splenda

    1/3 cup (145 g) almonds

    1/4 cup (40 g) minced onion

    1 clove garlic, crushed

    1 1/2 teaspoons Dijon mustard

    1/2 teaspoon soy sauce

    1/4 cup (15 g) minced fresh parsley, divided

    1 pound (455 g) flounder fillets, 4 ounces (115 g) each

Put 2 tablespoons (28 grams) of the butter, the lemon juice, orange extract, and Splenda in your slow cooker. Cover the slow cooker, set it to low, and let it heat while you fix your flounder rolls.

Put the almonds in a food processor with the S-blade in place and grind them to a cornmeal consistency. Melt 1 tablespoon (14 grams) of butter in a medium-sized heavy skillet and add the ground almonds. Stir the almonds over medium heat for 5 to 7 minutes or until they smell toasty. Transfer them to a bowl.

Now melt the final tablespoon (14 g) of butter in the skillet and sauté the onion and garlic over medium-low heat until the onion is just turning translucent. Add them to the almonds and stir them in. Now stir in the mustard, soy sauce, and 2 tablespoons (8 grams) of the parsley.

Lay the flounder fillets on a big plate and divide the almond mixture between them. Spread it over the fillets and then roll each one up and fasten it with a toothpick.

Take the lid off the slow cooker and stir the sauce. Place the flounder rolls in the sauce and spoon the sauce over them. Re-cover the pot and let the rolls cook for 1 hour. When they're done, spoon the sauce over the rolls and sprinkle the remaining parsley over them to serve.

Yield: 4 servings, each with: 285 calories, 19 g fat, 24 g protein, 5 g carbohydrate, 2 g dietary fiber, 3 g usable carbs.

Pantry Seafood Supper

This is convenient because, as the name strongly suggests, it uses seafood you've got sitting in your pantry. If you've got seafood sitting in your freezer, you can use it instead—just let it cook an extra 30 minutes or so to make sure it's thawed and cooked through.

1/4 cup (45 g) roasted red peppers jarred in oil, diced small (about 1 pepper)

1/3 cup (20 g) chopped parsley

1 cup (70 g) chopped mushrooms

3/4 cup (175 ml) chicken broth

3/4 cup (175 ml) dry white wine

2 tablespoons (20 g) minced onion

2 teaspoons dried dill weed

1/2 teaspoon paprika

1/2 teaspoon Tabasco sauce

1 cup (235 ml) Carb Countdown dairy beverage

1/4 cup (60 ml) heavy cream

Guar or xanthan

1 can (6 ounces, or 170 g) tuna, drained

1 can (6 ounces, or 170 g) crab, drained

1 can (6 ounces, or 170 g) shrimp, drained

Combine the red peppers, parsley, mushrooms, broth, wine, onion, dill, paprika, and Tabasco sauce in your slow cooker. Cover the slow cooker, set it to low, and let it cook for 3 to 4 hours.

When the time's up, stir in the Carb Countdown and cream and thicken the sauce to your liking with guar or xanthan. Now stir in the tuna, crab, and shrimp and let it cook for another 15 to 20 minutes.

Now you have a choice: You can eat this as a chowder, or you can serve it over *Cauli-Rice* (see recipe page 343) or low-carbohydrate pasta—or even over spaghetti squash. It's up to you.

Yield: 4 servings, each with: 269 calories, 9 g fat, 33 g protein, 4 g carbohydrate, 1 g dietary fiber, 3 g usable carbs.

Tuna-Noodle Casserole

Here's everybody's favorite childhood comfort food, decarbed.

8 ounces (225 g) mushrooms, coarsely chopped

3 cans (5 ounces, or 140 g each) tuna in water, drained well

1 cup (235 ml) heavy cream

1/2 teaspoon beef bouillon granules

1 tablespoon (15 ml) Worcestershire sauce

1/4 teaspoon salt or Vege-Sal

2 ounces (55 g) cream cheese

1/4 teaspoon pepper

1 cup (130 g) frozen peas NOT thawed

2 packages fettuccini-style tofu shirataki

Put the chopped mushrooms and drained tuna in your slow cooker. Stir together the cream, bouillon concentrate, Worcestershire sauce, salt, and pepper until the bouillon is dissolved. Pour this over the mushrooms and tuna and stir everything up. Now cut the cream cheese into a few chunks and settle them down into the tuna-mushroom mixture.

Dump the peas on top of everything and don't stir them in. Cover the pot, set it to low, and let it cook for 4 hours.

When suppertime rolls around, drain and rinse your shirataki and snip across them a few times with your kitchen shears. Put them in a microwaveable bowl and nuke them for 2 minutes on high. Drain them again, put them back in the bowl, nuke them for another 2 minutes, and then drain one more time. (You're getting the excess water out of your noodles so they don't make your casserole watery.)

While your noodles are in the microwave, take the lid off the slow cooker and stir everything together. See if it needs to be thicker—it may, because of the liquid cooking out of those mushrooms. Use your guar or xanthan shaker to thicken the sauce a bit if it needs it. When the noodles are drained for the third time, stir them in and serve. Alternatively, you can put the noodles on plates and serve the tuna mixture on top.

If you want something crunchy to replace the usual breadcrumb or potato chip topping, try crushed pork rinds or toasted slivered almonds, sprinkled over each serving right before you put them on the table.

Yield: 5 servings, each with: 339 calories, 23 g fat, 26 g protein, 8 g carbohydrate, 2 g dietary fiber, 6 g usable carbs.

chapter eight

Slow Cooker Crazy Mixed-up Meals

It's really very hard to organize a cookbook. Take, for instance, the recipes that follow. They really messed up my plan to organize this book largely by protein source. After backing and forthing, moving them around, I threw up my hands and gave them their own chapter.

Simple Meat Loaf

This is simple, but it's hardly boring! Because meat loaf takes at least an hour in the oven, many of you may have given up on it as a weeknight dinner. Baking it in your slow cooker works remarkably well, although it doesn't brown much.

1 pound (455 g) ground round

1 pound (455 g) pork sausage

1 medium onion, finely chopped

1 medium green pepper, finely chopped

1/4 cup (24 g) oat bran

1/2 teaspoon pepper

1/2 teaspoon salt or Vege-Sal

2 tablespoons (28 ml) Worcestershire sauce

2 eggs

1/2 cup (60 g) pork rind crumbs (Run pork rinds through your food processor or blender.)

Place all ingredients in a big mixing bowl and use clean hands to smoosh everything together until it's well blended.

Put a rack or a collapsible basket-style steamer in the bottom of your slow cooker. Fold two squares of foil into strips and criss-cross them on the rack or steamer and up the sides of the slow cooker. (What you're doing is making a sling to help you lift the loaf out of the slow cooker.) If the holes/slots in your rack are pretty big, put a sheet of foil over the criss-crossed strips and pierce it all over with a fork.

Place the meat mixture on top of this and form into an evenly-domed meat loaf, smoothing the surface with dampened hands. Cover the slow cooker, set it to low, and let it cook for 9 to 12 hours.

Use the foil strips to lift the meat loaf out of the slow cooker.

Yield: 8 servings, each with: 438 calories, 36 g fat, 23 g protein, 6 g carbohydrate, 1 g dietary fiber, 5 g usable carbs.

Morty's Mixed Meat Loaf

The combination of meats makes this loaf unusually tasty.

2 slices cooked bacon, crumbled

1 pound (455 g) ground round

1 pound (455 g) ground pork

1 pound (455 g) ground turkey

3 stalks celery, finely chopped

1/2 cup (30 g) finely chopped fresh parsley

1/2 cup (120 g) *Dana's No-Sugar Ketchup* (see recipe page 332) or purchased low-carb ketchup

1 teaspoon hot sauce

2 eggs

1/2 cup (60 g) barbecue-style pork rind crumbs (Just run them through your food processor.)

2 tablespoons (28 ml) Worcestershire sauce

1 teaspoon lemon juice

1/2 teaspoon dried marjoram

1 teaspoon salt or Vege-Sal

1/2 teaspoon pepper

Put a rack or basket-style steamer in the bottom of your slow cooker pot. Fold two squares of foil into strips and criss-cross them on the rack or steamer and up the sides of the slow cooker. (What you're doing is making a sling to help you lift the loaf out of the slow cooker.) If the holes/slots in your rack are pretty big, put a sheet of foil over the criss-crossed strips and pierce it all over with a fork.

Place all your ingredients in a big bowl and using clean hands, smoosh everything together really well. Form it into a round loaf on the rack in the slow cooker. Cover the slow cooker, set it to low, and let it cook for 8 to 10 hours.

Use the strips of foil to lift the loaf out of the slow cooker.

Yield: 8 servings, each with: 453 calories, 30 g fat, 37 g protein, 7 g carbohydrate, 2 g dietary fiber, 5 g usable carbs.

Louisiana Meat Loaf

I totally made this up out of my head. I just threw in all the Louisiana flavors I could think of, starting with the holy trinity of onion, green pepper, and celery, and it came out great.

> 1 pound (455 g) ground chuck
>
> 1 pound (455 g) pork sausage or turkey sausage
>
> 1/2 medium onion
>
> 1 celery rib, including leaves
>
> 1/2 green bell pepper
>
> 1 can (14 1/2 ounces, or 410 g) tomatoes with green chiles, drained
>
> 3 cloves garlic, crushed
>
> 1 tablespoon (1 g) dried basil
>
> 4 teaspoons (12 g) Creole seasoning (I used Tony Cachere's.)
>
> 1/2 cup (60 g) pork rind crumbs
>
> 1 egg

This is your basic meat loaf procedure: Dump your meat in a mixing bowl. Throw your onion, celery, and green pepper in your food processor with the S-blade in place and pulse until they're chopped medium-fine. Dump them in with the meat.

Add everything else. Smoosh it all up really well with clean hands.

Take two pieces of heavy-duty foil, long enough to reach down into your slow cooker, across the bottom, and back up the other side and fold each into a strip about 2 inches (5 cm) wide. Put your basket steamer in the slow cooker and criss-cross the foil strips across it, going around the stem in the middle.

Dump the meat in the slow cooker and form it into a nice, even loaf on the steamer. Cover the slow cooker, set to low, and let the whole thing cook for 6 to 7 hours.

Use the foil strips to lift the meat loaf out onto a platter and serve.

Yield: 6 servings, each with: 588 calories, 49 g fat, 28 g protein, 7 g carbohydrate, 1 g dietary fiber, 6 g usable carbs.

⌂ Pub Loaf

Why is it Pub Loaf? It's because I imagine this is the sort of thing you might get in an English pub. Never having been to England, I can imagine anything I like. Plus, it's got beer in it!

4 slices bacon

4 ounces (115 g) chopped mushrooms

1 pound (455 g) ground chuck

1 pound (455 g) ground turkey

1 medium carrot

1 celery rib

1/2 medium onion

1 cup (115 g) shredded Cheddar cheese

2 teaspoons salt or Vege-Sal

1/2 teaspoon pepper

1 cup (120 g) pork rind crumbs

1 egg

1/2 cup (120 ml) light beer

In your big, heavy skillet, cook the bacon until crisp. Remove from the skillet and reserve.

Start the mushrooms frying in the bacon grease. In the meantime, put the meats in a big mixing bowl. Shred your carrot and chop your onion fine and add them, too, along with the cheese, salt, pepper, pork rind crumbs, and beer. When the mushrooms are soft, throw them in, too. Use clean hands to smoosh it all together really well.

Take two pieces of heavy-duty foil, long enough to reach down into your slow cooker, across the bottom, and back up the other side and fold each into a strip about 2 inches (5 cm) wide. Put your basket steamer in the slow cooker and criss-cross the foil strips across it, going around the stem in the middle.

Dump the meat in the slow cooker and form it into a nice, even loaf on the steamer. Cover the slow cooker, set to low, and let the whole thing cook for 6 to 7 hours.

Use the foil sling to remove your meat loaf from the slow cooker, place it on a platter, and serve.

Yield: 8 servings, each with: 333 calories, 23 g fat, 26 g protein, 3 g carbohydrate, 1 g dietary fiber, 2 g usable carbs.

Tuscan-ish Meat Loaf

Okay, I haven't been to Tuscany any more than I've been to England. I'm provincial, so sue me. But I saw a recipe for a Tuscan meat loaf, and it looked good, so I whacked out the carbs and subbed for some hard to get ingredients, and it was tasty, so here it is. And I'll start thinking of tax deductible ways to get to Europe. I could jot down ideas for recipes, right?

1 pound (455 g) ground chuck

1 pound (455 g) pork sausage

1 pound (455 g) ground chicken

3 eggs

1 1/2 medium onions (or one big one)

1 large carrot

1 large celery rib, leaves included

4 cloves garlic

1/2 teaspoon nutmeg

1 1/2 teaspoons salt or Vege-Sal

1/2 teaspoon pepper

3/4 cup (75 g) grated Parmesan cheese

1 cup (120 g) pork rind crumbs

Throw all your meats in a big mixing bowl, along with the eggs. Chop your veggies fairly fine and throw them in, too, along with everything else. Use clean hands to smoosh it all up really well.

Take two pieces of heavy-duty foil, long enough to reach down into your slow cooker, across the bottom, and back up the other side and fold each into a strip about 2 inches (5 cm) wide. Put your basket steamer in the slow cooker and criss-cross the foil strips across it, going around the stem in the middle.

Dump the meat in the slow cooker and form it into a nice, even loaf on the steamer. Cover the slow cooker, set to low, and let the whole thing cook for 7 to 8 hours.

Use the sling to lift the meat loaf out of the slow cooker to a platter and serve.

Yield: 10 servings, each with: 510 calories, 37 g fat, 36 g protein, 4 g carbohydrate, 1 g dietary fiber, 3 g usable carbs.

Pizza-ish Meat Loaf

Here you've got your pizza sauce, you got your cheese, and you got your Italian sausage and onions and peppers. I do not, however, recommend trying to throw it in the air.

1 pound (455 g) ground chuck

1 pound (455 g) Italian sausage, hot or sweet, as you prefer

⅓ cup (40 g) pork rind crumbs

1 tablespoon (6 g) Italian seasoning

1 cup (245 g) no-sugar-added pizza sauce, divided

1 medium onion, chopped fairly fine

1 medium green pepper, chopped fairly fine

½ teaspoon salt

¼ teaspoon pepper

4 cloves garlic

1 egg

½ cup (60 g) shredded mozzarella cheese

This is your basic meat loaf procedure: Dump the two meats, the pork rind crumbs, the Italian seasoning, ½ cup (123 g) of the pizza sauce, the onion, green pepper, salt, pepper, garlic, and egg in a big mixing bowl and use clean hands to squish it together really well.

Take two pieces of heavy-duty foil, long enough to reach down into your slow cooker, across the bottom, and back up the other side and fold each into a strip about 2 inches (5 cm) wide. Put your basket steamer in the slow cooker and criss-cross the foil strips across it, going around the stem in the middle.

Dump the meat in the slow cooker and form it into a nice, even loaf on the steamer. Cover the slow cooker, set to low, and let the whole thing cook for 6 to 7 hours.

Open the slow cooker, sprinkle the mozzarella over the top, and re-cover the pot for just ten minutes to let the cheese melt. In the meantime, warm the rest of the pizza sauce. Use the foil sling to lift the meat loaf out of the slow cooker to a platter. Serve each slice of meat loaf with a tablespoon (15 g) of pizza sauce on it.

Yield: 8 servings, each with: 419 calories, 33 g fat, 23 g protein, 5 g carbohydrate, 1 g dietary fiber, 4 g usable carbs.

Pizza Stew

Here's a slow cooker meal for your pizza-craving family. Maria gets the credit for perfecting this one. It wasn't quite right the way I originally conceived it. Maria gave me feedback, we went with her suggestions, and success was ours!

> 1 pound (455 g) bulk Italian sausage
>
> 1 pound (455 g) ground round
>
> 1 green bell pepper, diced
>
> 1/4 cup (40 g) diced onion
>
> 14 ounces (390 g) no-sugar-added pizza sauce (Ragu makes one.)
>
> 2 cups (230 g) shredded mozzarella cheese
>
> 1/2 cup (40 g) shredded Parmesan cheese

In a big, heavy skillet, brown and crumble the sausage and beef together. Drain them well and transfer them to your slow cooker. Add the pepper and onion and stir. Stir in the pizza sauce. Cover the slow cooker, set it to low, and let it cook for 5 to 6 hours.

Now uncover the slow cooker and top the stew with the mozzarella cheese. Re-cover the slow cooker and let it cook for another 30 to 45 minutes to melt the cheese. Serve with the Parmesan cheese sprinkled on top.

Yield: 6 servings, each with: 626 calories, 49 g fat, 37 g protein, 8 g carbohydrate, 2 g dietary fiber, 6 g usable carbs.

Beef and Sausage Stew

This combination of beef and smoked sausage is great.

> 2 pounds (900 g) beef chuck
>
> 1 pound (455 g) smoked sausage
>
> 2 tablespoons (28 g) bacon grease
>
> 4 cups (600 g) cubed turnip
>
> 1¹/₂ medium onions (or maybe 1 big one)
>
> 2 celery ribs
>
> ¹/₂ cup (120 ml) beef broth
>
> 1 teaspoon beef bouillon granules
>
> 2 teaspoons thyme
>
> 1 can (14¹/₂ ounces, or 410 g) diced tomatoes

Cut your beef into cubes and slice your sausage about ¹/₂-inch (13 mm) thick. Put your big heavy skillet over medium-high heat and throw in the bacon grease. Brown the beef cubes—you'll want to do them in a couple of batches to avoid crowding—and transfer them to your slow cooker. Add more bacon grease if you need it and also brown your sausage slices a bit on both sides.

Are you up for some multitasking? While you're browning your meat, peel your turnips and cube them—I used three smallish ones. Peel and dice your onions, too.

But don't let your sausage slices burn! When they're browned, transfer them to the pot, too.

Slice the celery crosswise, thinly. Throw all the veggies in the pot.

Dump the beef broth in the skillet you browned the meat in and add the bouillon concentrate and thyme. Stir it around until the bouillon dissolves, along with all the tasty brown bits on the bottom of the skillet. Pour this over all the stuff in the pot. Add the tomatoes, give everything a stir, and whack on the lid. Set it for low and let it go for 7 to 8 hours.

Yield: 8 servings, each with: 502 calories, 38 g fat, 28 g protein, 11 g carbohydrate, 2 g dietary fiber, 9 g usable carbs.

Albondigas en Salsa Chipotle

Here are some Mexican meatballs! Yummy.

1/2 medium onion, chopped

1 tablespoon (15 ml) oil

1 teaspoon ground cumin

1 teaspoon ground coriander

3 cloves garlic, crushed

1 teaspoon dried oregano

1 teaspoon dried thyme

1 can (14 1/2 ounces, or 410 g) tomatoes with green chiles, drained

1 cup (235 ml) chicken broth

1/2 teaspoon chicken bouillon concentrate

1 chipotle chile canned in adobo sauce, or more to taste

1 pound (455 g) ground round

1 pound (455 g) ground turkey

1 egg

1 teaspoon pepper

1/2 teaspoon ground allspice

1/2 teaspoon ground cumin

1/2 teaspoon ground coriander

1 teaspoon dried oregano

2 teaspoons salt or Vege-Sal

1/2 medium onion, finely chopped

3 cloves garlic, crushed

2 tablespoons (28 ml) olive oil

1 teaspoon guar or xanthan

In a big, heavy skillet, sauté 1/2 onion in the 1 tablespoon (15 ml) oil over medium-high heat until translucent. Add the 1 teaspoon ground cumin, 1 teaspoon ground coriander, 3 cloves garlic, 1 teaspoon oregano, and 1 teaspoon thyme and sauté for another minute or two. Transfer the mixture to your blender or food processor.

Add the tomatoes, broth, bouillon, and chipotle. Blend until smooth and pour into your slow cooker. Cover the slow cooker, set it to low, and start it cooking as you make the meatballs.

Place the beef, turkey, egg, pepper, allspice, 1/2 teaspoon ground cumin, 1/2 teaspoon ground coriander, 1 teaspoon oregano, salt or Vege-Sal, 1/2 onion, and 3 cloves garlic into a big bowl and use clean hands to smoosh it all together. Form it into meatballs.

In the skillet, heat 2 tablespoons (28 ml) oil over medium-high heat and brown the meatballs on all sides. Transfer the meatballs to the slow cooker, re-cover, and let the whole thing cook for 3 to 4 hours.

Scoop the meatballs out with a slotted spoon and put them in a serving bowl. Thicken the sauce to taste with the guar or xanthan and pour the sauce over the meatballs.

Yield: 8 servings, each with: 297 calories, 20 g fat, 23 g protein, 5 g carbohydrate, 1 g dietary fiber, 4 g usable carbs.

Low-Carb Slow Cooker Paella

Maria, who tested this, rates it a 10. She added, "While this won't fool a purist, the flavor is quite good. For those who can't afford saffron, turmeric is an acceptable substitute. For an authentic presentation, which is important, put the 'rice' in a paella pan or flat casserole, mix it with the veggies, and arrange the chicken and shrimp artistically on top." Do look for Spanish chorizo, rather than Mexican chorizo, for this dish.

6 chicken leg and side quarters (about 3 pounds, or 1.4 kg)

1/4 cup (60 ml) olive oil

1 cup (160 g) chopped onion

1 clove garlic, crushed

1 green bell pepper

6 ounces (170 g) chorizo links or diced ham

1 can (141/2 ounces, or 410 g) tomato wedges, drained

1/2 teaspoon saffron threads

1 cup (235 ml) chicken broth

1 teaspoon chicken bouillon concentrate

6 ounces (170 g) shrimp

1/2 cup (73 g) fresh snow pea pods, cut into 1/2-inch (13 mm) pieces

1 head cauliflower

In a big, heavy skillet, brown the chicken in the oil.

While that's happening, put the onion, garlic, and green pepper in your slow cooker. When the chicken is brown, transfer it to the slow cooker as well.

If using chorizo, slice it into rounds and brown it in the same skillet and then transfer it to the slow cooker. If using ham, you can simply add it directly to the slow cooker. Place the tomatoes on top of that.

In a bowl, mix together the saffron, broth, and bouillon and pour it into the slow cooker. Cover the slow cooker, set it to low, and let it cook for 6 hours.

When the time's up, turn the slow cooker to high. Add the shrimp and snow peas to the slow cooker, re-cover, and cook for another 30 minutes.

While that's happening, shred the cauliflower in your food processor, put it in a microwavable casserole dish with a lid, add a few tablespoons (45 to 60 ml) of water, cover, and microwave it on high for 8 to 9 minutes. Serve with the paella.

Yield: 8 servings, each with: 599 calories, 42 g fat, 46 g protein, 8 g carbohydrate, 1 g dietary fiber, 7 g usable carbs.

Brunswick Stew

This is an old favorite, decarbed and updated for your slow cooker.

> 1 large onion, sliced
>
> 2 pounds (900 g) skinless chicken thighs
>
> 1 1/2 cups (225 g) ham cubes, cooked
>
> 1 teaspoon dry mustard
>
> 1 teaspoon dried thyme
>
> 1/2 teaspoon pepper
>
> 1 cup (180 g) canned diced tomatoes
>
> 1 can (14 ounces, or 390 g) chicken broth
>
> 3 cloves garlic, crushed
>
> 1 tablespoon (15 ml) Worcestershire sauce
>
> 1/4 teaspoon hot sauce, or to taste
>
> 1 cup (172 g) canned black soybeans, drained

Place the onion in your slow cooker first. Add the chicken and ham.

In a bowl, mix together the dry mustard, thyme, pepper, tomatoes, broth, garlic, Worcestershire sauce, and hot sauce. Pour the mixture over the chicken and ham. Cover the slow cooker, set it to low, and let it cook for 8 hours.

When the time's up, stir in the soybeans and let the whole thing cook for another 20 minutes or so.

Yield: 6 servings, each with: 212 calories, 10 g fat, 21 g protein, 9 g carbohydrate, 3 g dietary fiber, 6 g usable carbs.

Slow Cooker Soups

If there's a type of dish for which the slow cooker seems custom-made, it's soups. How wonderful to come home tired on a cold evening to a pot of hot, hearty, homemade soup!

Bone Broth for Busy People

This is more a rule than a recipe. Save all of your chicken bones in a sack in the freezer. Save your steak and other beef bones in a separate sack. Don't worry that these bones are picked clean; totally naked bones will make amazingly good broth.

When you have enough bones to fill your slow cooker, whatever its size, you're ready to make broth. Dump your bones into the slow cooker—you don't have to bother to thaw them, just dump them in. Cover them with water and add maybe a teaspoon of salt for a smallish slow cooker or two for a big one, plus a couple of tablespoons (28 ml) of vinegar, any kind. Cover the slow cooker, set it to low, and forget about it. I mean, for a long time. I let mine go for a good 36 hours.

Turn your slow cooker off, let the broth cool, then strain, throw away the bones, and either make soup with your broth or freeze it in snap-top containers for all future brothy needs. If you're going to freeze it, do yourself a favor and pay attention to how much your containers hold. Then, when you're looking at a recipe that calls for, say, 6 cups (1.4 L) of broth, you'll know how much you've got.

No hard and fast nutritional stats on this one, but unless you add onion or celery or something, it should be pretty much carb-free.

Black Bean Soup

One of the few carb-y dishes I sometimes miss is legume soup, especially black bean soup. This is my decarbed version.

1 can (28 ounces, or 785 g) black soybeans

1 can (14 ounces, or 390 g) black beans

2 cups (475 ml) chicken broth

1 medium onion, cut into chunks

4 cloves garlic, crushed

1 medium carrot, shredded

2 medium stalks celery, finely diced

1 teaspoon salt or Vege-Sal

1/2 teaspoon pepper

1 tablespoon (15 ml) liquid smoke flavoring

2 teaspoons hot sauce

2 cups (300 g) ham cubes

Using your food processor with the S-blade in place, puree the soybeans and black beans. Place them in your slow cooker. Stir in the broth.

Place the onion in the food processor. Add the garlic, carrot, and celery. Pulse the food processor until everything is finely chopped. Add to the soup.

Stir in the salt or Vege-Sal, pepper, liquid smoke flavoring, hot sauce, and ham. Cover the slow cooker, set it to low, and let it cook for 9 to 10 hours.

When the time's up, stir the soup up (it'll have settled out some) and check to see if it needs more salt and pepper. (This will depend on how salty your ham is.)

Yield: 8 servings, each with: 218 calories, 9 g fat, 19 g protein, 17 g carbohydrate, 9 g dietary fiber, 8 g usable carbs.

Mexican Beef and Bean Soup

You know the family will love this!

        12 ounces (340 g) ground round

        1 medium onion, chopped

        2 cloves garlic, crushed

        1 medium green bell pepper, diced

        1 quart (950 ml) beef broth

        1 teaspoon beef bouillon concentrate

        1 can (14½ ounces, or 410 g) tomatoes with green chiles

        1 can (15 ounces, or 425 g) black soybeans

        2 teaspoons ground coriander

        1 teaspoon ground cumin

        4 tablespoons (4 g) chopped cilantro

        6 tablespoons (90 g) sour cream

In a big, heavy skillet, brown and crumble the ground beef. Drain it well and transfer it to your slow cooker.

Add the onion, garlic, bell pepper, broth, bouillon, tomatoes, soybeans, coriander, and cumin and stir. Cover the slow cooker, set it to low, and let it cook for 7 to 8 hours.

Top each bowlful with cilantro and sour cream.

Yield: 6 servings, each with: 296 calories, 16 g fat, 25 g protein, 14 g carbohydrate, 5 g dietary fiber, 9 g usable carbs.

Pho

This Vietnamese-style beef noodle soup is so wonderful! I had never had it before I made some, but it was instantly soothing and comforting, as if I'd been eating it all my life. The gelatin is just to add some body to the beef broth, assuming you're using store-bought. If you've made your own *Bone Broth* (see recipe page 256), it will have plenty of gelatin in it.

6 cups (1.4 L) beef broth

2 teaspoons unflavored gelatin—optional

2 teaspoons beef bouillon concentrate

2 whole star anise

1 cinnamon stick

1 tablespoon (6 g) fresh ginger root, minced

1 teaspoon chili garlic sauce

1/4 cup (60 ml) fish sauce

12 ounces (340 g) beef round

2 packages shirataki noodles

1 cup (104 g) mung bean sprouts

4 scallions, sliced thin, including the crisp part of the green

1/4 cup (10 g) minced fresh basil

1/4 cup (4 g) minced fresh cilantro

If you are using the gelatin, sprinkle it over 1 cup (235 ml) of the beef broth to soften for five minutes.

In the meantime, put the rest of the broth in the slow cooker with the beef bouillon concentrate, anise, cinnamon stick, minced ginger, chili garlic paste, and fish sauce. Turn the slow cooker on to low.

Slice your beef as thinly as possible across the grain—having it half-frozen makes this

easier. Cut those strips into smaller ones, no more than an inch or two in any direction. Add to the broth. Stir in the broth with the gelatin, too, if you're using it. Cover and let it cook for 5 to 6 hours.

It's time for supper! Drain your shirataki and snip across them a few times. Stir them into your pho, along with the mung bean sprouts. Re-cover and let it cook just another 15 minutes or so while you slice the scallions thin and mince the basil and cilantro. Don't let the bean sprouts get too wilted.

Serve with scallion, basil, and cilantro on each bowlful.

Notes: Fish sauce runs about 6 grams of carb per fluid ounce; you can slice 6 grams out of this recipe by using half fish sauce, half soy sauce. Or perhaps you'll find you like it less salty and use less of both.

Yield: 4 servings, each with: 348 calories, 14 g fat, 39 g protein, 21 g carbohydrate, 5 g dietary fiber, 16 g usable carbs.

I prefer traditional shirataki to the tofu shirataki in this dish, spaghetti or angel hair width.

Bollito Misto

All this Italian soup-stew needs with it is a green salad and maybe some crusty bread for the carb-eaters.

> 1 large onion, sliced
>
> 2 carrots, cut 1/2-inch (13 mm) thick
>
> 3 stalks celery, cut 1/2-inch (13 mm) thick
>
> 2 pounds (900 g) beef round, cubed
>
> 1/2 teaspoon salt
>
> 1/2 teaspoon pepper
>
> 2 tablespoons (8 g) chopped fresh parsley
>
> 1 bay leaf
>
> 3 teaspoons (18 g) chicken bouillon concentrate
>
> 1 quart (950 ml) chicken broth
>
> 2 pounds (900 g) boneless, skinless chicken thighs, cubed
>
> 1 pound (455 g) Italian sausage links
>
> 1/2 cup (130 g) purchased pesto sauce

Put the onion, carrots, and celery in your slow cooker. Season the beef with the salt and pepper and place them on top. Add the parsley and bay leaf. Stir the bouillon into the chicken and pour it into the slow cooker. Cover the slow cooker, set it to low, and let it cook for 5 to 6 hours.

Add the chicken, turn the heat up to high, and let the whole thing cook another hour.

While it's cooking, pour yourself a glass of Chianti and put out some vegetables and dip for the kids. In a big, heavy skillet, place the sausages, cover with water, slap a lid on, and simmer for 20 minutes over medium heat. Remove the skillet from the heat and leave the sausages in the water, with the lid on.

When the slow cooker's time is up, drain the sausage and cut it into 1-inch (2.5 cm) chunks. Stir the sausage into the stuff in the slow cooker. Remove the bay leaf. Now ladle the whole thing into soup bowls and top each serving with a tablespoon (15 g) of pesto.

Yield: 8 servings, each with: 599 calories, 43 g fat, 44 g protein, 6 g carbohydrate, 1 g dietary fiber, 5 g usable carbs.

Italian Sausage Soup

This is perfect on a chilly, rainy evening!

> 1 pound (455 g) Italian sausage links
>
> 1 medium onion
>
> 1 green pepper
>
> 1 celery rib
>
> 1¹/₂ teaspoons oregano
>
> 1¹/₂ teaspoons Italian seasoning
>
> 3 cloves garlic
>
> 8 cups (1.9 L) chicken broth
>
> 2 cups (475 ml) heavy cream

Put your big, heavy skillet over medium heat and brown the sausage all over. Let it cool a little so you can handle it.

While it's cooling, chop your onion, pepper, and celery.

Transfer your sausage to your cutting board and throw the veggies in the skillet. Add a splash of olive oil if needed. Sauté the the veggies for a few minutes while you move on to the next step.

Slice your sausage. Dump it in the slow cooker. Throw the sautéed vegetables in, too. Add the oregano and Italian seasoning and crush in the garlic.

Pour a cup or two (235 to 475 ml) of the broth into the skillet and stir it around to deglaze. Add to the slow cooker, along with the rest of the broth. Cover the slow cooker and cook for five or six hours.

At dinnertime, stir in the cream. Let it heat another 10 to 15 minutes and serve.

Yield: 6 servings, each with: 604 calories, 55 g fat, 19 g protein, 8 g carbohydrate, 1 g dietary fiber, 7 g usable carbs.

Sausage and Green Bean Soup

Read the labels on the smoked sausage—they vary a lot in carb content.

1 pound (455 g) smoked sausage

1 tablespoon (15 g) coconut oil

1 small onion, chopped

1 can (14¹/₂ ounces, or 410 g) diced tomatoes

6 cups (1.4 L) chicken broth

1 pound (455 g) frozen cross-cut green beans, thawed

1 tablespoon (6 g) Italian seasoning

1 teaspoon cumin

¹/₂ teaspoon red pepper flakes

4 cloves garlic, crushed

Split the sausage lengthwise and slice into half-rounds about ¹/₄-inch (6 mm) thick. Put your big heavy skillet over medium-low heat and start browning the sausage in the coconut oil. (I gave mine a squirt of nonstick cooking spray first and needed only to rinse and wipe when done.) Unless your skillet is bigger than mine, this will take a couple of batches.

While the sausage is browning, chop the onion. When the sausage is all browned, throw it in the slow cooker and add the onion to the skillet. Sauté until it's translucent. Dump it in the slow cooker, too.

Add everything else, cover the cooker, and set it to low for 6 to 8 hours or on high for 4 to 6 hours.

When it's done, taste to see if it needs a little salt and pepper—mine didn't need a thing!—then serve.

Yield: 5 servings, each with: 441 calories, 32 g fat, 21 g protein, 18 g carbohydrate, 3 g dietary fiber, 15 g usable carbs.

Vegetable Beef Soup

This is serious comfort food!

3 pounds (1.4 kg) beef soup bones—meaty ones!

8 cups (1.9 L) water

5 teaspoons (30 g) beef bouillon concentrate

1 can (14 1/2 ounces, or 410 g) diced tomatoes

1 can (8 ounces, or 225 g) tomato sauce

1/2 cup (120 ml) dry red wine

2 celery ribs, diced

2 medium carrots, peeled and sliced

1 medium onion, chopped

3 cloves garlic, crushed

12 ounces (340 g) frozen cross-cut green beans or Italian beans, thawed

1 cup (130 g) frozen peas, thawed

1 large turnip, peeled and diced

2 tablespoons (2 g) dried basil

1 tablespoon (2 g) dried oregano

2 bay leaves

1 teaspoon pepper

Preheat your oven to 400°F (200°C, or gas mark 6) and let it heat while you throw your soup bones in a roasting pan. Slide them into the oven and give them about 40 minutes; you want them browned all over.

Put your browned bones in the slow cooker and add the water and beef bouillon concentrate. Turn it on to low while you gather/open/peel/cut up/measure everything else and add it all to the pot. Cover and let the whole thing cook for a good eight hours.

Fish out the bones with tongs or slotted spoon. The meat will be falling off the bone, so it should be very easy to take it off, chop it up, and throw it back in the pot. Remove the bay leaves, stir it up, and serve!

Yield: 8 servings, each with: 17 g carbohydrate, 4 g dietary fiber, 13 g usable carbs. It's hard to get a clear calorie and protein count on this because it will depend on how meaty your bones are. If they're not meaty enough for your tastes, feel free to throw in some diced beef—chuck or rump would do fine.

Cauliflower, Cheese, and Spinach Soup

Maria's family gave this raves. It's easy, too!

> 6 cups (600 g) cauliflower florets, cut into 1/2-inch (13 mm) pieces
>
> 1 quart (950 ml) chicken broth
>
> 1/2 cup (80 g) minced red onion
>
> 5 ounces (140 g) bagged baby spinach leaves, pre-washed
>
> 1/4 teaspoon cayenne
>
> 1/2 teaspoon salt or Vege-Sal
>
> 1/4 teaspoon pepper
>
> 4 cloves garlic, crushed
>
> 3 cups (360 g) shredded smoked Gouda cheese
>
> 1 cup (235 ml) Carb Countdown dairy beverage
>
> Guar or xanthan

In your slow cooker, combine the cauliflower, broth, onion, spinach, cayenne, salt or Vege-Sal, pepper, and garlic. Cover the slow cooker, set it to low, and let it cook for 6 hours or until the cauliflower is tender.

When the time's up, stir in the Gouda, a little at a time, and then the Carb Countdown. Re-cover the slow cooker and cook for another 15 minutes or until the cheese has thoroughly melted. Thicken soup a little with guar or xanthan.

Yield: 8 servings, each with: 214 calories, 14 g fat, 17 g protein, 7 g carbohydrate, 2 g dietary fiber, 5 g usable carbs.

Tavern Soup

Here's a cheese soup with beer! Don't worry about the kids, the alcohol cooks off.

1¹/₂ quarts (1.4 L) chicken broth

¹/₄ cup (30 g) finely diced celery

¹/₄ cup (38 g) finely diced green bell pepper

¹/₄ cup (28 g) shredded carrot

¹/₄ cup (15 g) chopped fresh parsley

¹/₂ teaspoon pepper

1 pound (455 g) sharp cheddar cheese, shredded

12 ounces (355 ml) light beer

¹/₂ teaspoon salt or Vege-Sal

¹/₄ teaspoon Tabasco sauce

Guar or xanthan

Combine the broth, celery, green pepper, carrot, parsley, and pepper in your slow cooker. Cover the slow cooker, set it to low, and let it cook for 6 to 8 hours, and even a bit longer won't hurt.

When the time's up, either use a hand-held blender to puree the vegetables right there in the slow cooker or scoop them out with a slotted spoon, purée them in your blender, and return them to the slow cooker.

Now whisk in the cheese a little at a time until it's all melted in. Add the beer, salt or Vege-Sal, and Tabasco sauce and stir till the foaming stops. Use guar or xanthan to thicken your soup until it's about the texture of heavy cream. Re-cover the pot, turn it to high, and let it cook for another 20 minutes before serving.

Yield: 8 servings, each with: 274 calories, 20 g fat, 18 g protein, 3 g carbohydrate, trace dietary fiber, 3 g usable carbs.

Cream of UnPotato Soup

I never cease to marvel at the versatility of cauliflower. This really does taste like potato soup.

1 quart (950 ml) chicken broth

1/2 head cauliflower, chunked

1/2 cup (80 g) chopped onion

1/2 cup (50 g) Ketatoes mix

1/2 cup (120 ml) heavy cream

1/2 cup (120 ml) Carb Countdown dairy beverage

Guar or xanthan (optional)

5 scallions, sliced

Put the broth, cauliflower, and onion in your slow cooker. Cover the slow cooker, set it to low, and let it cook for 4 to 5 hours.

I use a hand blender to purée my soup right in the slow cooker, but you may transfer the cauliflower and onion, along with a cup of broth, into your blender or food processor instead. Either way, purée until completely smooth and then blend in the Ketatoes. If you have removed the cauliflower from the slow cooker to purée, pour the purée back in and whisk it into the remaining broth.

Stir in the cream and Carb Countdown. Thicken it a bit further with guar or xanthan if you feel it needs it. Add salt and pepper to taste and stir in the sliced scallions. Serve hot right away or chill and serve as vichyssoise.

Yield: 6 servings, each with: 190 calories, 11 g fat, 12 g protein, 13 g carbohydrate, 6 g dietary fiber, 7 g usable carbs.

German UnPotato Soup

This is worth the time you spend cutting things up! It's hearty and filling.

   1 head cauliflower, chunked

   2 stalks celery, sliced

   1 medium onion, chopped

   8 ounces (225 g) smoked sausage, sliced

   1 tablespoon (28 ml) oil

   4 cups (950 ml) beef broth

   2 tablespoons (28 ml) vinegar

   1 tablespoon (1.5 g) Splenda

   1/4 teaspoon celery seed

   1/2 teaspoon dry mustard

   1/4 teaspoon pepper

   2 cups (140 g) bagged coleslaw mix

Place the cauliflower, celery, and onion in your slow cooker.

In a big, heavy skillet, brown the sausage a bit in the oil. Transfer the sausage to the slow cooker, too.

Pour 1 cup (235 ml) of the broth into the skillet and stir it around a bit to dissolve the flavorful bits. Pour it into the slow cooker.

In a bowl, combine the rest of the broth with the vinegar, Splenda, celery seed, dry mustard, and pepper. Pour over the vegetables and sausage. Cover the slow cooker, set it to low, and let it cook for 8 hours.

When the time's up, stir in the coleslaw mix and let it cook for another 20 to 30 minutes.

Yield: 4 servings, each with: 344 calories, 22 g fat, 20 g protein, 17 g carbohydrate, 2 g dietary fiber, 15 g usable carbs.

Cream of Mushroom Soup

If you've only ever thought of mushroom soup as gooey stuff that came in cans and was used in casseroles, you need to try this! It has a rich, earthy flavor. Even my mushroom-phobic husband liked it.

8 ounces (225 g) mushrooms, sliced

¼ cup (40 g) chopped onion

2 tablespoons (28 g) butter

1 quart (950 ml) chicken broth

½ cup (120 ml) heavy cream

½ cup (115 g) light sour cream

Guar or xanthan (optional)

In a big, heavy skillet, sauté the mushrooms and onion in the butter until the mushrooms soften and change color. Transfer them to your slow cooker. Add the broth. Cover the slow cooker, set it to low, and let it cook for 5 to 6 hours.

When the time's up, scoop out the vegetables with a slotted spoon and put them in your blender or food processor. Add enough broth to help them process easily and purée them finely. Pour the puréed vegetables back into the slow cooker, scraping out every last bit with a rubber scraper. Now stir in the heavy cream and sour cream and add salt and pepper to taste. Thicken the sauce a bit with guar or xanthan if you think it needs it. Serve immediately.

Yield: 5 servings, each with: 176 calories, 15 g fat, 6 g protein, 5 g carbohydrate, 1 g dietary fiber, 4 usable carbs.

Chipotle Pumpkin Soup

This is so good! If you leave the diced chicken breast out of this, it would make a nice starter for Thanksgiving supper.

    1 leek
    2 tablespoons (28 g) butter
    3 cloves garlic, crushed
    1 can (15 ounces, or 425 g) pumpkin purée
    2 chipotle chiles canned in adobo—minced, plus a couple of teaspoons of
        the sauce
    6 cups (1.4 L) chicken broth
    1 teaspoon cumin
    1 bay leaf
    12 ounces (340 g) boneless, skinless chicken breast
    1 cup (235 ml) heavy cream
    2/3 cup (154 g) sour cream

Trim the top and root off your leek and then split it vertically. Wash well, making sure there's no dirt between the layers. Then slice it thin, across the curve.

In your big, heavy skillet, melt the butter over medium heat and sauté the leek until it's softened a bit. Transfer to the slow cooker.

Add the garlic, pumpkin purée, chopped chipotles, broth, cumin, and bay leaf to the slow cooker and turn it on to low. Cover the pot. Now go wash the hot pepper off your hands! Let it cook for at least 4 hours, and a couple more won't hurt.

Dice the chicken into 1/4-inch (6 mm) cubes—this is easier if the chicken is half-frozen. Stir this into the soup along with the heavy cream. Re-cover and let it cook another 45 minutes to an hour.

You can thicken it just a little with guar or xanthan at this point, if you like, but don't make it any thicker than cream, okay?

Serve with a couple of tablespoons (30 g) of sour cream floating in the middle of each bowlful.

Yield: 6 servings, each with: 369 calories, 27 g fat, 21 g protein, 12 g carbohydrate, 3 g dietary fiber, 9 g usable carbs.

⛫ Not~Pea Soup

I love split pea soup, always have! But despite authorities asserting that legumes are good carbs, they make me gain weight. So I came up with this soup, which is remarkably like split pea, except for the carb count.

1 onion

1 carrot

2 celery ribs

4 cloves garlic

1 teaspoon thyme

2 bay leaves

2 pounds (900 g) ham hocks or shanks

3 pounds (1.4 kg) frozen green beans, thawed

8 cups (1.9 L) water

1 tablespoon ham bouillion concentrate (Better Than Bouillon makes one.)

Guar or xanthan

1/2 teaspoon pepper or to taste

Salt or Vege-Sal, to taste

Hot sauce—optional

Peel your onion and whack it into chunks. Do the same for your carrot. Throw them both in your food processor with the S-blade in place and pulse until they're chopped pretty fine. Dump this in your slow cooker. Put the food processor bowl back on the stand and put the blade back in place. Whack your celery into chunks, including any fresh leaves, and throw it in the food processor; chop that pretty fine, too. (You could do the celery with the onion and carrot, but it's so much softer that it's likely to be pretty pulverized by the time the carrot is chopped.) Dump that in the slow cooker, too. Crush in the garlic and add the thyme and bay leaves.

Throw your hocks or shanks (shanks are meatier) on top of the seasoning vegetables. Dump in all of the green beans. Add the water, cover, and set to low. Let it cook for a good 6 to 8 hours until the green beans are soft and have changed color—they should look like canned green beans, sort of dull green.

Use a slotted spoon to fish out the hocks or shanks and put them on a plate. Let them cool to the point where you can handle them.

In the meantime, use a stick blender to purée the soup until it's smooth. Now blend in the ham bouillon concentrate.

Use your guar or xanthan shaker and the stick blender to thicken up the soup to your taste. Salt and pepper to taste, too. I like a few dashes of Louisiana-style hot sauce—Tabasco, Frank's, or the like—in this, too, but go with your own taste.

Yield: 8 servings, each with: 370 calories, 22 g fat, 29 g protein, 16 g carbohydrate, 6 g dietary fiber, 10 g usable carbs.

Chicken and Vegetable Soup with Thai Spices

This soup is light, fragrant, and wonderful.

> 2 tablespoons (28 ml) oil
>
> 2 carrots, thinly sliced
>
> 4 stalks celery, thinly sliced
>
> 2 cups (140 g) sliced mushrooms
>
> 1/2 medium onion, thinly sliced
>
> 2 cloves garlic, crushed
>
> 1 1/2 pounds (680 g) boneless, skinless chicken breast, cut into 1/2-inch (13 mm) cubes
>
> 2 quarts (1.9 L) chicken broth
>
> 2 cups (248 g) frozen cross-cut green beans
>
> 1 tablespoon (8 g) grated ginger root
>
> 9 teaspoons (45 g) chili paste
>
> 1 tablespoon (15 ml) lemon juice
>
> 1 tablespoon (15 ml) lime juice
>
> 1/8 teaspoon anise seed, ground
>
> 1/4 teaspoon ground cardamom
>
> 1/4 teaspoon ground cinnamon
>
> 1/2 teaspoon ground cumin
>
> 1/4 teaspoon ground coriander
>
> 1 tablespoon (15 ml) fish sauce
>
> Fresh cilantro

Heat the oil in a big, heavy skillet over medium-high heat and sauté the carrots, celery, mushrooms, and onion until the onion is starting to get translucent. Transfer

them to your slow cooker, adding the garlic. Now add the chicken to the skillet and sauté just until it's sealed on the outside. Transfer it to the slow cooker, too.

Pour in the broth and add the green beans, ginger, chili paste, lemon juice, lime juice, anise seed, cardamom, cinnamon, cumin, coriander, and fish sauce. Stir, cover the slow cooker, set it to low, and let it cook for 6 to 8 hours.

Scatter a little cilantro over each bowlful before serving.

Yield: 8 servings, each with: 209 calories, 8 g fat, 25 g protein, 9 g carbohydrate, 2 g dietary fiber, 7 g usable carbs.

Chicken Soup with Wild Rice

Wild rice has more fiber and therefore fewer usable carbs than regular rice, either white or brown. And it adds a certain cachet to your soup!

> 2 quarts (1.9 L) chicken broth
> 2 carrots, thinly sliced
> 2 stalks celery, diced
> 1/2 cup (80 g) chopped onion
> 1 pound (455 g) boneless, skinless chicken breast, cut into 1/2-inch (13 mm) cubes
> 1/4 cup (40 g) wild rice
> 1 teaspoon poultry seasoning

Simply combine everything in your slow cooker, cover, set it to low, and let it cook for 6 to 7 hours.

Yield: 6 servings, each with: 182 calories, 4 g fat, 25 g protein, 10 g carbohydrate, 2 g dietary fiber, 8 g usable carbs.

Chicken Minestrone

Here's a decarbed version of the Italian favorite. You'll never miss the pasta!

> 3 slices bacon, chopped
>
> 1 medium onion, chopped
>
> 2 medium turnips, cut into 1/2-inch (13 mm) cubes
>
> 1 medium carrot, thinly sliced
>
> 2 small zucchini, quartered and sliced
>
> 2 stalks celery, thinly sliced
>
> 3 tablespoons (45 ml) olive oil
>
> 1 1/2 quarts (1.4 L) chicken broth
>
> 1 1/2 pounds (680 g) skinless chicken thighs, boned and cubed
>
> 1 tablespoon (6 g) Italian seasoning
>
> 1 can (14 1/2 ounces, or 410 g) diced tomatoes, undrained
>
> 1 can (15 ounces, or 425 g) black soybeans

Spray a big, heavy skillet with nonstick cooking spray and then start the bacon frying over medium heat. As some grease cooks out of the bacon, add as many of the vegetables as will fit and sauté them until they soften just a bit. Transfer the vegetables to your slow cooker and continue sautéing the rest of the vegetables, adding oil as needed, until all the vegetables are softened a bit and in the slow cooker.

Place the broth, chicken, Italian seasoning, tomatoes, soybeans, and salt and pepper to taste in the slow cooker. Cover the slow cooker, set it to low, and let it cook for 7 to 8 hours.

Yield: 6 servings, each with: 294 calories, 16 g fat, 21 g protein, 18 g carbohydrate, 6 g dietary fiber, 12 g usable carbs.

So Totally Inauthentic Malaysian-oid Pumpkin-Chicken-Tomato Soup

This started with a recipe for a Malaysian noodle dish called laksa. That wasn't happening, but the flavors looked really good, so I turned it into a soup, substituting for a few hard-to-get ingredients. The result is stellar!

1¹/2 pounds (680 g) boneless, skinless chicken thighs (or breasts, but I like the thighs here)

1 quart (950 ml) chicken broth

1 can (15 ounces, or 425 g) pumpkin purée

8 cloves garlic

3 tablespoons (24 g) grated ginger root

1 can (14¹/2 ounces, or 410 g) tomatoes with green chiles

1 can (13¹/2 ounces, or 380 ml) coconut milk

¹/4 cup (60 ml) fish sauce

2 tablespoons (28 ml) lemon juice

This is so simple! Cube the chicken and throw it in the slow cooker. Add everything else, whisk it all up, cover the slow cooker, and set it to low. Let it cook for 4 to 5 hours.

Yield: 5 servings, each with: 244 calories, 9 g fat, 27 g protein, 16 g carbohydrate, 3 g dietary fiber, 13 g usable carbs.

Spicy Chicken and Mushroom Soup

This is exotic and delicious.

> 3 tablespoons (45 g) butter
>
> 1 leek, thinly sliced (white part only)
>
> 8 ounces (225 g) sliced mushrooms
>
> 1 clove garlic, crushed
>
> 2 teaspoons *Garam Masala* (see recipe page 340) or purchased garam masala
>
> 1 teaspoon pepper
>
> 1/4 teaspoon cayenne
>
> 1/4 teaspoon ground nutmeg
>
> 1 quart (950 ml) chicken broth
>
> 12 ounces (340 g) boneless, skinless chicken breasts, cut into thin strips
>
> 1/2 cup (120 ml) Carb Countdown dairy beverage
>
> 1/2 cup (120 ml) heavy cream
>
> 3 tablespoons (3 g) chopped fresh cilantro (optional)

Melt the butter in a big, heavy skillet, over medium heat, and sauté the leek with the mushrooms until they both soften. Stir in the garlic, *Garam Masala*, pepper, cayenne, and nutmeg and sauté for another minute or two. Transfer to your slow cooker. Pour in the broth and add the chicken. Cover the slow cooker, set it to low, and let it cook for 6 to 7 hours.

When the time's up, use a slotted spoon to scoop roughly two-thirds of the solids into your blender or food processor. Add a cup (235 ml) or so of the broth and purée until smooth. Stir the purée back into the rest of the soup. (You may want to rinse the blender or food processor out with a little broth to get all of the purée.) Stir in the Carb Countdown and cream. Re-cover the pot and let it cook for another 30 minutes. Serve with cilantro on top. Or not, if you prefer—it's nice without it, too!

Yield: 6 servings, each with: 243 calories, 16 g fat, 18 g protein, 6 g carbohydrate, 1 g dietary fiber, 5 g usable carbs.

Chicken and Fennel Soup

If you haven't tried fennel, you really should. It has an enchanting mild licorice flavor, and it is a favorite in Italian cuisine, especially. It looks sort of like celery with feathery leaves and a swollen bulb at the bottom. Be aware that some stores mislabel it as anise.

2 quarts (1.9 L) chicken broth

2 teaspoons chicken bouillon concentrate

2 fennel bulbs

1 onion

4 tablespoons (55 g) butter

6 cloves garlic

2 pounds (900 g) boneless, skinless chicken breast

1 can (14½ ounces, or 410 g) diced tomatoes, preferably petite diced

½ teaspoon pepper

1 star anise

Dump the chicken broth in the slow cooker and turn it on to high; you may as well start it heating while you assemble everything else. Add the chicken bouillon concentrate, too, to start it dissolving.

Put your big, heavy skillet over medium heat and start melting the butter. Whack the stems off the fennel (save some tops for garnish) and trim the bottoms. Then cut them into chunks and throw them in your food processor with the S-blade in place. Peel your onion and chunk it and throw it in there, too. Pulse until everything's chopped medium-fine. Then dump it in the skillet. Sauté, stirring often, until everything's softened a bit.

While your veggies are sautéing, crush your garlic—you can add it to the fennel and onion or just throw it in the broth. You also want to cut your chicken into bite-sized pieces.

Okay, your veggies are softened. Scrape them into the slow cooker and stir in the chicken, too. Open the tomatoes and stir them in—don't drain them first—and add the juice, too.

Stir in the pepper, toss in the star anise, and re-cover the pot. Turn it back to low, let it all cook for 5 to 6 hours, and then serve with a garnish of fennel fronds.

Yield: 6 servings, each with: 352 calories, 14 g fat, 43 g protein, 13 g carbohydrate, 4 g dietary fiber, 9 g usable carbs.

Turkey Sausage Soup

This is a great, filling family soup for a cold night.

1¹/2 pounds (680 g) bulk turkey sausage

1 can (14¹/2 ounces, or 410 g) diced tomatoes

1 can (8 ounces, or 225 g) sliced mushrooms

1 turnip, diced

1 cup (100 g) cauliflower, diced

¹/2 cup (80 g) chopped onion

1 cup (150 g) chopped green bell pepper

1 quart (950 ml) chicken broth

2 teaspoons chicken bouillon concentrate

1 teaspoon dried basil

2 teaspoons prepared horseradish

1 cup (235 ml) heavy cream

In a large, heavy skillet, brown and crumble the sausage. Pour off the fat and put the sausage in your slow cooker. Add the tomatoes, mushrooms, turnip, cauliflower, onion, and green pepper.

In a bowl, stir the broth and bouillon together. Stir in the basil and horseradish. Pour the mixture into the slow cooker. Cover the slow cooker, set it to low, and let it cook for 7 to 8 hours.

When the time's up, stir in the cream and let it cook for another 10 to 15 minutes.

Yield: 6 servings, each with: 666 calories, 61 g fat, 17 g protein, 12 g carbohydrate, 2 g dietary fiber, 10 g usable carbs.

⊙ Macadangdang

Long-time readers know that I'm a big fan of Peg Bracken and her cookbooks. This is my decarbed version of Macadangdang Spinach Medley, which appeared in Peg's *I Hate To Cook Almanac*. It's named for her Aunt Henry Macadangdang, who married a Filipino gentleman of that name. I found the name so charming and euphonious, I thought I'd just call this version Macadangdang. My husband rates this a perfect 10, and I like it, too!

1/2 head cauliflower

10 ounces (280 g) frozen chopped spinach, thawed and drained

2 tablespoons (28 g) butter

1/2 cup (80 g) chopped onion

1 clove garlic, crushed

4 eggs

1/2 cup (120 ml) Carb Countdown dairy beverage

1 1/2 teaspoons salt or Vege-Sal

1/4 teaspoon pepper

1/2 cup (50 g) grated Parmesan cheese

1 cup (115 g) shredded mozzarella cheese

Run the cauliflower through the shredding blade of your food processor. Place the resulting *Cauli-Rice* in a mixing bowl. Drain the thawed frozen spinach really well (I actually squeeze mine) and add it to the *Cauli-Rice*.

Melt the butter in a medium skillet, over medium-low heat, and sauté the onion until it's just translucent. Add the garlic, sauté for another minute or two, and then dump the whole thing in the bowl with the cauliflower and spinach.

Add the eggs, Carb Countdown, salt or Vege-Sal, pepper, and Parmesan and stir the mixture up quite well. Put it in a 1 1/2 to 2 quart glass (1.4 to 1.9 L) casserole dish that you've sprayed with nonstick cooking spray. Cover the dish with foil and place it in your slow cooker. Pour water around it up to 1 inch of the rim. Cover the slow cooker, set it to low, and let it cook for 2 1/2 hours.

Open the slow cooker and remove the foil. Sprinkle the mozzarella over your *Macadangdang*, put the foil back on, recover the pot, and let it cook for another 20 minutes to melt the cheese. Then turn off the pot, uncover it, take off the foil, and let the whole thing cool just to the point where you can remove it from the water bath without scalding yourself, around 20 more minutes.

Yield: 6 servings, each with: 198 calories, 14 g fat, 13 g protein, 5 g carbohydrate, 2 g dietary fiber, 3 g usable carbs.

Broccoli with Bacon and Pine Nuts

This is quite special. Don't cook your broccoli any longer than 2 hours!

> 1 pound (455 g) frozen broccoli, unthawed
>
> 1 clove garlic, crushed
>
> 3 slices cooked bacon, crumbled
>
> 1 tablespoon (28 g) butter
>
> 1 tablespoon (15 ml) oil
>
> 2 tablespoons (18 g) pine nuts (pignolia), toasted

Place the broccoli in your slow cooker. Stir in the garlic and crumble in the bacon. Cover the slow cooker, set it to low, and let it cook for 2 hours.

Before serving, stir in the butter and oil and top with the pine nuts.

Yield: 3 servings, each with: 184 calories, 15 g fat, 8 g protein, 8 g carbohydrate, 5 g dietary fiber, 3 g usable carbs.

⌂ Braised Leg of Lamb

This is a great company dish, and it feeds a crew.

　　　5 pounds (2.3 kg) leg of lamb

　　　Olive oil—a few tablespoons (45 to 60 ml) or as needed

　　　1 large onion, sliced

　　　1 carrot, shredded

　　　1 bay leaf

　　　1 cup (235 ml) beef broth

　　　1/2 cup (120 ml) dry red wine

　　　6 cloves garlic, crushed

　　　1 teaspoon chicken bouillon concentrate

　　　1/2 teaspoon pepper

　　　11/2 tablespoons (5 g) dried rosemary, or several sprigs fresh

　　　Salt and pepper to taste

In your big heavy skillet, over medium-high heat, start searing the lamb in the olive oil; you want it brown all over.

In the meantime, slice your onion and put half of it in the bottom of the slow cooker. Shred the carrot and put all of it in there. Add the bay leaf, too.

When the lamb is browned on all sides, transfer it to the slow cooker and put it on top of the onion and carrot. Now mix together everything from the broth through the rosemary and stir until the bouillon concentrate is dissolved. Pour this over the roast. Make sure at least half of the crushed garlic winds up in the bottom of the pot, but you do want some on top of the roast, too.

Scatter the remaining onion over the roast. Cover the pot, set to low, and cook for a good 6 to 7 hours.

When it's done, fish out the roast and put it on a platter. Use a slotted spoon to pile the cooked onion from the bottom of the pot on top. Thicken the pot juices with your guar or xanthan shaker, salt and pepper to taste, and serve as gravy.

Yield: 8 servings or more; Assuming 8, each will have: 549 calories, 38 g fat, 42 g protein, 4 g carbohydrate, 1 g dietary fiber, 3 g usable carbs.

Lamb Stew Provençal

I turned this recipe over to my sister to test. She's mad for French food, especially from Provence. She gave this the thumbs-up.

3 pounds (1.4 kg) lamb stew meat—shoulder is good, cubed. (Have the meat guys cut it off the bone.)

3 tablespoons (45 ml) olive oil

1 whole fennel bulb, sliced lengthwise

1 medium onion, sliced lengthwise

4 cloves garlic, crushed

1 bay leaf

1 teaspoon dried rosemary, whole needles

1 can (15 ounces, or 425 g) black soybeans, drained

1 cup (235 ml) beef broth

1 teaspoon chicken bouillon concentrate

1/2 teaspoon dried basil

1/2 teaspoon dried marjoram

1/2 teaspoon dried savory

1/2 teaspoon dried thyme

Guar or xanthan

Season the lamb with salt and pepper. In a big, heavy skillet, heat the oil and brown the lamb on all sides over medium-high heat.

Place the fennel, onion, and garlic in the bottom of your slow cooker. Add the bay leaf and rosemary. Dump the soybeans on top of that. When the lamb is browned, put it on top of the vegetables.

In a bowl, stir together the broth, bouillon, basil, marjoram, savory, and thyme. Pour the mixture over the lamb. Cover the slow cooker, set it to low, and let it cook for 8 to 9 hours.

When it's done, thicken the liquid to the texture of heavy cream with guar or xanthan.

Yield: 8 servings, each with: 348 calories, 17 g fat, 41 g protein, 8 g carbohydrate, 4 g dietary fiber, 4 g usable carbs.

Lamb Shanks Osso Bucco Style

Osso Bucco is traditionally made with veal shank, but I like lamb better. These are wonderful.

2 slices bacon

2 tablespoons (28 g) bacon grease

4½ pounds (2 kg) lamb shanks

1 medium onion

1 medium carrot

½ cup (120 ml) dry white wine

1 can (14½ ounces, or 410 g) diced tomatoes

1 teaspoon dried rosemary

1 teaspoon dried oregano

1 teaspoon chicken bouillon concentrate

1 teaspoon beef bouillon concentrate

5 garlic cloves, crushed

½ teaspoon pepper

1 bay leaf, whole

In your big heavy skillet, cook your bacon crisp. (Alternately, you can microwave your bacon and use bacon grease you've previously saved to brown the meat.) Remove the bacon from the pan and reserve. Add extra bacon grease to equal about 2 tablespoons (28 ml). Start browning the lamb shanks in it; you want them browned all over.

In the meantime, slice the onion and the carrot and put in your slow cooker. When your shanks are browned, use tongs to transfer them to the slow cooker.

Add the wine, tomatoes, rosemary, oregano, chicken bouillon concentrate, beef bouillon concentrate, garlic, and pepper to the skillet and stir it over the heat, deglazing the pan, until the bouillon concentrates are dissolved. Pour over the shanks. Add the bay leaf.

Cover the pot, set to low, and let it cook for a good 7 to 8 hours. Remove the bay leaf. Thicken the sauce a little with your guar or xanthan shaker and serve.

Yield: 6 servings, each with: 650 calories, 42 g fat, 52 g protein, 9 g carbohydrate, 1 g dietary fiber, 8 g usable carbs.

Seriously Simple Lamb Shanks

Simple is good!

> 3 pounds (1.4 kg) lamb shank
>
> 2 tablespoons (28 ml) olive oil
>
> 1 cup (235 ml) chicken broth
>
> 1 teaspoon beef bouillon concentrate
>
> 2 teaspoons paprika
>
> 5 cloves garlic, crushed
>
> Guar or xanthan

Season the lamb all over with salt and pepper. In a big, heavy skillet, over medium-high heat, sear the lamb in the oil until it's brown all over. Transfer the lamb to your slow cooker.

In a bowl, mix together the broth and bouillon. Pour the mixture over the lamb. Sprinkle the paprika and garlic over the lamb. Cover the slow cooker, set it to low, and let it cook for 6 to 7 hours.

Remove the lamb with tongs and put it on a serving plate. Pour the liquid in the slow cooker into a 2-cup (475 ml) glass measuring cup and let the fat rise to the top. Skim the fat off and discard and then thicken up the remaining liquid using guar or xanthan. Serve the sauce with the shanks.

Either *Cauli-Rice* (see recipe page 343) or *Fauxtatoes* (see recipe page 343) would be nice with this, but it's fine with just a simple salad or vegetable side.

Yield: 4 servings, each with: 627 calories, 44 g fat, 52 g protein, 2 g carbohydrate, trace dietary fiber, 2 g usable carbs.

Green Bean Casserole

28 ounces (785 g) frozen green beans, unthawed

1 cup (70 g) chopped mushrooms

1/4 cup (45 g) roasted red pepper, diced

1/4 cup (40 g) chopped onion

2 teaspoons dried sage

1 teaspoon salt or Vege-Sal

1 teaspoon pepper

1/2 teaspoon ground nutmeg

1 cup (235 ml) beef broth

1 teaspoon beef bouillon concentrate

1/2 cup (120 ml) heavy cream

Guar or xanthan

3/4 cup (83 g) slivered almonds

1 tablespoon (14 g) butter

Combine the green beans, mushrooms, red pepper, and onion in your slow cooker.

In a bowl, mix together the sage, salt or Vege-Sal, pepper, nutmeg, broth, and bouillon. Pour the mixture over the vegetables. Stir the whole thing up. Cover the slow cooker, set it to low, and let it cook for 5 to 6 hours.

When the time's up, stir in the cream and thicken the sauce a bit with guar or xanthan. Re-cover the slow cooker and let it stay hot while you sauté the almonds in the butter until golden. Stir them into the beans.

Yield: 8 servings, each with: 191 calories, 14 g fat, 7 g protein, 12 g carbohydrate, 4 g dietary fiber, 8 g usable carbs.

Creamy, Cheesy Mustard Green Beans and Mushrooms

Try this with a roasted ham!

    4 ounces (115 g) mushrooms, chopped

    1/4 medium onion, chopped

    1 pound (455 g) frozen green beans, thawed

    1/4 cup (45 g) jarred roasted red pepper, diced

    1 cup (115 g) shredded Cheddar cheese

    1 cup (235 ml) heavy cream

    1 teaspoon beef bouillon granules

    1/8 teaspoon pepper

    1 1/2 teaspoons spicy brown mustard

Coat your slow cooker with nonstick cooking spray, dump in the mushrooms, onion, green beans, roasted red peppers, and cheese, and stir it up.

Combine the cream, beef bouillon concentrate, pepper, and mustard and stir until the bouillion is dissolved. Pour over the veggies.

Cover the slow cooker, set to low, and let it cook for 4 hours. Stir before serving.

Yield: 6 servings, each with: 247 calories, 21 g fat, 7 g protein, 9 g carbohydrate, 3 g dietary fiber, 6 g usable carbs.

Maria's New England Clam Chowder

This one is from my tester and dear friend Maria. She says, "This was so good that I called my brother Peter over and made him try it. He was very impressed. He's a big clam chowder fan, and he said that our grandmother would approve."

4 slices bacon, diced

1 medium onion, chopped

1 large turnip, cut in 1/2-inch (13 mm) cubes

1 can (16 ounces, or 455 g) clams, undrained

3 cloves garlic, crushed

1 teaspoon salt

1/2 teaspoon pepper

2 cups (475 ml) heavy cream

2 tablespoons (28 g) butter

In a big, heavy skillet, sauté the bacon, onion, and turnip until the onion is golden. Drain and put it on the bottom of your slow cooker.

Pour the clam liquid into a 2-cup (475 ml) measuring cup and add enough water to make 2 cups (475 ml). In a bowl, combine the liquid and water mixture, the clams, garlic, salt, and pepper. Pour the mixture into the slow cooker. Cover the slow cooker, set it to low, and let it cook for 5 hours or until the turnips are tender. Blend in the cream and butter during the last 45 minutes of cooking.

Yield: 5 servings, each with: 550 calories, 44 g fat, 27 g protein, 11 g carbohydrate, 1 g dietary fiber, 10 g usable carbs.

Seafood Chowder

My sister Kim, who tested this for me, said that you don't have to stick to shrimp. You could use crab, chunks of lobster tail, or even a cut-up firm-fleshed fish fillet. Don't use fake seafood—Delicaseas and such. It has a lot of added carbs.

1½ cups (150 g) shredded cauliflower

⅓ cup (37 g) shredded carrots

1 teaspoon dried thyme

1 clove garlic

1 tablespoon (9 g) finely minced green bell pepper

⅛ teaspoon cayenne

¼ teaspoon pepper

3 cups (700 ml) chicken broth

1 cup (235 ml) Carb Countdown dairy beverage

¼ cup (60 ml) heavy cream

8 ounces (225 g) shrimp, shells removed

1 tablespoon (5 g) Ketatoes mix

¼ cup (25 g) scallions, thinly sliced

Guar or xanthan

Combine the cauliflower, carrots, thyme, garlic, green pepper, cayenne, pepper, and broth in your slow cooker. Cover the slow cooker, set it to low, and let it cook for 4 hours.

Turn the slow cooker to high and stir in the Carb Countdown and cream. Re-cover the slow cooker and let it cook for another 30 to 45 minutes. If your shrimp are big, chop them coarsely during this time, but little, whole shrimp will look prettier, of course!

Stir in the Ketotoes mix. Now stir in the shrimp and re-cover the pot. If your shrimp are pre-cooked, just give them 5 minutes or so to heat through. If they're raw, give them 10 minutes. Stir in the scallions and salt to taste. Thicken the broth with the guar or xanthan.

Yield: 5 servings, each with: 164 calories, 8 g fat, 17 g protein, 7 g carbohydrate, 2 g dietary fiber, 5 g usable carbs.

Tangy Beans

4 cups (496 g) frozen green beans, unthawed

¼ cup (40 g) chopped onion

¼ cup (38 g) chopped green bell pepper

¼ cup (60 ml) cider vinegar

2 tablespoons (3 g) Splenda

⅛ teaspoon black pepper

Combine everything in your slow cooker. Stir to distribute evenly. Cover the slow cooker, set it to low, and let it cook for 5 hours.

Serve with a pat of butter and a little salt.

Yield: 4 servings, each with: 50 calories, trace fat, 2 g protein, 12 g carbohydrate, 4 g dietary fiber, 8 g usable carbs.

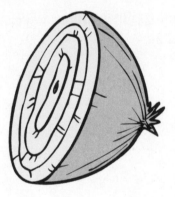

Festive Green Beans

The jarred roasted red pepper and Alfredo sauce make this a whole lot easier than it tastes. Read the labels on the Alfredo sauce to find the lowest carb brand.

> 1 pound (455 g) frozen green beans, cross-cut
>
> 1/2 medium onion, chopped
>
> 1/3 cup (60 g) jarred roasted red pepper, drained and chopped
>
> 1/2 cup (125 g) jarred Alfredo sauce
>
> 1/4 cup (30 g) coarsely crushed pork rinds

Don't thaw the green beans, unless you want to speed the whole thing up by at least an hour. Throw everything but the pork rinds in your slow cooker and stir to combine. Cover and cook on low for 5 to 6 hours.

Coarsely crush the pork rinds and sprinkle over green beans just before serving.

Yield: 5 servings, each with: 148 calories, 8 g fat, 10 g protein, 9 g carbohydrate, 3 g dietary fiber, 6 g usable carbs.

Spinach Parmesan Casserole

This is a lot like creamed spinach, only less—well, creamy.

>   20 ounces (560 g) frozen chopped spinach, thawed and drained*
>
>   1/3 cup (80 ml) heavy cream
>
>   1/2 cup (40 g) shredded Parmesan cheese
>
>   1 clove garlic, crushed
>
>   2 tablespoons (20 g) minced onion
>
>   1 egg
>
>   1/2 teaspoon salt

Place all ingredients in a mixing bowl. Stir it to blend very well. Spray a 6-cup (1.4 L) glass casserole dish with nonstick cooking spray. Put the spinach mixture in the casserole, smoothing the top.

Place the casserole dish in your slow cooker and carefully pour water around it up to 1 inch of the rim. Cover the slow cooker, set it to low, and let it cook for 4 hours.

Uncover the slow cooker and turn it off at least 30 minutes before serving time so the water cools enough that you can remove the dish without scalding yourself.

*Make sure your spinach is very well drained. It's best to put it in a colander and press it as hard as you can, turning it several times.

Yield: 6 servings, each with: 109 calories, 8 g fat, 7 g protein, 5 g carbohydrate, 3 g dietary fiber, 2 g usable carbs.

Basic Artichokes

2 artichokes

¼ cup (60 ml) lemon juice

Using kitchen shears, snip the pointy tips off the artichoke leaves. Split the artichokes down the middle, top to bottom, and scrape out the chokes.

Fill your slow cooker with water, add the lemon juice, and put in the artichokes. Cover the slow cooker, set it to high, and let it cook for 3 to 4 hours.

Drain the artichokes.

Serve the artichokes with the dipping sauce of your choice, such as lemon butter, mayonnaise, aioli, chipotle mayonnaise, whatever you've got. If you have a big slow cooker, feel free to cook more artichokes!

Yield: 2 servings, each with: 68 calories, trace fat, 4 g protein, 16 g carbohydrate, 7 g dietary fiber, 9 g usable carbs.

Maria's Slow Cooker Asparagus

Here's another recipe contributed by my pal and recipe tester Maria.

1 pound (455 g) asparagus spears

1 teaspoon dried rosemary

1 clove garlic, crushed

1 tablespoon (15 ml) lemon juice

Cut off woody ends of the asparagus. Place trimmed asparagus on the bottom of your slow cooker. (If you're using a round cooker, you may need to cut them to fit.) Sprinkle the asparagus with the rosemary and garlic and pour the lemon juice on top. Cover the slow cooker, set it to low, and let it cook for 2 hours or until the asparagus is tender.

Yield: 4 servings, each with: 17 calories, trace fat, 1 g protein, 4 g carbohydrate, 1 g dietary fiber, 3 g usable carbs.

Cheddar-Barbecue Fauxtatoes

My husband was crazy about these!

> $^1/_2$ head cauliflower, cut into florets
>
> $^1/_2$ cup (120 ml) water
>
> $^1/_2$ cup (58 g) shredded cheddar cheese
>
> 2 teaspoons *Classic Rub* (see recipe page 338) or purchased barbecue rub
>
> 2 tablespoons (10 g) Ketatoes mix

Put the cauliflower in your slow cooker, including the stem. Add the water. Cover the slow cooker, set it to high, and let it cook for 3 hours. (Or cook it on low for 5 to 6 hours.)

When the time's up, use a slotted spoon to scoop the cauliflower out of the slow cooker into your blender or your food processor (have the S-blade in place) and purée it there, or you can drain off the water and use a hand-held blender to purée the cauliflower right in the pot. Either way, drain the cauliflower and purée it!

Stir in everything else until the cheese has melted.

Yield: 3 servings, each with: 120 calories, 7 g fat, 8 g protein, 6 g carbohydrate, 3 g dietary fiber, 3 g usable carbs.

🍲 Fluffy, Savory Pumpkin

What a fantastic side dish this is! Serve this in place of the potatoes, and everyone will rave, even the carbivores.

> 1 large onion, chopped
>
> 4 tablespoons (55 g) butter
>
> 1 can (29 ounces, or 810 g) pumpkin purée
>
> 2 eggs
>
> 3/4 cup (195 g) ricotta cheese
>
> 3/4 cup (175 ml) heavy cream
>
> 1 teaspoon salt or Vege-Sal
>
> 1/2 teaspoon pepper

Slowly sauté your chopped onion in the butter until it's soft and turning golden brown. Transfer to a big mixing bowl.

Add everything else and whisk it up until everything is well-mixed.

Coat your slow cooker with nonstick cooking spray. Spoon the pumpkin mixture into it and level the top. Cover, set the slow cooker to low, and cook for 4 to 5 hours.

Yield: 8 servings, each with: 225 calories, 18 g fat, 6 g protein, 11 g carbohydrate, 3 g dietary fiber, 8 g usable carbs.

Fauxtatoes

Fauxtatoes is the now nearly-universal name for cauliflower puree, used by low-carbers everywhere as a substitute for mashed potatoes. To make plain Fauxtatoes as a side dish to serve with a slow-cooked main dish, see recipe page 343. These are slow cooked *Fauxtatoes* with truly tasty additions.

Place the cauliflower in your slow cooker. Add the broth, Italian seasoning, and garlic. Cover the slow cooker, set it to low, and let it cook for 5 to 6 hours. (Or cook it on high for 3 hours.)

When the time's up, either remove the cauliflower with a slotted spoon and put it in your blender or food processor (with the S-blade in place) and purée it or drain the broth out of the slow cooker and use a hand-held blender to purée your cauliflower in the pot. Add the cream cheese and stir till melted.

The mixture will still be a little watery. Stir with a whisk as you use guar or xanthan to thicken it up a bit.

Yield: 3 servings, each with: 46 calories, 4 g fat, 2 g protein, 2 g carbohydrate, 1 g dietary fiber, 1 g usable carbs.

Ranch and Green Onion Fauxtatoes

This is great with anything with a barbecue flavor.

> 1 head cauliflower, cut into florets
> 1 cup (235 ml) water
> 1 cup (100 g) Ketatoes mix
> 6 teaspoons (18 g) ranch-style dressing mix
> 4 scallions, thinly sliced

Place the cauliflower in your slow cooker with the water. Cover the slow cooker, set it to low, and let it cook for 5 hours. (Or cook it on high for 3 hours.)

When the time's up, the easiest thing to do is use a hand blender to purée the cauliflower right in the slow cooker. Don't bother to drain the water first. Whisk in the Ketatoes, ranch dressing mix, and scallions.

Yield: 6 servings, each with: 170 calories, 3 g fat, 14 g protein, 23 g carbohydrate, 11 g dietary fiber, 12 g usable carbs.

Chipotle Fauxtatoes

This is killer with a grilled steak or barbecued brisket.

> 1/2 head cauliflower
>
> 1 chipotle chili canned in adobo
>
> 2 tablespoons (28 ml) olive oil
>
> 2 tablespoons (28 ml) half and half
>
> 6 garlic cloves
>
> 2 ounces (55 g) cream cheese

Whack your cauliflower into smallish chunks and throw it in the slow cooker.

Chop up your chipotle. Mix it, plus a couple of teaspoons of the adobo sauce from the can, with the olive oil, half and half, and garlic. Pour this over the cauliflower and toss to coat. Plunk the block of cream cheese on top.

Cover the slow cooker and cook for 3 hours on high or 5 to 6 hours on low.

When the time's up, uncover the slow cooker and use your stick blender to purée the cauliflower and mix in the cream cheese; then serve.

Yield: 5 servings, each with: 115 calories, 10 g fat, 3 g protein, 5 g carbohydrate, 2 g dietary fiber, 3 g usable carbs.

Italian Garlic and Herb Fauxtatoes

> 1/2 head cauliflower, cut into florets
>
> 1/2 cup (120 ml) chicken broth
>
> 1 teaspoon Italian seasoning
>
> 1 clove garlic, crushed
>
> 1 ounce (28 g) cream cheese
>
> Guar or xanthan

Garlic-Onion Fauxtatoes

Our tester Maria said her kids were particularly impressed by this!

    1 head cauliflower, cut into florets
    1/2 cup (80 g) chopped onion
    3 cloves garlic, crushed
    2/3 cup (150 ml) water
    2/3 cup (67 g) Ketatoes mix
    3 tablespoons (45 g) butter

Place the cauliflower in your slow cooker. Add the onion, garlic, and water. Cover the slow cooker, set it to high, and let it cook for 2 1/2 to 3 hours. (Or cook it on low for 5 to 6 hours.)

When the time's up, use a hand-held blender to purée the cauliflower, onion, and garlic right there in the slow cooker. Alternatively, scoop it all into a food processor to purée, but you'll want the water in the pot, so if you transfer the vegetables, put the purée back in the pot with the water when you're done. Now stir in the Ketatoes, butter, and salt and pepper to taste.

Yield: 6 servings, each with: 162 calories, 8 g fat, 9 g protein, 15 g carbohydrate, 7 g dietary fiber, 8 g usable carbs.

Easy (But Really Slow) Rutabagas

We adore rutabaga, but it can take a long time to cook soft. What better job for a slow cooker? This is how I cooked my rutabaga for Thanksgiving this year.

    4 tablespoons (55 g) butter
    1 large rutabaga
    Salt and pepper

Throw the butter in the slow cooker and turn it on to low. Cover and let the butter melt.

Peel the rutabaga and cut it into 1/2-inch (13 mm) cubes. This takes a big sharp knife and some tough talk.

Dump the rutabaga cubes in the slow cooker—by now your butter should be melted. Toss the cubes to coat with the butter. Cover the slow cooker and let them cook for a minimum of 12 hours, and 14 isn't too much.

Toss with salt and pepper and serve.

Yield: 6 servings, each with: 76 calories, 8 g fat, trace protein, 2 g carbohydrate, 1 g dietary fiber, 1 g usable carbs.

Bonus Recipe: Make Rutabaga Hash Browns! If you have any rutabaga left over, the next day you chop a little onion and throw it in your big, heavy skillet with the leftover rutabaga cubes and plenty of melted butter. Fry them, chopping up the rutabaga more with your spatula, and keep cooking until they're getting brown and crusty. YUMMY!

Maple-Mustard Turnips

4 medium turnips

2 tablespoons (28 g) bacon grease, melted

2 tablespoons (40 g) sugar-free pancake syrup

1 tablespoon (11 g) brown mustard

1/2 teaspoon salt or Vege-Sal

1/4 teaspoon pepper

2 dashes Tabasco sauce or other Louisiana-style hot sauce

Peel and cube the turnips and throw them in the slow cooker. Drizzle in the bacon grease and toss to coat.

Mix together everything else, drizzle over the turnips, and toss to coat again. Cover the pot, set to low, and cook for 5 hours.

Yield: 6 servings, each with: 67 calories, 5 g fat, 1 g protein, 6 g carbohydrate, 2 g dietary fiber, 4 g usable carbs. (Analysis does not include the polyols in the sugar-free pancake syrup.)

Cheesy Neeps

This would make a great holiday side dish. If you're serving buffet style, just plug in the slow cooker and they'll even stay warm for you. (In case you're wondering, *neeps* is an old Scots term for turnips.)

2 large turnips

6 ounces (170 g) Swiss cheese (Gruyère is even better, if you can find it.)

1/2 medium onion

3 tablespoons (45 g) butter

1 teaspoon salt or Vege-Sal

1/2 teaspoon pepper

Peel the turnips, whack them into hunks, and run them through your food processor's shredding blade. Run the Swiss cheese through, too. Chop your onion pretty fine—I find my shredding disc doesn't work for this, so I just used a knife and a cutting board, but you could swap out the shredding disc for the S-blade and use it to chop your onion fine, if you like.

Coat your slow cooker with nonstick cooking spray. Put the turnips, cheese, and onion in there and sprinkle the salt and pepper over it all. Toss until everything is well-combined.

Smooth the top. Now cut your butter into little bits and dot the top of the turnip mixture evenly with it. Cover the pot, set to low, and let it all cook for 5 hours or so.

Yield: 6 servings, each with: 172 calories, 14 g fat, 9 g protein, 4 g carbohydrate, 1 g dietary fiber, 3 g usable carbs.

Mashed Turnips

2 large turnips, cubed

1/4 cup (40 g) chopped onion

3/4 cup (175 ml) beef broth

Put the turnips and onion in your slow cooker and add the broth. Cover the slow cooker, set it to low, and let it cook for 6 to 7 hours.

I like to mash these right in the pot with my hand-held blender, but if you prefer, you can transfer them to your food processor or regular blender.

If you're going to serve these plain, you might add some butter, salt, and pepper, but if you're serving them with a gravy, they're great as is.

Yield: 4 servings, each with: 31 calories, trace fat, 3 g protein, 5 g carbohydrate, 1 g dietary fiber, 4 g usable carbs.

The Simplest Slow Cooker Mushrooms

You want simple? We got simple.

> 1 pound (455 g) sliced mushrooms (You'll buy them that way, right?)
> 8 ounces (225 g) cream cheese with chives and onions
> 2 cloves garlic crushed

Dump everything in the slow cooker. Cover the pot. Set to low. Cook for 5 to 6 hours. Stir. Serve.

Yield: 8 servings, each with: 110 calories, 9 g fat, 3 g protein, 5 g carbohydrate, 1 g dietary fiber, 4 g usable carbs.

Lemon-Parmesan Mushrooms

> 8 ounces (225 g) mushrooms
> 1/2 cup (125 ml) chicken broth
> 1/4 cup (60 ml) lemon juice
> 1/2 cup (40 g) shredded Parmesan cheese
> 1/4 cup (15 g) chopped fresh parsley

Wipe the mushrooms clean with a damp cloth or paper towel and put them in your slow cooker. Pour the broth and lemon juice over them. Cover the slow cooker, set it to low, and let it cook for 6 to 8 hours.

Remove the mushrooms from the slow cooker with a slotted spoon and put them on serving plates. Sprinkle with the Parmesan and parsley.

Yield: 4 servings, each with: 65 calories, 3 g fat, 6 g protein, 5 g carbohydrate, 1 g dietary fiber, 4 g usable carbs.

Blue Cheese Mushrooms

These are perfect next to a steak or slab of prime rib.

> 8 ounces (225 g) fresh mushrooms
>
> 1/4 cup (30 g) crumbled blue cheese
>
> 2 ounces (55 g) cream cheese
>
> 1 clove garlic

Wipe or rinse your mushrooms and throw them in a slow cooker. Sprinkle the blue cheese over them and add the cream cheese cut into little hunks, so you can distribute it a bit. Crush the garlic and throw it in, too. Give it all a quick stir. Then cover, set to high, and cook for 2 hours or set to low and cook for 4 hours.

Yield: 3 servings, each with: 126 calories, 10 g fat, 5 g protein, 4 g carbohydrate, 1 g dietary fiber, 3 g usable carbs.

Spinach-Mushroom Gratin

Mushrooms, spinach, and cheese—what's not to like? This is great with take-out grilled or rotisserie chicken.

> 1/2 head cauliflower
>
> 1 onion, chopped
>
> 4 tablespoons (55 g) butter
>
> 8 ounces (225 g) sliced mushrooms
>
> 3 cloves garlic, crushed
>
> 10 ounces (280 g) frozen chopped spinach, thawed
>
> 1 teaspoon thyme
>
> 1 teaspoon oregano
>
> 2 teaspoons salt or Vege-Sal
>
> 1 teaspoon pepper
>
> 1/2 teaspoon red pepper flakes
>
> 1 1/2 cups (173 g) shredded Cheddar cheese

Chop the onion. Melt the butter in your big heavy skillet and start sautéing the onions with the mushrooms; use the edge of your spatula to break the sliced mushrooms up into smaller pieces as they cook—you want them in chunks a little bigger than a pea.

Run your cauliflower through the shredding blade of your food processor.

Drain the spinach very well—I dump mine a colander in the sink and use my hands to squeeze it dry.

When the onion is translucent and the mushrooms have changed color, stir in the crushed garlic and then put all the vegetables in your slow cooker.

Add the thyme, oregano, salt, pepper, red pepper, and cheese. Stir it all up until it's well-combined. Cover, set to low, and let it cook for 4 hours.

Yield: 8 servings, each with: 169 calories, 13 g fat, 8 g protein, 7 g carbohydrate, 3 g dietary fiber, 4 g usable carbs.

Mushrooms Stroganoff

Even That Nice Boy I Married, not a mushroom fan, loved this. He actually asked for the leftovers to take for lunch! This is great over steak or chicken, but try it in omelets, too.

> 1 1/2 pounds (680 g) sliced mushrooms, button, crimini, and portobello
> 1 cup (235 ml) heavy cream
> 1/4 cup (60 ml) Worcestershire sauce
> 1/2 teaspoon salt or Vege-Sal
> 1/2 teaspoon pepper

I used 1/2 pound (225 g) of each kind of mushroom, but just one or two kinds is fine. Buy them sliced—so much easier! Dump all your mushrooms in the slow cooker, and if you're using different kinds, stir them together.

Stir everything else together, pour over the mushrooms, cover the pot, and set to low. Cook for 5 to 6 hours.

Yield: 12 servings, each with: 87 calories, 8 g fat, 2 g protein, 4 g carbohydrate, 1 g dietary fiber, 3 g usable carbs.

Curried Mushrooms Malabar

This recipe is for fans of the exotic.

> 1½ pounds (680 g) sliced mushrooms—portobello, crimini, button, or a combination
>
> 1 can (13½ ounces, or 380 ml) coconut milk
>
> 3 cloves garlic, crushed
>
> 1 tablespoon (8 g) grated ginger root
>
> 1 tablespoon (11 g) mustard seed
>
> 2 teaspoons ground coriander
>
> 2 teaspoons ground cumin
>
> 1 teaspoon ground turmeric
>
> 1 teaspoon salt or Vege-Sal

Dump the mushrooms in the slow cooker. Measure everything else and stir it together well. Pour it evenly over the mushrooms, cover the pot, and set to low. Cook for 4 hours and then serve.

Yield: 12 servings, each with: 92 calories, 8 g fat, 2 g protein, 5 g carbohydrate, 1 g dietary fiber, 4 g usable carbs.

Baked Beans

This has a classic baked bean flavor and will be appreciated at any barbecue. I wouldn't attempt this recipe without a slow cooker. Do you have any idea how long it takes to cook soybeans soft? But with your slow cooker, you can just forget about them for 12 hours. If your health food store can't get you black soybeans (they're lower carb than white soybeans), you can order them from www.locarber.com.

> 2 cups (372 g) dry black soybeans
>
> 2 cups (475 ml) water
>
> 1/2 cup (80 g) chopped onion
>
> 1/2 tablespoon blackstrap molasses
>
> 3 tablespoons (45 g) low-carb ketchup (see recipe page 332)
>
> 1 tablespoon (9 g) dry mustard
>
> 2 tablespoons (3 g) Splenda
>
> 2 cups (475 ml) water
>
> 3/4 pound (340 g) smoked ham hocks

Put the soybeans in a big, nonreactive bowl and cover with the first 2 cups (475 ml) of water. Let them sit until the water is absorbed. Then put your soaked beans in the freezer overnight. (The freezing water will help break cell walls in the soybeans, making them soften faster when you cook them.)

When you want to cook the soybeans, thaw them and pour off any soaking water. Put them in your slow cooker. Add the onion, molasses, ketchup, dry mustard, and Splenda. Pour the additional 2 cups (475 ml) of water over all and stir it up. Now dig a hole in the center with a spoon and plunk the ham hock down in it. Cover the slow cooker, set it to low, and let cook for 12 hours.

Fish out the ham hock with tongs, remove and discard the skin and bone. Chop the meat and stir it back into the beans before serving.

Yield: 10 servings (5 cups total), each with: 286 calories, 15 g fat, 8 g protein, 12 g carbohydrate, 11 g dietary fiber, 1 g usable carbs.

Slow Cooker "Risotto" with Mushrooms and Peas

Okay, it's not really risotto. But it's got a lot of the same flavors, and it cooks while you do something else.

8 ounces (225 g) mushrooms, crimini or portobello, sliced

1 medium onion, chopped

2 tablespoons (28 g) butter

2 tablespoons (28 ml) olive oil

1 tablespoon (2 g) dried oregano

1/2 head cauliflower

1 cup (100 g) grated Parmesan cheese

1 1/2 cups (195 g) frozen peas

1/2 teaspoon pepper

1/3 cup (80 ml) dry white wine

2 teaspoons chicken bouillon granules

1 cup (235 ml) heavy cream

1 tablespoon (15 ml) balsamic vinegar

2 ounces (55 g) cream cheese

Start the mushrooms and chopped onion sautéing in the butter and olive oil. Use the edge of your spatula to break the mushrooms up into smaller pieces as you sauté them. When the onion is translucent and some liquid has cooked out of the mushrooms, stir in the oregano. Remove from heat.

Run the cauliflower through the shredding blade of your food processor.

Coat your slow cooker with nonstick cooking spray. Dump in the cauliflower, mushrooms and onion, peas, Parmesan, and pepper. Stir to combine.

In a 2-cup (475 ml) glass measuring cup, measure the wine. Add the cream, bouillon concentrate, and balsamic vinegar and whisk until the bouillon concentrate is dissolved. Pour this mixture into the cauliflower mixture and stir the whole thing up. Now pack it down and smooth the top. Put the cream cheese on top.

Cover the slow cooker, set to low, and let cook for 4 hours. When it's done, stir in the cream cheese until everything's evenly coated and serve.

Yield: 6 servings, each with: 362 calories, 31 g fat, 10 g protein, 11 g carbohydrate, 3 g dietary fiber, 8 g usable carbs.

Bavarian Cabbage

This is great with the *Sauerbrauten* on page 126!

> 1 head red cabbage
>
> 1 medium onion, chopped
>
> 1 medium Granny Smith apple, chopped
>
> 6 slices cooked bacon, crumbled
>
> 2 teaspoons salt
>
> 1 cup (235 ml) water
>
> 3 tablespoons (4.5 g) Splenda
>
> 2/3 cup (160 ml) cider vinegar
>
> 3 tablespoons (45 ml) gin

Whack your head of cabbage in quarters and remove the core. Then whack it into biggish chunks. Put it in a big mixing bowl. Add the onion, apple, and bacon to the cabbage. Toss everything together. Transfer the mixture to your slow cooker. (This will fill a 3-quart [2.8 L] jobbie just about to overflowing! I barely got the top on mine.)

In a bowl, mix together the salt, water, Splenda, vinegar, and gin. Pour the mixture over the cabbage. Cover the slow cooker, set it to low, and let it cook for 6 to 8 hours.

Yield: 6 servings, each with: 80 calories, 3 g fat, 2 g protein, 7 g carbohydrate, 1 g dietary fiber, 6 g usable carbs.

Apricot Custard

Don't go increasing the quantity of apricot preserves here. They're the biggest source of carbs. This dessert is yummy, though!

> 1/3 cup (107 g) low-sugar apricot preserves
>
> 2 tablespoons (28 ml) lemon juice
>
> 2 teaspoons Splenda
>
> 1 1/2 cups (355 ml) Carb Countdown dairy beverage
>
> 1/2 cup (120 ml) heavy cream
>
> 4 eggs
>
> 2/3 cup (16 g) Splenda
>
> 1/2 teaspoon almond extract
>
> 1 pinch salt

Whisk together the preserves, lemon juice, and the 2 teaspoons of Splenda. Spread them over the bottom of a 6-cup (1.4 L) glass casserole dish you've sprayed with nonstick cooking spray. Set aside.

Whisk together the Carb Countdown, cream, eggs, 2/3 cup (16 g) Splenda, almond extract, and salt. Pour into the prepared casserole gently, so as not to mix in the apricot preserves.

Place the casserole dish in your slow cooker. Pour water around the casserole to within 1 inch of the rim. Cover the slow cooker, set it to low, and let it cook for 4 hours.

When the time's up, turn off the slow cooker, uncover it, and let it cool until you can remove the casserole dish without risk of scalding. Chill well before serving.

Yield: 6 servings, each with: 165 calories, 12 g fat, 7 g protein, 7 g carbohydrate, trace dietary fiber, 7 g usable carbs.

Peaches with Butterscotch Sauce

These are delectable. You can serve them as is, with a little heavy cream, with *Whipped Topping* (see recipe page 342)—or, the Big Casino, with a scoop of low-carb vanilla ice cream.

> 1 pound (455 g) frozen, unsweetened, sliced peaches
>
> 2 teaspoons lemon juice
>
> 1/3 cup (8 g) Splenda
>
> 2 tablespoons (42 g) sugar-free imitation honey
>
> 1/2 teaspoon blackstrap molasses
>
> 2 tablespoons (28 ml) heavy cream
>
> 1/4 teaspoon cinnamon
>
> 2 tablespoons (28 g) butter, melted
>
> Guar or xanthan

Place the peaches in your slow cooker. (I didn't even bother to thaw mine.)

In a bowl, stir together the lemon juice, Splenda, honey, molasses, cream, cinnamon, and butter. Pour the mixture over the peaches. Cover the slow cooker, set it to low, and let it cook for 6 hours.

Thicken the sauce to a creamy consistency with a little guar or xanthan and serve hot.

Yield: 6 servings, each with: 86 calories, 6 g fat, 1 g protein, 9 g carbohydrate, 2 g dietary fiber, 7 g usable carbs. (Analysis does not include polyols in the imitation honey.)

Cauli-Rice

I give thanks to Fran McCullough for this recipe! I got this idea from her book *Living Low-Carb*, and it's served me very well indeed.

1/2 head cauliflower

Simply put the cauliflower through your food processor using the shredding blade. This gives a texture that is remarkably similar to rice. You can steam this, microwave it, or even sauté it in butter. Whatever you do, though, don't overcook it! I usually put mine in a microwaveable casserole with a lid, add a couple of tablespoons (28 to 45 ml) of water, and microwave it for 7 minutes on high.

Yield: This makes about 3 cups, or at least 3 to 4 servings. Assuming 3 servings, each with: 24 calories, trace fat, 2 g protein, 5 g carbohydrate, 2 g dietary fiber, 3 g usable carbs.

Fauxtatoes

This is a wonderful substitute for mashed potatoes if you want something to put a fabulous sour cream gravy on! Feel free, by the way, to use frozen cauliflower instead. It works quite well here.

1 head cauliflower or 1 1/2 pounds (680 g) frozen cauliflower

4 tablespoons (55 g) butter

Steam or microwave the cauliflower until it's soft. Drain it thoroughly and put it through the blender or food processor until it's well puréed. Add the butter and salt and pepper to taste.

Yield: 6 servings, each with: 72 calories, 8 g fat, trace protein, 1 g carbohydrate, trace dietary fiber, trace usable carbs. (This makes six generous servings.)

The Ultimate Fauxtatoes

I'm not crazy about Ketatoes by themselves, but added to pureed cauliflower *Fauxtatoes*, they add a potato-y flavor and texture that is remarkably convincing! This is a killer side dish with many of your slow cooker main dishes.

1/2 head cauliflower

1/2 cup (50 g) Ketatoes mix

1/2 cup (120 ml) boiling water

1 tablespoon (14 g) butter

Trim the bottom of the stem of your cauliflower and whack the rest of the head into chunks. Put them in a microwaveable casserole dish with a lid. Add a couple of tablespoons (28 to 45 ml) of water, cover, and microwave on high for 8 to 9 minutes.

While that's happening, measure your Ketatoes mix and boiling water into a mixing bowl and whisk together.

When the microwave beeps, pull out your cauliflower—it should be tender. Drain it well and put it in either your food processor, with the S-blade in place, or in your blender. Either way, purée the cauliflower until it's smooth. Transfer the puréed cauliflower to the mixing bowl and stir the cauliflower and Ketatoes together well. Add the butter and stir till it melts. Add salt and pepper to taste and serve.

Yield: 4 servings, each with: 140 calories, 5 g fat, 10 g protein, 14 g carbohydrate, 8 g dietary fiber, 6 g usable carbs.

Acknowledgments

A few quick thank you's here:

To my darling friend Maria Vander Vloedt, who tested many, many recipes for this book. She's the perfect tester: She's smart and funny and reliable, she knows how to cook, she can follow instructions but make constructive suggestions when they're needed, she eats low-carb, and she has a husband and five kids to try my recipes out on! Thanks, Maria.

Also to my sister Kim, who is always up for a new recipe, and my pal Ray Stevens, who tested a bunch when crunch time rolled around: Thanks, guys!

As always, to my husband, Eric Schmitz. Thank God I married him, I could never find another person with his combination of skills in the open job market. All this, and he's nice to have around the house, too.

And to my editor, Holly, for browbeating me into writing this book. It's been a lot cooler than I expected.

About the Author

Dana Carpender is a best-selling author and radio host who was startled to discover that limiting her carbohydrate intake not only helped her control her weight, but produced the health and vitality a low-fat diet had promised but never delivered. More than fifteen years later, she laughs at people who say "You can't eat that way long-term." Her nine cookbooks are the result of her realization that the key to permanent dietary change is the answer to the age-old question, "What's for supper?" To date they have sold over a million copies worldwide. Dana blogs about low-carb nutrition at www.HoldtheToast.com; her weekly blog digest goes out to over 20,000 readers. She is also managing editor of CarbSmart Magazine at www.CarbSmart.com, as well as a featured staff writer. She launched her internet radio show and podcast, Dana's Low Carb For Life, in January 2011. Dana lives in Bloomington, Indiana, with her husband and a menagerie of pets, all of whom are well and healthily fed.

Mockahlua

This recipe originally appeared in *500 Low-Carb Recipes*, but because I've included it in some recipes in the dessert chapter I thought I'd better repeat it! This recipe makes quite a lot, but don't worry about that; 100-proof vodka's a darned good preservative. Your *Mockahlua* will keep indefinitely.

2¹/₂ cups (570 ml) water

3 cups (75 g) Splenda

3 tablespoons (18 g) instant coffee granules

1 teaspoon vanilla extract

1 bottle (750 milliliters) 100-proof vodka (Use the cheap stuff.)

In a large pitcher or measuring cup, combine the water, Splenda, coffee granules, and vanilla extract. Stir until the coffee and Splenda are completely dissolved.

Pour the mixture through a funnel into a 1.5 or 2 liter bottle. (A clean 1.5 liter wine bottle works fine, so long as you've saved the cork.) Pour in the vodka. Cork and shake well.

Yield: 32 servings of 1¹/₂ ounces (42 ml)—a standard "shot," each with: 53 calories, 0 g fat, trace protein, trace carbohydrate, 0 g dietary fiber, trace usable carbs.

Whipped Topping

I keep repeating this recipe, but then, it's a wonderful, classic whipped cream topping for any dessert.

1 cup (235 ml) heavy cream, chilled

3 teaspoons (15 g) sugar-free vanilla instant pudding mix

Simply whip the cream with the pudding mix. Use your electric mixer, or if you like, a whisk—neither a blender nor a food processor will work. Stop whipping as soon as your topping is nice and thick, or you'll end up with vanilla butter!

If you make this ahead of time, refrigerate it until you're ready to serve dessert.

Yield: 8 servings, each with: 104 calories, 11 g fat, 1 g protein, 1 g carbohydrate, 0 g dietary fiber, 1 g usable carbs.

Sugar-Free Chocolate Sauce

This is as good as any sugar-based chocolate sauce you've ever had, if I do say so myself. Which I do. Don't try to make this with Splenda; it won't work. The polyol sweetener somehow makes the water and the chocolate combine. It's chemistry, or magic, or some darned thing. You very likely will need to order maltitol. Just do a Web search under "low carbohydrate," and you'll find dozens of websites ready to ship anything your heart desires. My favorite is carbsmart (www.carbsmart.com).

1/3 cup (80 ml) water

2 ounces (55 g) unsweetened baking chocolate

1/2 cup (100 g) maltitol

3 tablespoons (45 g) butter

1/4 teaspoon vanilla

Put the water and chocolate in a glass measuring cup and microwave on high for 1 to 1 1/2 minutes or until the chocolate has melted. Stir in the maltitol and microwave on high for another 3 minutes, stirring halfway through. Stir in the butter and vanilla.

Note: This works beautifully with maltitol. However, when I tried to make it with other granular polyols—erythritol, isomalt—it started out fine but crystallized and turned grainy as it cooled. I'd stick with maltitol.

Yield: Makes roughly 1 cup, or 8 servings of 2 tablespoons, each with: 75 calories, 8 g fat, 1 g protein, 2 g carbohydrate, 1 g dietary fiber, 1 g usable carbs. (Analysis does not include the maltitol.)

Cajun Seasoning

This New Orleans–style seasoning, originally from *500 Low-Carb Recipes*, is good sprinkled over chicken, steak, pork, fish—just about anything. It will also work in any recipe in this book that calls for Cajun seasoning. But if you'd rather use purchased seasoning, go for it.

2½ tablespoons (18 g) paprika

2 tablespoons (36 g) salt

2 tablespoons (18 g) garlic powder

1 tablespoon (6 g) pepper

1 tablespoon (7 g) onion powder

1 tablespoon (5 g) cayenne

1 tablespoon (3 g) dried oregano

1 tablespoon (4 g) dried thyme

Combine all ingredients thoroughly and store in an airtight container.

Yield: Makes ⅔ cup. The whole batch contains: 187 calories, 4 g fat, 8 g protein, 37 g carbohydrate, 9 g dietary fiber, 28 g usable carbs. (Considering how spicy this is, you're unlikely to use more than a teaspoon or two at a time. One teaspoon has 1 gram of carbohydrate, with a trace of fiber.)

Adobo Seasoning

Adobo is a popular seasoning in Latin America and the Caribbean. It's available at many grocery stores, in the spice aisle or the international aisle. But if you can't find it, it sure is easy to make.

    10 teaspoons (30 g) garlic powder
    5 teaspoons (5 g) dried oregano
    5 teaspoons (10 g) pepper
    2¹/₂ teaspoons (8 g) paprika
    5 teaspoons salt

Simply measure everything into a bowl, stir, and store in a lidded shaker jar.

Yield: Makes a little over ¹/₂ cup, or about 48 servings of ¹/₂ teaspoon, each with: 3 calories, trace fat, trace protein, 1g carbohydrate, trace dietary fiber, 1 g usable carbs.

Garam Masala

This is an Indian spice blend used in several of the curries in this book. You may well be able to buy perfectly lovely garam masala already made at a local Asian market or big grocery store—I can! But if you can't, you can easily make your own.

    2 tablespoons (14 g) ground cumin
    2 tablespoons (12 g) ground coriander
    2 tablespoons (12 g) ground cardamom
    1¹/₂ tablespoons (9 g) black pepper
    4 teaspoons (8 g) ground cinnamon
    ¹/₂ teaspoon ground cloves
    1 teaspoon ground nutmeg

Simply combine everything and store in an airtight container.

Yield: Makes roughly 9 tablespoons, each with: 19 calories, 1 g fat, 1 g protein, 4 g carbohydrate, 1 g dietary fiber, 3 g usable carbs.

Hoisin Sauce

Hoisin sauce is sort of Chinese barbecue sauce, and it customarily contains a lot of sugar. It also doesn't usually have peanut butter in it, but it works quite well here. This is a repeat from *500 Low-Carb Recipes*, by the way.

> 4 tablespoons (60 ml) soy sauce
>
> 2 tablespoons (32 g) natural peanut butter
>
> 2 tablespoons (3 g) Splenda
>
> 2 teaspoons white vinegar
>
> 1 clove garlic
>
> 2 teaspoons dark sesame oil
>
> 1/8 teaspoon five-spice powder

Just assemble everything in your blender and blend till it's smooth. Store it in a tightly lidded jar in the fridge. Feel free to double or triple this, if you like.

Yield: Makes roughly 1/3 cup, or 6 servings of about 1 tablespoon, each with: 52 calories, 4 g fat, 2 g protein, 2 g carbohydrate, trace dietary fiber, 1 g usable carbs.

Low-Carb Teriyaki Sauce

There's now commercial low-carb teriyaki sauce on the market, but I like this better, and it's so easy to make, why wouldn't I? Why wouldn't you?

> 1/2 cup (120 ml) soy sauce
>
> 1/4 cup (60 ml) dry sherry
>
> 1 clove garlic, crushed
>
> 2 tablespoons (3 g) Splenda
>
> 1 tablespoon (8 g) grated ginger root

Combine all the ingredients. Refrigerate until ready to use.

Yield: Makes 3/4 cup, or 12 servings of 1 tablespoon, each with: 13 calories, trace fat, 1 g protein, 1 g carbohydrate, trace dietary fiber, 1 g usable carbs.

Classic Rub

This barbecue rub first appeared in *The Low-Carb Barbecue Book*, and it's a great choice in any recipe that calls for barbecue rub.

¹/4 cup (6 g) Splenda

1 tablespoon (18 g) seasoned salt

1 tablespoon (9 g) garlic powder

1 tablespoon (15 g) celery salt

1 tablespoon (7 g) onion powder

2 tablespoons (14 g) paprika

1 tablespoon (8 g) chili powder

2 teaspoons pepper

1 teaspoon lemon pepper

1 teaspoon ground sage

1 teaspoon mustard

¹/2 teaspoon thyme

¹/2 teaspoon cayenne

Simply stir everything together and store in an airtight container.

Yield: Makes 13 tablespoons of rub, each with: 13 calories, trace fat, 1 g protein, 2 g carbohydrate, 1 g dietary fiber, 1 g usable carbs.

Dana's "Kansas City" Barbecue Sauce

This recipe, from *The Low-Carb Barbecue Book*, is it—what most of us think of when we think of barbecue sauce: tomato-y, spicy, and sweet. It's unbelievably close to a top-flight commercial barbecue sauce—and my Kansas City–raised husband agrees. If you like a smoky note in your barbecue sauce, add 1 teaspoon of liquid smoke flavoring to this. (Note: If you can get it locally, commercially-made low-carb barbecue sauce is likely to be lower carb than this recipe.)

> 2 tablespoons (28 g) butter
>
> 1 clove garlic
>
> 1/4 cup (40 g) chopped onion
>
> 1 tablespoon (15 ml) lemon juice
>
> 1 cup (240 g) *Dana's No-Sugar Ketchup* (page 332) or purchased low-carb ketchup
>
> 1/3 cup (8 g) Splenda
>
> 1 tablespoon (20 g) blackstrap molasses
>
> 2 tablespoons (28 ml) Worcestershire sauce
>
> 1 tablespoon (8 g) chili powder
>
> 1 tablespoon (15 ml) white vinegar
>
> 1 teaspoon pepper
>
> 1/4 teaspoon salt

Combine everything in a saucepan over low heat. Heat until the butter melts, stir the whole thing up, and let it simmer for 5 minutes or so. That's it!

Yield: Roughly 13/4 cups, or 14 servings of 2 tablespoons each, each with: 45 calories, 3 g fat, 1 g protein, 7 g carbohydrate, 1 g fiber, 6 g usable carbs.

Piedmont Mustard Sauce

This bright-yellow sauce, heavy on the mustard, but completely free of tomato, is typical of the Piedmont region of North Carolina. Try it on *Slow Cooker Pulled Pork* (see recipe page 188).

1/2 cup (88 g) yellow mustard

2 tablespoons (28 ml) lemon juice

2 tablespoons (3 g) Splenda

1 tablespoon (15 ml) white vinegar

1/4 teaspoon cayenne

Combine everything in a saucepan and simmer for 5 minutes over low heat.

Yield: Makes roughly 3/4 cup, or 6 servings of 2 tablespoons, each with: 17 calories, 1 g fat, 1 g protein, 2 g carbohydrate, 1 g dietary fiber, 1 g usable carbs.

Eastern Carolina Vinegar Sauce

This is the traditional Eastern Carolina sauce for pulled pork. It's just sweetened vinegar with a good hint of hot pepper. It'll be great with your *Slow Cooker Pulled Pork* (see recipe page 188)!

1/2 cup (120 ml) cider vinegar

1 1/2 tablespoons (2 g) Splenda

1/4 teaspoon blackstrap molasses

1 teaspoon red pepper flakes

1/4 teaspoon cayenne

Combine everything in a saucepan and simmer for 5 minutes over low heat.

Yield: 6 servings, each with: 4 calories, trace fat, trace protein, 2 g carbohydrate, trace dietary fiber, 2 g usable carbs.

Cocktail Sauce

You'll need this for the *Easy Party Shrimp* on page 27!

> 1/2 cup (120 g) *Dana's No-Sugar Ketchup* (page 332) or purchased low-carb ketchup
>
> 2 teaspoons prepared horseradish
>
> 1/4 teaspoon Tabasco sauce
>
> 1 teaspoon lemon juice

Combine all ingredients in a bowl and mix well.

Yield: Makes about 1/2 cup. The whole batch contains: 142 calories, 1 g fat, 5 g protein, 36 g carbohydrate, 6 g dietary fiber, 30 g usable carbs. Good thing you'll be sharing it! You can drop this carb count considerably by using commercially-made low-carb ketchup.

Florida Sunshine Tangerine Barbecue Sauce

The name of this sauce is partly from the tangerine note, which is unusual and delicious, but the name is also from the fact that this sauce is at least as hot as the Florida sun! It's especially good on poultry. You can use this in any of the recipes that call for barbecue sauce, or you can use the Kansas City–style sauce on the following page—this one's lower carb, but less traditional. Or for that matter, you can use the newly available bottled low-carb barbecue sauce. You won't hurt my feelings.

12 ounces (355 ml) Diet Rite Tangerine Soda

1/4 cup (6 g) Splenda

1 tablespoon (8 g) chili powder

2 teaspoons black pepper

1 teaspoon ginger

1 teaspoon dry mustard

1 teaspoon onion salt

4 cloves garlic, crushed

1/2 teaspoon cayenne

1/2 teaspoon coriander

1/2 teaspoon red pepper flakes

1 bay leaf

1/2 cup (120 ml) cider vinegar

1 tablespoon (20 g) sugar-free imitation honey

1 tablespoon (15 ml) Worcestershire sauce

3/4 cup (180 g) *Dana's No-Sugar Ketchup* (page 332) or purchased low-carb ketchup

Pour the soda into a nonreactive saucepan and turn the heat under it to medium-low. While that's heating, measure the other ingredients into the sauce. By the time you get to the ketchup, it should be simmering. Whisk everything together until smooth and let it simmer over lowest heat for a good 10 to 15 minutes.

Yield: Makes about 3 cups, or 24 servings of 2 tablespoons, each with: 11 calories, trace fat, trace protein, 3 g carbohydrate, trace dietary fiber, 3 g usable carbs. (Analysis does not include the polyols in the imitation honey.)

Index